THROUGH
THE
WHIRLWIND

Also by William Houston

Meltdown
Riding the Business Cycle

THROUGH THE WHIRLWIND

William Houston

LITTLE, BROWN AND COMPANY

A *Little, Brown* Book

First published in Great Britain in 1997
by Little, Brown and Company

Copyright © William Houston 1997

The moral right of the author has been asserted.

All rights reserved.
No part of this publication may be reproduced,
stored in a retrieval system, or transmitted, in any
form or by any means, without the prior
permission in writing of the publisher, nor be
otherwise circulated in any form of binding or
cover other than that in which it is published and
without a similar condition including this
condition being imposed on the subsequent purchaser.

A CIP catalogue record for this book
is available from the British Library.

ISBN 0 316 88018 3

Typeset by Solidus (Bristol) Limited
Printed and bound in Great Britain by
Clays Ltd, St Ives plc

UK companies, institutions and other organisations wishing
to make bulk purchases of this or any other book
published by Little, Brown should contact their local
bookshop or the special sales department at the address below.
Tel 0171 811 8000. Fax 0171 911 8100.

Little, Brown and Company (UK)
Brettenham House
Lancaster Place
London WC2E 7EN

To Averil

CONTENTS

List of Illustrations — viii
Acknowledgements — ix
Preface — xi

1. If You Cannot Avoid the Whirlwind Then Prepare for the Vortex — 1
2. The Cycles Shaping Our Lives — 9
3. Finessing the Long Wave With the Business Cycle — 30
4. Strategies for the Kondratieff Long Wave — 41
5. Competitive Tactics During the Business Cycle — 67
6. The Cycles of Failure and Action to Accelerate Recovery — 72
7. Third-generation Techniques for 'Flattening' the Organisation — 94
8. Policies for the Downwave — 113
9. Managing Investments in Turbulent Markets — 139
10. Ending the Eunuchs' Reign — 165
11. The Cycles of Warfare and Internal Conflict — 207
12. The Battle Between Mutating Bug Cycles and Modern Medicine — 225
13. The Cycles of Technology and Innovation — 248
14. Through the Whirlwind to Recovery — 277

Further Reading List and Useful Addresses — 298
Index — 301

LIST OF ILLUSTRATIONS

1	Historical events related to the 179-year cycle	14
2	Cyclical indicators associated with the business cycle	32
3	Table of indicators used by the Foundation for the Study of Cycles	37
4	The Kitchin and Kondratieff cycles	38
5	Business cycle indicators from 1964 to 1995	39
6	Summary of management attitudes during the long wave	65
7	Phases of the business cycle	68
8	Percentage of listed UK industrial companies at risk	78
9	Number of insolvencies and reconstructions	78
10	Market action during K1	144
11	Market action during K2	146
12	Market action during K3	148
13	Market action during K4	150
14	J Pugsley's Deadly Anomaly	164
15	Historical events associated with K1	173
16	Historical events associated with K2	175
17	Historical events associated with K3	177
18	Historical events associated with K4	180
19	Summary of cycles influencing politicians during the long wave	187
20	Comparison of cycle synthesis with actual battles	223

ACKNOWLEDGEMENTS

This book would have been impossible to write without the help and encouragement of a great number of people. I am particularly indebted to: Larry Acker, Martin Armstrong, Stephen Bamford, John Barraclough, Teddy Butler-Henderson, Robert Dallek, Richard Dent, Willem Foks, Evelyn Garriss, Harold Hayward, Stephen Hill, Simon Hollington, Simon Hunt, Stephen Lewis, Sophie Schubert, Jane Malcomson, Gareth Price, William Rees-Mogg, Christeen Skinner, Guenter Steinwitz, Richard Taffler, Peter Warburton, David Whately, Michael White and Martin Whitehill. All in their way have provided valuable help or ideas; any errors in the book are entirely mine. Where feasible all the reference documents have been mentioned in the text or in the bibliography.

I am also very grateful to Richard Mogey and his team at the foundation for the Study of Cycles, who, as always, have provided me with invaluable help and data. I have also received much encouragement and help from Dick Fox and Christopher Woodward, who have been particularly helpful with suggestions and reading proofs. I have also received much encouragement and guidance from Alan Samson of Little, Brown, and from my agent Doreen Montgomery. Finally I am indebted to my wife Averil who has given me much encouragement and has taken time and effort from her own busy life to be an assiduous proof reader.

William Houston, Datchworth, April 1996

PREFACE

We are entering one of the most interesting periods of modern history and few people, least of all politicians and public servants, have any idea what is going to happen, for they are relying on the principle that tomorrow will be much like yesterday. It will not. It will be full of discontinuities first covered in *Riding the Business Cycle* and now detailed in *Through the Whirlwind*. Evidence is growing that the major climatic and economic cycles are working as in the past. These must be understood and new policies implemented. The next few years will be hard, though very satisfying, for those who understand these rhythms; it will be devastating for those who do not.

Mankind has recovered from difficult situations in the past and will do so again – supported by knowledge of the past and possibly with the help of the scenarios described in this book. The most important probable result will be not the *whirlwind* itself but how we deal with the next upwave, for that will be quite different from anything experienced over the last 300 years. Darby, Newcomen, Watt and others triggered the Industrial Revolution; later, sciences such as biogenetics and cold fusion have spawned a whole range of innovations making the post-industrial society not only fascinating but extremely rewarding. The individual could be provided with a sense of freedom, a renewed faith and a dignity only possible for the minority back in the industrial age.

This is a hands-on practical book. Initially it reminds the reader about prevailing cycles, then it describes how they give rise to strategy and tactics covering a wide range of human affairs; from managing a business through to investment, politics, housing, warfare, technology and disease. The whole is brought together in the last chapter, providing a bird's-eye view of the most likely events implicit in the cycles and the personal qualities needed to solve the problems successfully.

CHAPTER ONE

IF YOU CANNOT AVOID THE WHIRLWIND THEN PREPARE FOR THE VORTEX

Pilots are taught to evade cumulonimbus thunderclouds wherever possible because the danger from turbulence and icing conditions can be fatal. If they cannot be avoided, then those in command should stow everything movable and tighten seatbelts to improve safety in the extreme turbulence; they should also turn on cabin lighting to reduce blindness from lightning and switch on de-icing equipment. Most importantly, they are warned never to make a turn, since the uneven lift from ice-covered wings can cause an uncontrollable spin.

Unlike thunderclouds, cycles cannot be avoided. They can be understood of course – which was the whole point of writing *Riding the Business Cycle* – but carrying out the correct drill in adversity is an amalgam of historical perception, research and practical application. But just as an aeroplane emerges from a cumulonimbus cloud into still air, so do people survive difficult times and find the next golden era. These are the themes of this book.

The Big Picture

Every age has its big picture. In the 16th and 17th centuries England was dominated by overseas growth, the Spanish threat and fears of popery. In the 18th century the main enemy was France, but by then financing conflicts was easier, with the wealth generated from iron, coal, cotton and steam – the essentials of the Industrial Revolution. The French threat ended in 1815 but was replaced by German unification in 1870 which triggered two world wars and so exhausted Britain that the torch was passed to America. The post-war power of the United States then overcame the threat of communism.

Is the fall of socialism now the 'end of history' as described by Francis Fukuyama? The Harvard academic postulated that because the Anglo-Saxon democracies and free-market economies had overcome the totalitarian threat, the liberal victory had been won and we could look forward to a more certain future without discontinuities. Does this mean that China can now grow only if it adopts the successful western systems? Can Islamic republics ever be viable?

The important cycles of the 1990s and the next century are about discontinuities – changes that could usher in one of the most unusual periods of history for some 500 years. These rhythms are described in *Riding the Business Cycle* which was completed in early 1994 before the main cycles started to work in earnest. There are three fundamental rhythms: the first is a drought cycle; next is a sequence of booms and busts; finally there is a 500-year era which coincides with the period after the Industrial Revolution. This is briefly how history is repeating itself.

There are several *drought cycles* caused by influences within the solar system ranging from 11.2 years to 179 years. Historically these have upset the ability of nations to survive and have changed existing patterns – leading to civil or limited wars which also run in rhythms. Climatic changes upset crop yields which is why the 1995 corn crop in the USA was some 25% down on the previous year and the grain carry-over stocks of forty-nine days are some of the lowest on record.

More worrying was the extreme cold of the winter of 1995–6 where temperatures of minus 60 degrees Fahrenheit were recorded in the Canadian central provinces; the cold was due to the exceptionally low sunspots (the heat emitted from the sun) plus the sun's rays being diffused by the atmospheric debris of volcanic action. The extreme cold will have damaged the winter wheat crop in North America. In Russia it was known by the spring of 1996 that the excessively low temperatures had destroyed swathes of winter wheat. In China 15 million acres of wheat were destroyed and 100,000 people were near starvation from the blizzard-stricken area of Qinghai province. Historically, sunspots remain low after the

179-year cycle which is normally accompanied by increased volcanic activity.

We should also be aware of the downwave section of a *long wave* which has dominated economics and politics since at least 1792. There have been three complete cycles which have all followed a similar pattern of up- and downwaves. The latest rhythm started around 1942 and was responsible for the almost continuous boom until the crash of 1975. There followed a period of some fifteen years when the cycle entered a stage of frenzied growth accompanied by a dramatic rise in government and private borrowing. Then in 1990 came the start of the downwave that is being felt around the world.

The first to feel the effect of collapsing debt was Japan, after the stock-market crash created huge losses for the interlinked shareholding common in the country. The next to be hit was the property market, which was excessively overborrowed and succumbed to the typical downwave action where the value of assets falls faster than loans can be repaid – graphically described as a credit vortex. The government attempted to regain the upward momentum of the economy by lowering interest rates – which failed in an earlier cycle when the Americans tried it in the 1930s. Maynard Keynes described it as 'pushing on a string'. In short, Japan settled into a deflation with short periods of upturn.

Other countries are being affected. Germany, the former driving force in Europe, has such high social security and other costs that firms like Daimler Benz have been obliged to manufacture in places like Poland or cease production. While foreign investment has risen rapidly, internal spending has collapsed. When the downwave hit the country in early 1996, the rate of unemployment started to rise rapidly to a post-war peak of 9.6% in western Germany and 17.5% in the east; the figures probably understate the position, for they do not include the prematurely retired, most of whom have given up looking for work. The true unemployment figure is estimated to be nearer 7 million than the official total of 4.27 million.

France is repeating its folly of the early 1930s when, by holding on to the gold standard, the politicians applied such a squeeze on prices that wages were also driven down to create a spiral of social unrest. Then in June 1936 the socialist Front Populaire under Léon Blum was elected, which forced up wages and prices. The result was a run on the franc and a collapse of internal finances. The French government is making exactly the same mistake in the 1990s by tracking the German Deutschmark, a policy which is creating rising unemployment and social unrest.

Other countries are showing similar symptoms to those of over sixty years ago. In the fight for the Republican leadership in the United States Pat Buchanan (like Perot in 1992) delivered themes from the 1930s of job creation through tariff protection, normally the territory of the Democrats. By early 1996, there was the same frenetic stock-market rise as in 1929, encouraged by companies that increase profitability by laying off workers and a spending demand weakened by falling personal incomes.

We are also influenced by a *500-year cycle* that has regularly created major discontinuities every half-millennium as shown in Chapter 2. This time we are entering the post-industrial age described by Alvin Toffler as the Third Wave; it is also known as the Cybernetic Revolution. Companies are subcontracting a wide range of manufacturing and services, and employing information technology to remove tiers of management and supervision. The Organisation for Economic Cooperation and Development (OECD) is already forecasting that only 50% of the working population in developed countries will be in full-time employment by 2005 compared to about 90% in 1996. This may be optimistic. Michael White, an international consultant, believes that into the next century the USA will only have 8% employed in manufacturing, 2% in agriculture and 30% in service industries; the remainder will have only part-time employment. There will be similar proportions in most western countries.

Governments will be of little help. The downwave that started in 1990 has created a credit vortex where the value of assets declines faster than the collateral borrowings. But this is not understood by most politicians who still believe that the old rules of increasing public spending and lowering interest rates can revive economies. Japan is trying to energise their economy with public works programmes and low interest rates as America did in the 1930s. They will almost certainly fail until all the bad public and private debts have been purged and a new cycle allowed to start.

As the downwave continues, the taxed revenue of most governments will continue to fall as many more people become self-employed and are able to offset expenses against their income. The authorities will also find it difficult to collect tax from the increasing amount of transactions carried out on systems like the Internet. In desperation they might try to increase indirect taxation but this will hit the poorest in society and be very unpopular. Western countries are also caught in the trap of having an ageing population, where beyond the year 2010 it is estimated that those working will need to be taxed at above 70% to pay the present levels of state pensions. Here the worst hit countries will be Germany, France, Italy and Japan, which have a low level of private pensions.

By early 1996 the political pretence of 'business as usual' has caused governments to increase their debts massively in the hope of keeping the welfare state alive, but they are worried. Countries such as Sweden, France, Germany, Italy, the United States, Canada and Britain are attempting to cut back benefits amidst great political controversy. As taxed revenue falls, countries will try to borrow more but lenders will become progressively more anxious about debt repayment and demand increasingly higher rates. Interest rates will be forced lower in an attempt to avoid this.

However, in addition to the downwave, politicians are likely to be faced with rising food prices as growing conditions remain difficult – so forcing up the cost of living. This is known as stagflation, a very dangerous condition which causes widespread bankruptcies and failures. Caught between the dilemma of rising inflation and economies slowing in the downwave, governments could be driven to monetise their debts through buying their own securities by newly created money before facing a financial crisis. With the rising level of insolvencies and governments unable to raise funds, politicians will be forced to dismantle the Welfare State around the turn of the century.

This evidence may not yet be conclusive but the lessons of the 1930s and other periods in history remind us that by the time cycles are confirmed it may be too late; businesses will have failed, capital and jobs will have been lost. Of course, one can always continue in ignorance of cycles, but would it not be better to know about these processes and the eventual recovery described in later chapters of this book?

Even for those accustomed to cycles much of the material in this book will be unfamiliar, hence it is organised into separate parts. Chapter 2 is a recapitulation of the cycles outlined in *Riding the Business Cycle* followed by a short description of how these rhythms have worked in the past. Then there is a chapter on a shorter-term business cycle enabling us to finesse with some accuracy the timing of longer-term waves.

As most of a nation's wealth is generated from business, the next five chapters are devoted to describing how cycles can shape management strategies and tactics. Moving through each phase, one becomes aware that although managers cannot 'buck the cycle' they can make it work for them – just in the way a judo artist takes advantage of an opponent's weaknesses and nullifies their strengths. There are also chapters on the cycles of insolvency and management action to help businesses weather very difficult trading conditions.

An important chapter follows devoted to investment, covering what will undoubtedly be a roller-coaster in the commodity, bond, currency and stock markets. These have followed closely the Kondratieff long wave described earlier and there will be considerable confusion as the cycles work out their gyrations. Readers should be aware of what to look for and the appropriate actions at each stage. Housing is also very vulnerable to similar turbulence and we have to re-learn the lessons of the early 1930s in America to avoid large numbers of family homes being repossessed.

Cycles have influenced politics for at least 200 years, primarily in the United States but also elsewhere in the west. Chapter 10 describes how the present political parties were set up in the industrial era, when capital wrestled with labour as each sought to gain the upper hand. In the post-industrial age both management and unions will decline as new parties are formed to represent the individual. The new breed of politicians will then negotiate with the electorate the privatisation of state provisions such as health, education, pensions and social security. The rump state will be left with defence, the legal system, criminal investigation (but probably not crime prevention) and protection of the currency – which could once again be backed by gold.

The next three chapters are devoted to the cycles of warfare, disease and technology which will have a dominating influence in the next few years. There are several cycles tracking warfare – the two most powerful probably being the 179-year and long-wave rhythms described earlier. However, conflicts are unlikely to be on a global scale in the next century but may arise either from the collapse of the Russian empire, or from food shortages in areas like central Africa. Historically, dry conditions in the steppes of central Asia have triggered mass movements of people to the west and south which could once again become a danger. Similar conditions could further encourage nationalistic governments in Russia and China that are unfriendly to the west.

A factor increasingly considered by medical journals is the problem of mutating bacteria, which make some diseases very difficult to treat. Already strains of gonorrhoea, malaria and tuberculosis are not responding to standard drugs, forcing a renewed battle between drug research and the microbes. The researchers will not be helped by people becoming more susceptible to disease through malnutrition in the expected climatic changes. The dangers will increase. By the year 2000 cities such as Bombay, Calcutta, Rio de Janeiro and Jakarta (probably without adequate sewage and fresh water) will house half the world's population. Modern communications have dramatically increased the mobility of disease carriers which will force individual states to tighten their migration procedures.

The third leg of the trilogy is concerned with the cycles of technology that economists like Joseph Schumpeter believed were responsible for the Kondratieff long wave. He argued that a confluence of major breakthroughs such as Abraham Darby's iron smelting and Newcomen's steam-driven pump spawned a range of innovations that propelled the Industrial Revolution. When the existing techniques become stale, the boom ends and causes a recession. We can look forward to new technologies taking us into the next golden age.

The Bad News and the Good News

Each of the cycles described earlier would alone present considerable problems; in combination their impact could create very difficult conditions for managing a business, a government or one's own personal affairs. *Every difficult period has proved a jumping-off board for new opportunities, and the next century will be no exception.*

So many changes could occur that the likely outcome is outlined in the last chapter. A set of scenarios focuses on understanding a world quite different to that left behind in the 1980s. As the power of government declines so the scope for individuals will increase. It is difficult to look at the events of the downwave without seeing opportunities. For example, for every potential corporate collapse there will be entrepreneurs eager to purchase the component parts, often very cheaply. The dynamic new owner/managers will provide a tremendous economic stimulus to drive economies forward, taking advantage of low interest rates and a de-restricted trading system. Contributing to the impetus will be the expanding opportunities for individuals with new technologies supplying an increasing range of personal services. These new groups, located away from cities, will create the focus around which fresh communities will form to assume many of the responsibilities previously taken on by central and local governments. The Swiss system of communities within a canton will be widely copied.

As described earlier, the promise of inventions such as cold fusion could totally change the nature and application of energy well into the next century. In the mid-1990s the medical profession is confronted with resistant microbes, but in the next century sciences such as genetics will be capable of reducing inherited diseases and strengthening people's immunity to certain disorders.

One of the exciting realities to emerge from difficult times will be the renewed power, authority and freedom of individuals released from the expectation of being employees. It is true that not everyone will welcome the responsibility and many will find it difficult to adjust, but the logic of the cycles demands that we take note of the trends and make the most of them. The following chapters describe how it is likely to happen. The more one understands, the better one can cope!

CHAPTER 2

THE CYCLES SHAPING OUR LIVES

Politics, business, markets and our lives all work in cycles; some are long-term and measured in decades – even centuries – others span only a few years, or months. Most of these rhythms are created naturally from movements within the solar system, affecting the climate and people's attitudes, as a later chapter will explain. Others are man-made and have a duration of up to two generations which suggests that most of us find it difficult to learn from history. It would seem sensible for anyone in authority to understand cycles and, if wise enough, to harness them for the benefit of their countries or organisations.

Unfortunately, the knowledge is sparsely spread – otherwise business people and politicians would not make so many stupid mistakes. For example, the 1920s and 1980s occurred at a similar stage of a cycle, but this did not stop industrial and commercial leaders making exactly the same errors as their predecessors. There was rampant land speculation in both periods which attracted banks and institutions which were then forced to wipe billions off their balance sheets. In the politics of the 1990s only New Zealand seems to have learned from Neville Chamberlain's wise management of the British economy in the 1930s.

Most businesses are aware of the rhythms affecting sales or costs but not how these may relate to the business cycle as a whole. For example, investors know that the first sector to emerge from a recession is food distribution and the last is machine tools – the reverse is true going into a slowdown. Their timing would be greatly helped if they better understood the business cycle detailed in Chapter 3. The same applies to industrial and commercial managers who could take steps to stop their business failing prior to a recession.

That we are controlled by natural cycles should surprise no one. Our routines are fashioned by the rhythm of night and day and the seasons by the earth's passage around the sun. Although life on earth could not exist without the sun, the moon has double the gravitational pull, creating diurnal tides varying between springs and neaps over the lunar month. There are also several other cycles caused by movements within the solar system which affect economics through their impact on climate and hence the price of many commodities.

How these rhythms work in detail was explained in *Riding the Business Cycle*. This chapter aims at compressing this earlier work into its essentials by describing briefly the forces at work and their impact on earth.

The Driving Forces Behind Cycles

One of the most important rhythms likely to affect decisions during the 1990s and into the next decade is the 179-year sun retrograde cycle caused by an unusual alignment of the Sun, Jupiter and Saturn. Since the birth of Christ, whenever this cycle has reached a low point there has been a prolonged period of cool dry weather which has reduced crop yields and often changed the course of nations.

Although the sun's mass makes up 99.9% of the solar system, the movement of two large planets, Jupiter and Saturn, influences the sun's radiation and can unsettle the earth's structure. Jupiter is the biggest planet circling the sun, with an orbit of nearly twelve earth years, while Saturn, being even further out from the centre, takes over twenty-nine earth years to complete its trajectory. In all, the solar system forms its own centre of gravity around the sun called the barycentre; this orbits the sun's centre generally just outside its surface.

However, every 179 years or so the circuit does a sort of planetary somersault. Instead of going around the sun, the barycentre makes a turn inside its orbit which seriously upsets magnetic forces. These in turn affect the sun's radiation output through what are known as sunspots; these are dark areas on the surface which can be seen through a dark glass with the naked eye and which vary the heat emitted over a cycle lasting on average 11.2 years. Another important rhythm is the Hale (or drought) cycle whose length is twice the average sunspot cycle. Work done by Danish researchers shows that the observed so-called global-warming patterns have a very high correlation to the *duration* of the sunspot cycle. Both the Hale and sunspot cycles are closely aligned in length to Raymond Wheeler's war cycles described in Chapter 11.

Although the sun is 93 million miles from the earth, a small change in its surface temperature can vary the heat we experience by one or two degrees Fahrenheit. This may not sound much but an average drop of one degree Fahrenheit can make it feel like living 300 miles further towards the pole in the northern hemisphere. This could make a Londoner feel he is in Edinburgh and someone in the Scottish capital experience a climate similar to the Faroes. In the past, the long-term 179-year rhythm has caused the sunspot cycle to lengthen and the sun to give out less heat than normal.

Unfortunately the same somersault that reduces the sun's rays also disturbs the earth's crust, causing earthquakes and volcanic explosions: the first can cause appalling local damage – as we have seen from Japan's Kobe earthquake – but large eruptions can be even more dangerous in the longer term. A sizeable outburst ejects millions of tons of gas and dust into the stratosphere which shields the sun's rays – so cooling the earth more effectively than a reduction in sunspots. As we shall see, the 179-year sun retrograde cycle has caused seriously disruptive periods in history through economic and political chaos; it is also quite close to the 142-year war cycle described in Chapter 11.

Volcanoes are also triggered by the alignment of the sun and moon in relation to the earth. Every 8.85 years, the three bodies are not only in line but at their closest proximity. When this happens, great masses of water build up on the earth opposite this alignment; when these fall on the sensitive geological margins bordering the Pacific, they can upset the delicate balance causing earthquakes or eruptions in what is known as the 'ring of fire'. Some two thirds of all volcanoes are around this ocean, and these have included the largest volcanic explosions on record: Tambora went off in 1815 with the force of some hundred fusion detonations; later in 1883

Krakatoa went off with slightly less force. Krakatoa is in the Sunda Strait between Sumatra and Java, and Tambora is further east on North Sumbawa, part of the same chain of islands. The eruption at Krakatoa was heard in Adelaide, South Australia. There have been several smaller eruptions in this century. Pinatubo in the Philippines blew in June 1991; others are expected. The millions of tons of dust and droplets discharged into the stratosphere remain for months or years, reducing the earth's temperature and so cutting the radiation available for growing food. When Tambora erupted the price of wheat per bushel reached $6 in June 1816 – equivalent to nearly $100 today!

Most people living in the west take it for granted that there will be enough water and sunshine to grow food and provide us with a comfortable environment. Britons or Frenchmen may complain about the Atlantic climate but there are very few years when there is not enough rainfall and sunshine to grow and ripen crops. Compare this to the farmers living in west Kansas, where barely 12 inches of rain fall in a year, or in the Volga basin, which can suffer from extremes of drought or cold which over time drastically reduce harvest yields.

These seasons of scarcity and plenty have been responsible for many of the observable cycles since at least the 6th century BC. These are known, not from direct measurement of temperature and precipitation, but from climatic records available from measuring the thickness of tree rings. The annual accretion of bark, the thickness of which varies with the moisture available, have shown how climatic cycles have worked in the past and from this can be deduced the previous amount of impact of several cycles which coincide during the 1990s.

But Mankind is also Responsible

Since at least 1792, there have been three completely man-created cycles in the capitalist west, largely caused by the rise and subsequent collapse of excessive debt. As will be explained later, these rhythms have a duration of from 45 to 60 years and apart from debt, their cause has been put down to the cycles of technical and commercial innovation which over time have led to the 'bunching' of inventions – described in Chapter 13. For example, the railway age created the demand for such developments as high-grade steel for rails, construction techniques for bridges and tunnels, and evermore powerful locomotives.

However, there are a number of short-term cycles of around ten years' duration associated with the natural rhythms of a free economy. The most consistent of these (at least since 1920) has been a 9- to 11-year cycle named after a French economist called Clement Juglar, whose work in the 1860s identified debt as the main problem responsible for the booms and busts at the end of most decades. There is also the Kitchin – or inventory cycle – described in Chapter 3.

These cycles and others described later all reach their low point in the last decade of this century, making it one of the most unusual periods for five hundred years. Remember the old Chinese curse – 'may you live in interesting times'.

The 179-Year Planetary Cycle

The sun retrograded last on 20 April 1990 which, as explained earlier, has in the past created a cooler climate accompanied by high grain prices. The more bracing weather usually creates greater personal energy (and also probably intolerance) which is why this could also be a time for the rebellions and civil wars described in Chapter 11. After the sun retrograded in 1632 there followed the Thirty Years War and also the English Civil War.

The next cycle reached a low point in 1811 which coincided with wars of liberation against Napoleon in Europe and a decade later most of Latin America declared independence from Spain. In the early 1990s there was the longest era of high sunspots since the 17th century which could rebound to an unusually cool period similar to the other 'minima' in 1632 and 1811 – both were periods of considerable turbulence. How this will affect our modern sophisticated society is a matter of acute interest, but at least we can be guided by the way people have behaved in the past.

During the 1930s and into the 1950s, two researchers, Elsworth Huntington and Raymond Wheeler, conducted a considerable amount of empirical research which is described in *Riding the Business Cycle*. It seems that when it becomes cooler we are more inclined to be restless, to seek independence; we resent those who rule us and are liable to revolt against governments. As it grows warmer and more humid, people are more cooperative, tolerant, creative and prepared to be led; unfortunately, the creativity is often turned to wars of expansion and previously benevolent rulers then become tyrants. Figure 1 shows the pattern since 1200 AD.

It was warm during the creative times of great Gothic architecture in the early 13th century and then again during the Italian Renaissance two centuries later; this itself was followed by the English Renaissance in the 16th century. The next warm period included the Industrial Revolution, which began in Britain before spreading through Europe and the USA. It was warm in the booming post-First World War decade of the 1920s, which turned to tyranny, depression and wars of aggression during the hot 1930s. It has also been unusually warm in the latter part of the 20th century.

Cool periods are also distinctive; not only do they break up the existing order but very often something happens which makes possible the advance in the next warm spell. One example was the terrible famine in northern Europe during 1317–18 followed thirty years later by the Black Death; although many died, this ended serfdom in England when the survivors demanded their independence. The next cool

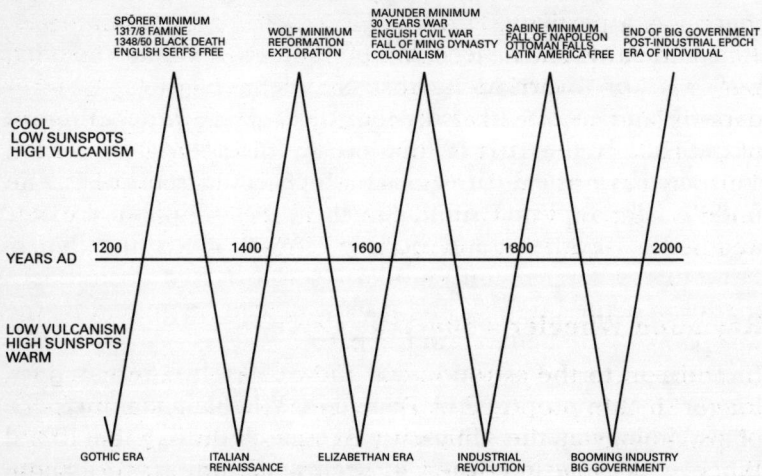

Figure 1. Historical events related to the 179-year drought and plenty cycle.

period provided the impetus for Ferdinand and Isabella of Spain to expel the Moors and to be the first, with Portugal, to seek overseas possessions; the Tudor dynasty in England, which led to the Elizabethan Renaissance, started in the same cool spell. The English Civil War and liberation of Europe from Napoleon occurred in the next cool periods which coincided with the Latin American Spanish and Brazilian colonies declaring independence early in the 19th century.

Other Weather Rhythms – The Kuznets and Hale Cycles

In addition to planetary movements around the sun, the moon makes a variable orbit of the earth which swings north and south with a periodicity of 18.6 years – the point where it exerts its maximum gravitational pull. We have already seen the powerful influence the moon has on precipitating volcanic action around the Pacific 'ring of fire'. Dr Iben Browning, who did extensive work on the relationship between tidal forces and volcanic action, calculated a 179-year cycle by combining the 18.6-year lunar cycle and the 8.85-year rhythm described earlier.

As with all disruptions of the earth's crust, the volcanic eruptions caused by the Kuznets cycle cool the climate, which in turn causes poor crops through changing weather patterns: there was a particularly dry spell in 1919, another in 1937, 1955 and 1974. The next season of poor crops was due in 1992, but this was overridden by some most unusual weather patterns and is quite likely to coincide with the next low point of the Hale cycle – part of the sunspot cycle described earlier. This rhythm was held responsible for the Dust Bowl in the middle west of the United States in 1930–1, and the dry weather in 1952, 1974 and again in 1995–6.

Raymond Wheeler's 500-Year Cycle

In addition to the astronomical 179-year cycle, there is a yet longer rhythm proposed by Dr Raymond Wheeler, a professor of psychology at the University of Kansas during the 1930s. Wheeler became interested in the impact of climate on the affairs of mankind and with a team of researchers collected many thousands of weather-related historical facts. His work was enormously helped by Charles Douglas whose research into relating climate to tree rings was closely correlated with historical data extending to before 1500 years BC.

Wheeler also believed there was evidence of a geographical switch of power every 500 years whereby the dominant civilisation changed the world's culture between the east and west. Although the evidence is not well defined there could be such a shift and there is certainly no doubt about western domination from around 1500 AD onwards. This is a precis of Wheeler's work:

500 BC to AD: This 500 years belonged to the west. By 300 BC the glory of classical Greece had declined with the disintegration of Alexander's empire, but a new force was rising. Rome dominated the Mediterranean at the time of Christ's birth and then went on to govern much of Europe with the most sustainable legal, military and administrative system the world had ever seen. Meanwhile in China, the Han Dynasty replaced the Ch'ing Empire which had flourished after the 'warring states' had fragmented the country.

AD to 500 AD: Wheeler claimed that the east dominated this period but the honours are probably even. Rome reached its zenith before it too became lost in bureaucracy and was sacked in 410 by the Visigoths. China prospered under the Han Dynasty but this was replaced by the Hsiung-nu; this warlike tribe from the north came from the same group of peoples as the Huns who triggered the devastation of Europe and the fall of the Roman Empire.

500 AD to 1000: Again the balance was probably equal if the Middle East is taken into account. While Europe was in the Dark Ages, the Muslim armies drove west into Spain to create the most dazzling court west of Constantinople at Cordoba, housing half a million Muslims, Christians and Jews. In the Middle East, on the Tigris, Baghdad, Caliph Harun al-Rashid's capital city, was probably the greatest city in the world. In China the T'ang Dynasty spread aggressively westwards to be beaten by Muslim warriors at the battle of the Salas River. But despite this setback, the T'ang built a modern city at Ch'ang-an laid out on a grid and housing two million people.

1000 AD to 1500: The period started with a split between the Rome and Byzantine churches, a divide that gave new vigour to the Orthodox faith. It was to be an unhappy time for the west with periods of prosperity sandwiched between the Mongol invasions, the Black Death, and the Hundred Years War between Britain and France – many believing in the passing of the Four Horsemen of the Apocalypse: famine, war, plague and death. China suffered even more from the Mongols than Europe did but eventually the Ming Dynasty was founded which started to repair the Mongol vandalism.

1500 AD to 2000: The west dominated this 500 years with voyages of exploration, conquest, acquisition, plunder and colonisation. The year 1500 also saw the beginning of a technological revolution that was the hallmark of modern states. Western domination was encouraged by Spain and Portugal who started exploration, followed by the Dutch, French and the English. In a succession of wars fought on sea and land, Europe and later America created empires throughout the world.

Identifying the Long Wave

As suggested earlier, there seems to be strong evidence of a 45 to 60-year economic and political cycle. This has been particularly evident in America, which has tracked the booms and busts of economic and political life at least since the early 1790s – but the rhythm probably goes back much further. Some statisticians are dubious about the way Kondratieff himself analysed his material but others have explained the waves as driven by innovation, investment or climatic change. The peaks and troughs of the cycle also have an association with international or civil conflicts.

There has been high volcanic action at each of the low points in the *long wave*, creating particularly dry growing conditions which may be either warm or cool: it was cool during the depressions of the 1790s and the 1840s, but the climate was becoming warmer for the economic downturns of the 1890s and 1930s. Coupled with the 179-year cycle considered earlier, the latter part of the 1990s could once again be cool and with the consequences for people's behaviour described earlier.

The Kondratieff long wave is named after its originator, a Russian economist working at the Agricultural Academy in Moscow during the 1920s. Using interest rates, commodity and finished goods prices from Britain, the USA and France, he deduced a long wave of between 45 and 60 years. This he divided between three phases: the upwave, a time of expansion out of a deep recession; an in-between period called the plateau stage; and a downwave – a return to recession. Having correctly forecast the 1930s Depression he then predicted a recovery which was quite contrary to communist dogma and he died alone in Siberia. These are the phases in more detail.

The upwave: Each cycle begins with a recovery from the previous recession which accelerates to a euphoric climax before ending with an inflationary blow-off as the pent up pressures of the boom boil over with high interest rates and commodity prices. The recovery is not smooth because it is itself modulated by the 4-year business cycle described in Chapter 3 and the Juglar Cycle described later. The upwave varies with the cycle: the first, which started in the 1790s, was generated by the Napoleonic Wars and land speculation in the USA after the Louisiana Purchase in 1803. The second cycle which began around 1850 developed around the gold rush of 1857 and the third from the rapid industrialisation of America early in the 20th century.

Each upwave so far has ended in conflict: the first was the War of 1812 and the end of the Napoleonic supremacy, the second was the American Civil War in 1861 and the third was the First World War. It is likely that the Vietnam War was at least partly responsible for the build up of debt that exaggerated the panic of 1974 and the subsequent recession. Doubters might argue that wars are inflationary anyway but the timing could be governed by the Kuznets cycle described later.

Also associated with the ending of the upwave is the decoupling of a major currency from the gold standard. Britain went off the gold standard during the Napoleonic Wars, returning to it in the 1820s. America did the same during the Civil War when 'greenbacks' were issued unbacked by gold. Britain came off the gold standard again in 1913 and returned twelve years later at an unrealistic valuation only to be forced off once again in 1931. Although Roosevelt devalued the dollar against gold by 70% in 1934, it was not finally decoupled until 15 August 1971. Will history be repeated by the return of the gold standard in the late 1990s?

The crisis that marks the end of the upwave begins the *plateau phase* – a period that appears to be a continuation of the expansion but, in fact, creates the conditions for the eventual crash and deep recession. As suggested earlier, the plateau is often triggered either by a war or a rapid rise in commodities associated with one of the shorter cycles, followed by a brief deep recession – the ending of which marks the start of the next boom. The latter part of the plateau is the most dangerous stage of the whole cycle for it attracts all the speculators who are finally convinced that the boom will go on for ever, as in the late 1920s and 1980s.

The final speculation varies with each cycle. Farmland in America and railways in Britain were the targets in the first Kondratieff wave. The next wave was the railway boom in the United States opening up the west. The speculation in the late 1920s had mainly switched to the stock market but land was changing hands in Florida like shares on a bourse. The last plateau probably ended in 1989 when again there was frenzied leveraged buying of land and real estate which caused billions to be wiped off the balance sheets of banks and institutions. One can tell when the plateau has ended for there is usually a chorus from economists declaring the business cycle dead. This they did at the end of the 1920s and 1980s and were rewarded by a deflationary spiral and a downwave recession.

Each *downwave* from the 1830s onwards conforms to a pattern of collapsing credit, falling prices and steeply declining business activity. This continues in fits and starts until all the excess and bad loans are finally wrung out of the system just as they were in the 1840s, the 1890s and 1930s. The question is will it happen in the 1990s? Or have our clever politicians and central bankers finally ended the rhythm that has cleansed the financial system every fifty years or so since biblical times?

There have been three complete Kondratieff cycles since the 1790s. The first, called K1, started around 1792 and ended fifty-six years later in 1848. The next, K2, was shorter, reaching a peak in around 1860 then falling to a low point in 1896. K3, the last complete cycle, reached the plateau around 1919 and began its downwave in 1930, reaching the low point in 1941.

The latest cycle, K4, probably reached the end of the upwave in the early 1970s and started the downwave in 1990. We shall see; but by 1996, the total debt to gross domestic product (GDP) ratio in the United States is level with the peak it reached in 1931, probably confirming the 1990 timing.

During the *upwave* demand exceeds supply hence, to be successful, big organisations may be appropriate for attracting the appropriate human, financial and capital assets. The upwave also benefits disciplined economies such as those of Germany and Japan while the more individualistic nations such as America and Britain do less well. It may be also appropriate for banks and other institutions to have cross-linking shareholdings to cement successful relationships.

Everything changes in the *downwave* for the large high-cost organisations and big governments now lack the flexibility to react swiftly to different conditions. The changes undermine the institutions in the disciplined countries, which now start to lose confidence. Up to the 1970s Germany attracted investment capital from all over the world but in the late 1980s the high fixed costs of labour were forcing many German companies to set up plants in low-cost areas. This caused unemployment and additional demands on already stretched welfare and social security programmes.

Politicians react to the downwave by lowering interest rates in an attempt to re-start economies locked in recession. But what worked during the upwave is no longer successful as the Japanese discovered. The most successful policy in a credit cycle would be for politicians to lead and promote debt-for-equity conversion programmes; they could also encourage the break-up of large ailing corporations to increase flexibility engendered by having more individual managers owning their own businesses. The years into the next century will favour the more individualistic countries.

The Setting for the K4 Downwave

But the United States is not the most highly indebted nation in the developed world. Now Canada, Italy, Sweden and Belgium have government debt to GDP ratios in excess of 90% and the proportion of governments unable to balance their budgets is growing. The position is made more dangerous because, in an effort to reduce interest charges, central banks have reduced the maturity of their debt so that now the USA and Canada have to reissue nearly 40% of their debt every year; the maturity in Sweden and Italy forces their central banks to reissue their debt every twelve months.

While private debt was the major problem in the late 1920s it is still a difficulty now, particularly in the Anglo-Saxon nations who have increased their borrowing to make up an income shortfall during the early 1990s recession; in Britain the problem is compounded by the decline in house prices leaving numbers of mortgagors with negative equity. The private debt levels make it less easy to control economies through varying interest rates, so obliging the US central bank in particular effectively to 'print money' by buying government securities with newly-created cash.

Although the present position is much more sophisticated and complex than at the beginning of other downwaves, it is essentially the same as the previous crises when speculation either in farms, railways or the stock market (in the late 1920s) led to subsequent crashes. There followed widespread failures of private debt that built up during the final stages of the *plateau phase* described earlier. This time governments and private debtors could both default – destroying the savings of millions.

Apart from indebtedness there is the potential hazard of breaking down what are known as the derivative markets. As their name implies these are based on currency, the stock, bond and commodity markets but are traded separately. Derivatives are instruments – such as the forward markets, futures, options and swaps – which help those managing industry, investments and commerce to hedge an existing position or to trade against sudden reverses.

What were prudent measures to protect hedge positions in foreign exchange, commodities, the stock or interest markets became instruments of speculation. Lending is barely profitable during a recession so traders, such as Nick Leeson of Barings, were making a good proportion of their banks' profits. Apart from Barings, speculators are known to have lost nearly $75 billion from derivative trading, including Orange County in California ($1.7 billion), Metallgesellschaft ($4 billion) and Kidder Peabody ($3 billion).

By 1996 the situation is still dangerous, with several banks and institutions having an exposure worth many times their capital. Unfortunately, the potential liabilities are off the balance sheet, implying that third parties have little or no knowledge of the risks in lending to any one institution. The threat is also widespread with 40% of state governments, public retirement and private pension funds all using some form of derivatives. Over 40% of all trading is between dealers, considerably increasing the danger of a domino effect if a major player fails.

The losses in 1994–5 are but a foretaste of what could occur if central banks were forced to raise their interest rates sharply. If there were large reversals in the major stock markets then the losses in the derivative markets could be catastrophic for the world's economies. The total size of this market is estimated at over $45 trillion – some twice the size of the world's GDP.

As the decade continues, rising government debt and budget deficits have increased the market's reluctance to hold the national debt of countries like Sweden, Italy and Canada – quite apart from many developing countries. By 1996 we are now in a 'credit vortex' where any failures, public or private, make investors increasingly reluctant to hold bonds. A crisis could be triggered from several directions: a lack of confidence could cause serious falls in bond or derivative markets – as could a weather-related rise in commodity prices. At present most governments are working on the assumption that cycles no longer apply to them – a sentiment which could change rapidly once their ability to run a welfare state is seriously undermined.

Princeton Economics Approach to Cycles

Martin Armstrong, the chairman of Princeton Economics, has derived an empirical model which works directly on the cyclical patterns derived from the major panics between 1683 and 1907. There were twenty-six financial crises between these dates which work out to an average duration of 8.6 years – however, each crisis was not of equal magnitude and the turning points did not always coincide with other events such as wars. By making up a series of six 8.6-year cycles, Armstrong asserts there is an overall 51.6-year rhythm which can be traced back at least as far as 1854. As one major cycle ends and before the next series begins, there are five further panics each reaching a higher peak than the one before.

Starting in June 1854, the first six-series peak was the panic of 1878, which marked the beginning of the downwave of the second Kondratieff cycle. The next series peaked in October 1929 coinciding with the Great Crash and the beginning of the next downwave. After a low point in 1934, which Armstrong marks as the bottom of the 1930s Depression, the next series of six ended in April 1981 which was the point of maximum bond yield during the crisis of the early 1980s. The present series started in July of 1985, to reach the first peak in December of 1989. The next low point was in May 1996, heading for an expected crisis in late June 1998; this should end in the autumn of the year 2002. Intriguingly, Princeton Economics have labelled each successive period of 51.6 years as alternating between the influence of either the public or private sector. In Princeton's first cycle starting in 1854, investors had confidence in the government and were prepared to buy bonds. This switched to domination by the private sector until the crash of 1929 when confidence in the elected rulers once more dominated until the panic of 1981. Starting in January 1985, confidence has once again switched to the private sector which, in an era of rising debt, could provide a bleak future for most bond markets.

The Juglar Cycle

This shorter man-made cycle was mentioned earlier as a by-product of capitalism; every ten years or so there is a build up of debt that needs the regular purge of a financial crisis with collapsing bond prices and rising interest rates. There was alarm in 1920, and much greater chaos in 1930–1; war conditions controlled any panic in 1940 and 1950 but it started again in 1960 through to 1980 with interest rates rising progressively with each crisis. Curiously the huge build up of debt in many western nations did not create a panic in 1990, but as suggested earlier the crisis has almost certainly not been purged, only delayed.

There Could be Evidence for a Religious Cycle

The 500-year cycle mentioned earlier could also track momentous philosophical or religious events. Confucius and Buddha were born in the 6th century BC and Jesus Christ 500 years later. The next 1000 years are less clear. After Christ the most important events were the birth of Mohammed in 570 and the first jihad (or holy war) in 632 after his death.

The 500-year rhythm is clearer from 1000 AD to the present. Byzantium split from the Roman church in 1054 and the eastern empire collapsed nearly 400 years later when the Ottoman Turks captured Constantinople. Christendom was again split in 1517 when Luther nailed his ninety-five theses to the Castle church door at Wittenberg. It is likely that much of the vigour shown by the Dutch, British and Americans was generated from the increased individualism released when Protestant countries split from Rome.

Apart from momentous events every half-millennium it is also possible to discern a 700-year cycle starting from the birth of Christ. The Muslim faith was formed in the 7th century when Mohammed fled from Mecca to Medina (known as the Hegira). Subsequently the first jihad spread an Islamic crescent around the Mediterranean from Spain to Turkey. During the second jihad in the 14th century the Ottoman Turks conquered Anatolia, Constantinople, the Balkans, and then around the Black Sea including the Caucasian Chechnya enclave. Now in the 1990s with rising religious fervour, such as in evangelical Christianity and fundamentalist Islam, we could be at the foothills of another religious upheaval.

The Possibility of a 100-Year Weather and Nation Cycle

Professor Wheeler and a more recent researcher called George Modelski came independently to the conclusion that a 100-year cycle could be identified going back at least to before 1500 AD. Like many regular cycles it might be easier to identify trends in retrospect than to forecast the future, as there are some difficulties in deciding when Wheeler's warm and cool periods began or ended.

Wheeler postulated that over a hundred years the climate moves through four phases: the first is dry and cool which stimulates individual effort. This gives way to a warm/wet period of prosperity and benign government. Unfortunately it then becomes hot and dry when the affairs of state are taken over by despots and dictators, but they too are overthrown as it becomes cool and wet at the end of the cycle. Modelski's model follows a similar 100-year rhythm with one nation becoming dominant, then having to fight a major war before a period of peace.

Modelski describes his research into the rise and decline of national supremacy. Since around 1500 only four nations, out of the near dozen empires that waxed and waned, ever reached his criteria of durable states which flourished for one hundred years or more. The qualities exhibited by these nations are important because they provide a clue to how any new power might emerge in the 21st century. These ideas are explained in more detail in *Riding the Business Cycle*.

There are several reasons why Modelski believes that some states become dominant while others, like a shooting star, have only a short reign of brilliance. First, they should be difficult to invade – a factor which rules out most continental countries. Second, they should achieve a form of democracy that unites the will of the people. Next, the country should have the economic ability to sustain and win a war through what Modelski calls a 'global reach' – the ability to impose their will overseas. There have been four such nations: the Portuguese, Dutch, British and Americans.

Modelski also surmised that the possible decline of the United States as a world power into the next century may imply not the rise of a dominant *nation* but of an idea. For example, the Muslim empire was created, not by revolting against a power force, but by peoples touched by the word of Allah; other credos such as Confucianism or Christianity could also become paramount.

Achieving independence is the spur that fired many national ambitions. It was the impetus that gave Spain the vigour to defeat the Moors, the Portuguese and Dutch when breaking free from Spain, and the thirteen colonies of the newly formed United States in separating from Britain. Unification is another incentive. Germany achieved its greatest strength and became a threat to its neighbours when Bismarck created the First Reich. There have been times when China has blossomed under a benign leadership, allowing the natural strength of its peoples to develop. However, unity is not the sole criterion as Russians found under the Tsar or the Soviets; there has to be a genuine freedom of expression and individual independence before the whole becomes greater than the sum of the parts.

A new regime created France's domination and expansion under Louis XIV, and the Tudors provided new impetus for England. In Japan the Meiji took control after the humiliation of the Shogunate when the country was unable to resist Admiral Perry's demands in 1853.

Religion motivated the Ottoman Empire, possibly the most remarkable of all those of the last thousand years. Inspired by the Koran, the Seljuk Turks gained control of the Caliphate in the 11th century, then (as described earlier) they absorbed the Ottomans, overran Anatolia, crossed the Dardanelles and captured Constantinople. They went on to control the Balkans, Hungary, southern Russia around the Black Sea then east to the Caspian and along the old Byzantine territory in north Africa. Although totally undemocratic, the Caliphate rule allowed considerable local autonomy for further conquest or fighting invaders; the local Sultans could do almost what they liked, provided taxes were collected and remitted to the centre.

The forces of decline: Some countries have worn themselves out either through war or internal decline. The Portuguese suffered from an ill-fated foreign venture in Morocco and the Spanish took over their throne. The great empire of Louis XIV became enfeebled after supporting the American colonists against the British and then fell to the Revolution. Britain never really recovered from the First World War, and although it was significant in winning the Second World War the country was more content to accept the easy life than to revive itself – the losers, Germany and Japan, did the opposite.

Another cause of decline seems to be the distance of government, and the domination by bureaucrats, which inevitably leads to corruption. Roman rule became remote and corrupt, the people becoming soft through imperial handouts; China has suffered the same fate several times and perhaps this too will be the downfall of the European Union and even the United States.

Could we be Due for Another 'March of the Barbarians'?

One must pray not, but the researcher Dr Iben Browning, in his book *Climate and the Affairs of Man*, has identified an 800-

year climatic cycle based on tree rings and historical analysis. This tallies with the major migrations in history when it became impossible for nomadic people to stay in their homeland. The Hun invasion of Europe and China in the 5th century AD was part of this pattern as was the Mongol attack 800 years later.

Around 2000 BC the Indo-European people dwelling in southern Russia poured through the Caucasus; joined by the Hittites, they spread west to Greece and southern Italy, then east to Turkey and Persia where they became the ancestors of the Medes and Persians. The same peoples known as the Shang or Yin spread through China. It is thought that the Hyksos people who occupied Egypt for several hundred years from 1750 BC were from the same Semitic stock.

There was another mass movement from the Caucasus in the 12th century BC when men, women and children left their homeland and came south for food. Those living in the Levant or Egypt called them 'People of the Sea' because, although land based, they launched themselves over the seas to settle islands like Cyprus and Crete. These people also infiltrated latter-day Palestine where they became the Philistines; when they arrived in Egypt they were stopped by the armies of Rameses III. Other people moved as well; the Etruscans went into Italy, the Celts invaded England around 1195 BC and Moses led the Jews across the Red Sea in their flight from Egypt.

Eight hundred years later the Hallstatt culture which had become settled in eastern Europe was pushed west and south by steppe nomads, mounted warriors from north and east of the Danube. The Hallstatt, known as 'La Tene', went to the Ukraine, south to Turkey and south-west to Spain.

And now? If we are entering a particularly cool period, it could become impossible for the tough Turkic tribes to continue living in their traditional homeland of Central Asia and Mongolia and once again move both south and west. As in the past, the hungry people from central Russia could push westwards into western Russia, the Ukraine and eastern Europe. But it would not be a migration of mounted warriors as in the past. This time it could be the migration of over 65 million despairing people (after their displacement by Stalin in the 1930s) seeking to return either to their homeland or to find refuge and food in the west. Their numbers would swamp the states of central Europe, requiring the world to mount a relief operation on a scale never before attempted.

What Conclusions can be Drawn From These Cycles?

By 1996 it is becoming clear that the build up of debt in the plateau phase of the latest Kondratieff cycle is already hitting Japan and causing difficulties in other countries such as Canada, Sweden, Germany, France, Belgium and Italy. It is doubtful whether the politicians and central bankers can avoid a deep recession to purge bad debts from this system. On top of a debt deflation there are indications that the drier conditions expected from the sun's retrogration on 20 April 1990 are already present with the low crop yields and poor carry-over stocks. In the early 1990s there were the highest sunspots since the 17th century, followed by a steep decline, due to reach a low point in 1995–6. A series of low sunspots would confirm this cycle.

A climatic change would also be confirmed by rising volcanic and earthquake activity: there have been several eruptions such as Pinatubo in 1991 and Kliuschevsky in 1994, but not as yet an explosion on the scale of Tambora or Krakatoa. There have, however, been several earthquakes notably around Japan including the highly destructive one at Kobe.

By 1996 there were signs of unusual weather all over the world, in the trail of the longest series of *el Niños* on record; these are distortions in the ocean currents that have created excellent weather conditions in India and South America but almost desert conditions in Australia and southern Africa. There is also evidence of a North Atlantic Oscillation (NAO) which has for a while moved the westerly winds upwards over the Atlantic to give northern Europe unusually warm and wet conditions. By 1996 the NAO has now become negative, bringing rain to the parched conditions in Spain and the Mediterranean and cooler drier weather to northern Europe.

The Hale cycle mentioned earlier is also likely to create poor growing conditions similar to 1972–4, but could last much longer. Then, the grain prices were the first to rise, next the precious metals and shortly after that, oil. These were represented by the commodity index published by the Commodity Research Bureau (CRB) which recorded a rise of more than double from around 100 in 1970 to a peak of 230 in

1972. A repeat of the early to mid 1970s in the mid to late 1990s would see the price of a number of commodities rising rapidly: gold and precious metals could soar from currency instability and from the unsettled state of the world's economies. Others like coffee could rise from unusual frost conditions in Brazil and in west Africa. If the weather in North America, Russia and northern China became unusually dry the price rises could be relatively much greater than during the 1970s because of the low carry-over stocks mentioned earlier. These factors plus the possibility of a national default (outlined in more detail in the chapter on political cycles) would have a devastating impact on today's highly leveraged economies. How this affects heavily indebted nations will be covered in Chapter 9 dealing with investment cycles.

The good news: If the cycles follow previous patterns we could witness massive changes. Earlier half-millennia have seen the decline of institutions that are no longer relevant and the creation of new systems better suited to the people they aim to serve. By 1996 there is a growing awareness that governments can no longer support the Welfare State and, however reluctantly, many are being forced to seek their own solution. Matters will be brought to a head during the likely financial crisis; people will be forced to find their own solutions within family units and communities – just as they did before the Industrial Revolution forced the majority of people to become employees. Perhaps a crash is a price worth paying for the opportunity for individuals to return to principles of self-sufficiency, a basic faith and manners?

This short introduction to cycles should do two things: first it should encourage the reader to understand in a little more detail the forces likely to impinge on their business, investment and personal affairs. Secondly, it should stimulate an interest in an entirely new set of phenomena.

CHAPTER 3

FINESSING THE LONG WAVE WITH THE BUSINESS CYCLE

Late in the 1980s economists were declaring the business cycle dead – just when it was turning down. The noted economist Irving Fisher recommended buying in the stock market just before the crash of October 1929; he took his own advice and lost everything but then had the contrition to explain why he had been mistaken. These advisers should have known better because the business cycle was first measured in 1912 in New York after a report that a mathematician, working for the House of Rothschild, had devised a programme for plotting the movement of British consolidated stock. The New York group commissioning the study found the cyclical analysis worked well during the First World War; then later a Harvard professor called W. L. Crum discovered a cycle in commercial paper rates. At about the same time Joseph Kitchin, another Harvard professor, reported six other American and British series in commodity prices and interest rates. In 1939, Joseph Schumpeter gave Kitchin's name to what became known as the 40-month inventory cycle in his classic book, *Business Cycles*.

Although the study of cycles has been well developed they have proved less than reliable as a forecasting tool if used incorrectly. For example, many first heard about cycles from reading Robert Beckman's *Downwave*. This well-researched and illustrated book correctly defined the length of the *average* Kondratieff long wave cycle as 54 years but did not mention that this could vary between 45 to 60 years. Those unfortunately taking Beckman's advice would have sold their house and equity portfolio just when the boom started in 1984.

While there is powerful evidence for the existence of booms and busts in the Kondratieff long wave, it is actually quite difficult to judge the precise turning points, for each cycle is slightly different. This deficiency is remedied by the shorter business cycle described in this chapter which finesses the long wave. The Juglar cycle has also worked well since at least 1920 (with the exception of the war years) but this too could have been incorporated in other rhythms. Are there then other ways of accurately identifying periodical turns in time for these to be a helpful management tool? The American Institute for Economic Research (AIER) bulletin called 'Forecasting Business Trends' identifies three:

Informal GNP model: This is the name given to an unstructured technique developed by a renowned American statistician called Lawrence Klein. Using a highly tuned judgment, he was able to achieve quite accurate forecasts but unfortunately was unable to pass on his method in a form that could be consistent. Others such as Iben Browning, whose work is described in Chapter 2, had the same flair with climatology.

Econometric models: These are highly sophisticated computer-based programs employing hundreds of mathematical equations which attempt to model the major aspects of an economy. The data has been chosen to have a statistical correlation with historical patterns and the machine is entered with such variables as government spending, tax rates, interest rates, money supply, foreign trade etc. – the computer does the rest. For all its sophistication the method has not been reliable for forecasting the turning points in an economy – perhaps because the data entered into equations has been too highly smoothed.

Statistical indicators: These rely on the observation that data series such as commodities, interest rates and stock prices repeat themselves over time with a degree of regularity and in roughly the same order. Although Kondratieff and Juglar used a series going back to the 1790s, the AIER has some data going back to 1854 with additional information since the First World War. With this they have worked out thirty-two cycles until February 1994 with an average duration of four years and three months. The advantage claimed for the statistical method is that it relies on practical business data, such as millions of stock-market transactions a day, housing permits or money supply, for signalling the turning points of the economy.

The first statistical indicators were created by a Harvard group under Warren Persons who generated three curves representing distinct sectors of the economy. The first curve A measured stock prices, the second B tracked the number of cheques drawn (representing business activity) and the third measured short-term interest rates. Persons' work was continued by the National Bureau of Economic Research (NBER) and by the late 1930s twenty-one indicators had been selected from seventy-one which had been 'tolerably consistent in their timing'. They were used to signal the upturn in the American economy beginning in June 1938.

The twenty-one indicators divided into three series: fourteen led expansions or contractions by between one and six months, three were coincident with business activity and four lagged as shown in Figure 2. Although represented here as a sine wave, the actual series described later in the chapter are anything but regular and need careful interpretation. For example, there have been occasions when the turning of the

Movement of Business-Cycle Indicators

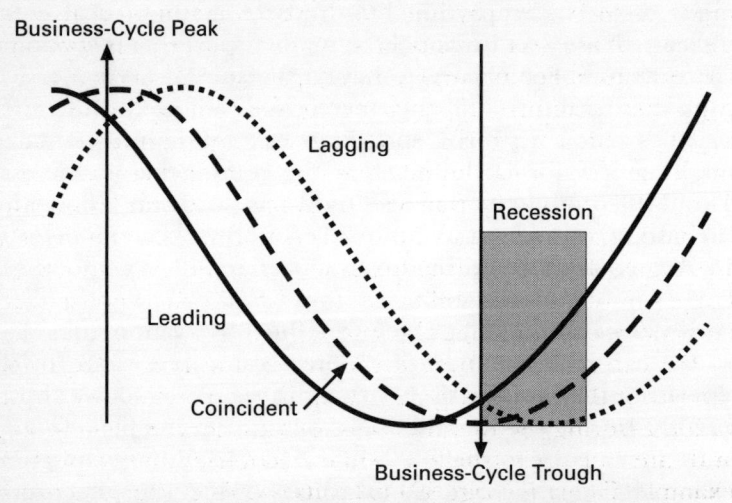

Figure 2. Cyclical indicators associated with the business cycle, showing the leading, coincident and lagging indicators. (From the American Institute for Economic Research,'Forecasting Business Trends'.)

leading indicator did not represent a change in trend and the wily interpreter would be prudent to wait until the coincident or lagging indicator itself gave the signal.

For business and investment purposes we must first track the Kondratieff long wave which determines overall business strategy. Within this, decisions can then be refined to take into account the shorter-term Kitchin cycle with its irregular duration of from 28 months in the early 1920s to 117 months in the late 1960s. However, some patterns emerge when judged against the 45 to 60-year Kondratieff cycle.

The Kitchin wave appears to have shorter cycles during the Kondratieff upwave than during the downwave. For example the recovery from 1896 until the plateau phase began in 1918 had five cycles with an average duration of 41 months; the recovery from 1940 to 1972 had an average length of 45 months. The plateau phases seem to have a consistently longer average duration of 82 months although there may be a distortion as they all coincided with major wars. The downwaves are also interesting. There were at least two long rhythms of 99 and 74 months in Kondratieff 2 (K2), a 64- and 63-month cycle in K3 and up to now, K4 has had three rhythms of over 55 months.

The cycles appear consistently repetitive unless an external input disturbs the rhythm. We have already noted that the plateau phase was unusually long due to war but there are other factors. For example, a major financial shock could be caused by a country defaulting on their debt, as did Germany in 1931 which triggered a cascade of bank failures; another might be a major earthquake around a major financial centre. The AIER point out that the unprecedented inflation after Richard Nixon removed America from the gold standard on 15 August 1971 has already made some indicators obsolete. For example, the stability of the US dollar against other currencies can no longer be guaranteed.

We can now fine tune the point in the long wave by the severity of the business cycle, taking into account earlier observations. During the upwave recessions are shorter than average and are relatively shallow while recoveries are rapid. For example, Figure 5 (page 39) exhibits two short sharp recessions but almost immediate recoveries. As noted earlier the plateau consists of two parts: a sharper recession than normal after a financial crisis then a steep and sustained recovery; a typical long plateau phase is shown in Figure 5. Conversely, the downwave recessions are more severe than those in the upwave and the recoveries more shallow. For example, the 1991 recession was much deeper and widespread than those during the 1960s: the recovery that started in 1992–3 was more shallow for countries with stubbornly high unemployment and a rising level of failures. If indeed the downwave started in 1990, the next downturn, signalled by the leading indicator in Figure 5 in 1994, could prove every bit as deep as during the early 1930s.

In the early 1990s the US Bureau for Economic Analysis (BEA) in the Department of Commerce had identified ninety-five criteria for creating leading, coincident and lagging indicators. They have been chosen because they are significant, the data flows in a consistent pattern and can be assembled into a series. Finally there are no significant time delays before being reported; this rules out company profits, which are reported two months after the quarter ends. It is also recognised that the majority of the indicators relate to the manufacturing sector (employing around 20% of the workforce) which in most advanced economies has been declining relative to the service sector which now accounts for the majority of employed persons.

To compile their own series the AIER have selected twenty-four economic items comprising twelve leading measures which precede events; there are six coincident indicators which run parallel with events and then six lagging items. In their pamphlet 'Forecasting Business Trends' the AIER publish a table showing how each indicator either leads, is coincident with or lags events:

> The *leading indicators* give on average seventeen months lead before a peak in the business cycle and four months before a trough.
> The average of the *rough coincident indicator* gives two months warning to the peak and only five days warning before a trough.
> The *lagging indicators* turn down just over two months from the peak and seven months from the trough.

The data used by the AIER is sourced from the monthly *Survey of Current Business* published by the US Department of Commerce, which provides time series on over 250 statistical indicators; some of these items are published during the month and have a considerable influence on the stock and bond markets. Once entered into the computer, the data is processed in several steps. First, *moving averages* are calculated using differing time scales of one to six months, depending upon whether the cyclical movements can be discerned through the irregular fluctuations. At most, a change of trend will be evident after three months. For example, money supply measures such as M1 and M2 are averaged per month while sensitive raw materials are averaged over six months. Next, the *change of direction* for each indicator is checked to determine whether a change of trend is likely, then the proportion in each leading, coincident or lagging group is noted. The *leading, coincident or lagging* groups together are then plotted to check whether a change in direction has occurred.

There are known relationships between, for example, commodity prices and bond yields which in turn affect interest rates and economic activity. If, through one of the drought cycles described in Chapter 2, a poor crop forced the cost of grains to rise, then this would be reflected by a fall in the bond market because inflation is likely to go up. Wars or international incidents have a similar impact on gold, silver and other commodity prices because of potential instability and shortages which again will impact on the economy. More can be read about these relationships in a paper entitled 'The 40-month Cycle Synchrony' by Richard Mogey in the *Cycles* magazine of March–April 1994.

These interlinking factors are evident in the three groups of indicators used by the AIER which have been carefully chosen for their reliability and their stability within their section. They comprise the following items:

Leading indicators include such series as the M1 and M2 money supplies which are an estimate of the cash balances at commercial banks, plus small denomination time deposits and interest-bearing cash held by brokers or dealers. The list also includes the changes in the price of sensitive basic materials, the value of new orders for consumer goods and the value of new contracts and building plant issued. The leading indicators also include the issued permits for new private housing. Other leading indicators include a rise or fall in manufacturing output in relation to inventories carried, and the increase or decrease in the speed of deliveries from manufacturers. The millions of transactions in common stocks as measured by the Standard & Poor's 500 shares is another leading indicator, as is the rise or fall of instalment credit measured as a percentage change from three months earlier. The list ends with the hours of production worked together with the initial claims for unemployment benefits.

> *Of these probably M2 money supply figures are the most sensitive, giving warning two or three months before troughs and four months before peaks. Expressed in another way, when the M2 and then M1 series dropped 1% they proved 100% accurate in forecasting either a trough or a peak.*

The AIER identify six *coincident indicators* which track the current cycle. They include the number of employees on non-agricultural payrolls, the index of industrial production (which is a measure of the physical volume of goods produced by the manufacturing and mining sectors plus power generation) and the personal income of manufacturing industries. Other coincident measures are the total sales of the manufacturing, distribution and retail sectors of the economy, the gross national product and a ratio of those employed to the working population.

> *Of the six indicators, a rise or fall in non-agricultural employment gives on average three or four months' warning before a cyclical turn. When either this or the GNP statistic fell 1%, it was 100% accurate in forecasting the change in trend.*

The *lagging indicators* used by AIER incorporate the average length of the working week, the size of total inventories of the manufacturing, distributive and retail sectors, and values of outstanding commercial and industrial loans. Other factors are the ratio of consumer instalment debt to personal income, the percentage change in manufacturing labour cost per unit of output and an amalgam of the rates on thirty and ninety commercial paper and prime banker acceptance yields.

> *The most sensitive lagging indicator before the troughs and peaks is the level of trade inventories. This plus the instalment credit ratio were accurate in recording the trend changes when they moved 3%.*

THROUGH THE WHIRLWIND

ECONOMIC INDICATORS

		1996 Jan	Feb	Mar	Apr	May	Jun	Cyclic Outlook
PRIMARY LEADING INDICATORS	Money Supply, M1*	−	−	+	−	−	−	↓
	Money Supply, M2*	+	+	+	−	−	+	↑
	Municipal Bonds, Bond Buyer 20 Bonds^	+	+	−	−	−	−	↓
	Corporate Bonds, Moody's AAA^	+	−	−	−	−	−	↓
	FHA Mortgage Applications (annual rate)*	+	+	−	+	+	+	↑
	Housing Permits, Total (annual rate)*	−	+	+	+	−	−	↑
	Housing Starts, Private (annual rate, thous.)*	+	+	−	+	−	−	↓
	Sensitive Materials (rate of change)	−	+	+	+	+	+	↑
	S&P 500 Index (1941–43 = 10)	−	+	−	+	+	+	↑
	Vendor Performance^	−	+	−	−	+	+	↑
	Business Failures, Liabilities (total)^	−	+	+	−	+	−	↓
	Average Hours Worked, Private, Non-farm*	−	+	+	−	−	+	↓
	Private Residential (bil $, annual rate)*	−	−	+	+	−	−	↓
	New Construction (bil $, annual rate)*	+	−	+	+	−	+	↑
	Mobile Home Shipments (annual rate, thous.)	+	−	+	+	−	+	↑
	Demand Deposits (total)	+	+	+	−	+	+	↑
	Time Deposits, Large and Small*	−	+	+	+	+	+	↑
	Construction Contracts, Plant and Equipment	+	+	+	+	+	+	↑
	Consumer Confidence, N.I.C.B.	−	+	+	+	−	−	↓
	Consumer Goods, New Orders (total)*	+	−	−	+	+	−	↓
	Durable Goods, Unfilled Orders (total)*	+	+	+	−	+	+	↑
	Unemployment, Initial Claims^	−	−	−	+	+	−	↑
	Consumer Debt, Change in	−	−	−	−	−	−	↓
	Total Rising (+)/Falling (−)	1	7	5	3	−1	1	13
	Percent Rising/Falling (smoothed) %	57%	59%	58%	59%	57%	56%	57%
PRIMARY COINCIDENT INDICATORS	Personal Income, Manufacturing (annual rate)*	−	+	−	+	+	+	↓
	Velocity of Money, Ratio (personal income/M2)	+	+	−	+	+	+	↑
	Manufacturing and Trade Sales (total)*	−	+	+	+	+	−	↑
	Employees, Non-farm Payrolls (mil)*	−	+	+	+	+	+	↑
	Cotton Consumption (thous. bales, 4-wk rate)	−	+	+	−	+	na	↑
	Capacity Utilization (total)	−	+	−	+	+	+	↓
	Industrial Production Index (total)*	−	+	+	+	+	+	↑
	Motor Vehicles, Passenger Cars, Retail Sales*	−	+	+	−	+	−	↑
	Retail Sales (total, estimated)*	+	+	+	−	+	−	↑
	Employment Population, Ratio*	+	+	+	+	+	+	↑
	Personal Consumption Expenditures (1987$)	−	+	+	+	+	−	↑
	Gross Domestic Product (annual rate)*	+	+	+	+	+	+	↑
	Total Rising (+)/Falling (−)	−6	12	4	4	12	3	10
	Percent Rising/Falling (smoothed) %	65%	68%	68%	72%	74%	70%	83%
PRIMARY LAGGING INDICATORS	Consumer Prices, Urban (1982 = 100)	+	+	+	+	+	+	↑
	Producer Prices (1982 = 100)	+	+	+	+	+	+	↑
	Unemployment Rate, Civilian Workers*^	−	+	−	+	−	+	↑
	New Incorporations*	na	na	na	na	na	na	↑
	CRB Index	−	+	−	+	+	−	↑
	Bank Assets	+	+	+	−	+	+	↑
	Manufacturing and Trade Inventories*	+	−	−	+	+	+	↑
	Unfilled Orders (total)*	−	−	+	+	+	+	↓
	T-Bills, New Issue, 90-day	−	+	+	+	+	+	↑
	Prime Lending Rate	−	−	+	+	+	+	↑
	Unemployment, Average Duration^	+	−	−	+	−	−	↑
	Installment Debt to Personal Income, Ratio	+	+	+	+	+	na	↑
	Consumer Installment Debt (total)*	+	+	+	+	+	+	↑
	Construction, Non-residential	+	−	−	+	−	+	↑
	Commercial Paper Rates, 6 month	−	−	+	+	+	+	↑
	Commercial, Industrial Loans Outstanding (mil 1982$)	+	+	−	−	+	+	↑
	Ratio of Inventories to Sales (bil 1982$)	+	−	−	−	−	na	↑
	Prices for Farm Products	+	−	+	−	+	+	↑
	Total Rising (+)/Falling (−)	4	−4	6	6	8	10	18
	Percent Rising/Falling (smoothed) %	66%	63%	63%	61%	63%	64%	95%

* Seasonally adjusted
^ Series inverted
na Data not available

Figure 3. Table of indicators used by the Foundation for the Study of Cycles. The monthly columns show the indicators by month rising or falling with the cyclical outlook arrow on the right. (Courtesy of the Foundation for the Study of Cycles.)

There are several versions of the business cycle. The AIER has twenty-four indicators but there are others, notably those maintained and published by the Foundation for the Study of Cycles, which incorporate fifty-six different indices listed in Figure 3; the table includes most of the indicators described earlier but in addition, items relating to the service trades such as consumer confidence, durable goods orders, retail sales and unfilled orders.

Using the Business Cycle

The business cycle is highly effective as a tactical indicator for management planning and action; but to be completely effective it should be used in conjunction with the long wave described in Chapter 2. It will be recalled that the long wave has exhibited three cycles with durations from 45 to 60 years from its first low point in 1792. Both the strategic and tactical implications of these two cycles are described in Chapters 4 and 5.

From the earlier description we know that the long wave starts from a deep recession and moves into an upwave. After a slow beginning, confidence gradually builds up as consumers start spending, factories are opened and houses are built. As the recovery consolidates, the impact of the business cycles is to create shallow recessions and rapid recoveries. For example, there were five business cycles from the Second World War until the end of the upwave in the early 1970s. The first cycle had a duration of 48 months ending in October 1949. The next rhythms lasted 55, 47, 34 and 117 months respectively.

The long wave plateau started with a sharp recession in

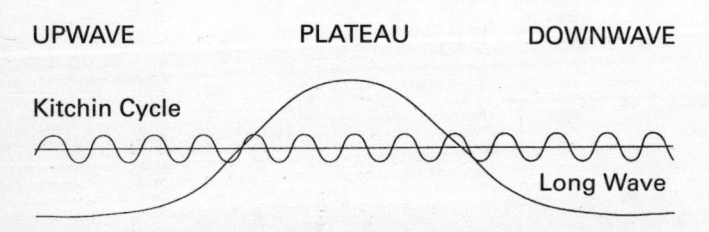

Figure 4. The Kitchin and Kondratieff cycles. An idealised long wave superimposed with the average 4.3 year business cycle. (Adapted from *Business Cycles* by Joseph Schumpeter.)

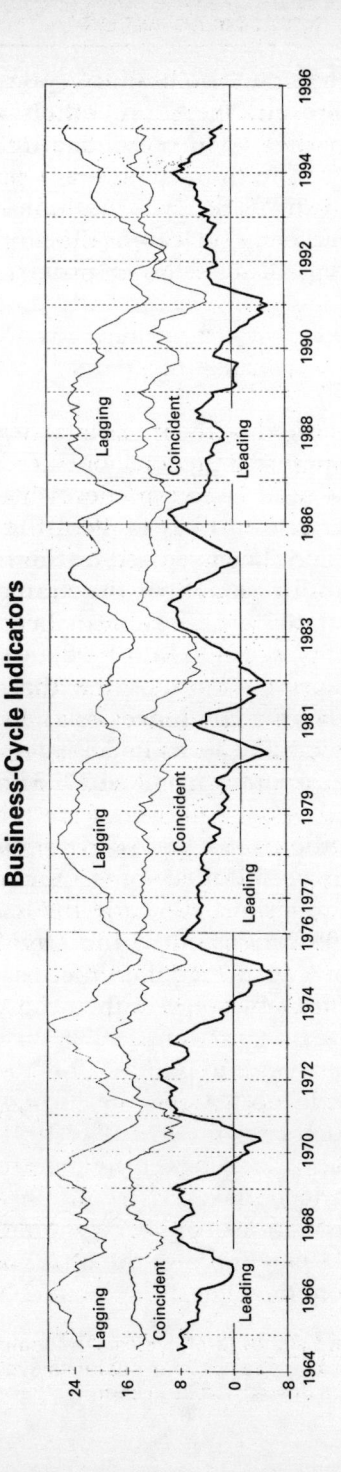

Figure 5. Business cycle indicators showing a combined index for the leading, coincident and lagging cycles in the US from 1964 to 1995. (Courtesy of The Foundation for the Study of Cycles.)

1975 coinciding with the low point of the business cycle. After a rhythm lasting 64 months, the next low point was in July 1980 followed by a very short cycle of 28 months. After a steep recovery to a peak in the third quarter of 1983, the leading indicators showed a dip which was not confirmed by coincident or lagging markers. The leading clue for the end of the plateau phase was signalled in the first quarter of 1986 and confirmed by the lagging indicator early in 1989. With the turndown of the leading indicator there was no excuse for any manager to continue speculating in real estate or housing after that time.

There is growing evidence that the downwave which started in 1990 was confirmed by the unusually steep recession in 1991 and followed by a slow, anaemic recovery. The leading indicator then turned down early in 1994 which, by the first quarter of 1996, has not been verified by the other two measures. There are growing signs that the classical Kondratieff downwave is now established in Mexico, Europe and Japan, suggesting a very deep recession into 1998, bottoming around 2002. A graphic representation of the three indicators is shown in Figure 5. Here a combined index has been plotted for each series showing the leads and lag for the peaks and troughs in the United States from mid-1964 with the cycles clearly defined.

A recovery from the trough of 1967 was pointed to by the leading indicator, to be followed quite quickly by the other two. However, this was a short cycle and the leading indicator turned down in 1968 confirmed by the lagging indicator in 1969. The series once again signalled the early 1970s' boom marking the end of the upwave, and then the sharp recession of 1975 as early as the first quarter of 1972; this was confirmed early in 1973. There was a pointer for the early 1980s' recession when the leading indicator turned down in late 1975, confirmed much later in 1978. The 1991 recession and later recovery was also flagged well in time for preventative management action to be taken. Now in 1997, business and investment strategists and managers should be planning forward for the late 1990s and into the next century. This will be considered in more detail in subsequent chapters.

CHAPTER 4

STRATEGIES FOR THE KONDRATIEFF LONG WAVE

The major weak link in the planning process – and in most decision taking – is the inadequate perception of the direction of future trends. If the banks and institutions on both sides of the Atlantic had known that the leading indicators in the United States had turned down in the first quarter of 1986 (described in Chapter 3) they would never have lost the billions from their real estate and acquisition portfolios in the early 1990s – so creating losses that seriously worried central bankers.

The planning process itself was not at fault because these prestigious institutions had the finest academic and business brains at their disposal. What they lacked was the understanding of business cycles. As we saw earlier, a study of the long cycle itself cannot provide a precise forecast because there are too many factors at work. What they can provide, however, are two major inputs into the planning and decision-making process. Firstly, they can provide foresight enabling planners to prepare sensible contingency schedules which can then be implemented if and when the leading indicators give the signal. Secondly, a knowledge of the business cycle provides the fine tuning for decision taking within the overall framework of the long wave. Creating a strategy now becomes a melding of academic disciplines with the dynamism of conflict, which this chapter expresses through the work of the Chinese general Sun Tzu.

The Contribution of Sun Tzu

About the same time as the conflict between Athens and Sparta in around 300 BC, a number of Chinese kingdoms were engaged in similarly mutual destruction. The conflicts were less polarised than in Greece, hence it was common to employ mercenary generals; one such was Sun Tzu who became renowned for his intelligence, guile and discipline. This last talent interested a king whose concubines were showing a marked lack of respect and the monarch gave Sun Tzu authority to restore discipline.

This he did by drilling the girls, who misjudged their tutor by giggling when ordered to move around the parade ground. Blaming himself for the initial lack of success he twice more tried to direct their movements, but failing the third time he ordered the king's favourite concubine to be beheaded. The monarch deeply regretted his general's action but he had given Sun Tzu the authority and had no choice. Thereafter however, neither Sun Tzu nor the king had any further insubordination.

Sun Tzu's principles have dominated eastern political and business thought for centuries, for they combine the wisdom and subtlety of the Chinese with the practicality of a successful soldier. There are some who believe that Sun Tzu's work was the driving force behind the Japanese Meiji revolution in the latter part of the 19th century and for the incredible success of post-war Japan. Warfare, like business, is dynamic so it is likely its principles can be readily adapted to an equally aggressive although less deadly contest. Some might liken the general's ideas to those of Machiavelli, the adviser to Cesare Borgia who wrote *The Prince* after working in a similar environment to Sun Tzu. But strategists are likely to feel closer to the general's thinking than the Italian's devious suggestions aimed at politicians.

Sun Tzu's most famous dictum advises his disciples 'to win without fighting' which is obviously attractive as a principle and might be considered a council of perfection until one starts to understand how he thought and how it can be related to business. Sun Tzu introduced a number of ideas particularly pertinent to executives who sometimes put action before thought. He believed that intelligence gathering and thoughtful planning should be carried out *before* a foot is put 'outside the encampment'; this would then render unnecessary much of the tactical manoeuvring which is part of implementing the strategic plan. A distillation of his work, in a military context, will be found at the end of the chapter.

Cycles and Strategy

Surprisingly none of the textbooks on business strategy listed under Further Reading mention cycles at all – let alone the specific rhythms described in earlier chapters. This is strange because the success of many of the strategic issues covered in the textbooks depend almost entirely upon catching the right economic climate. For example, one possible marketing strategy for a manufacturer wishing to get closer to the customer is to purchase his distributors; in this way he may learn more about the competition, increase margins and create a greater market share. This might make excellent sense in some phases of the cycle, but if the managers chose the wrong timing this policy could be a disaster. Three examples illustrate this point:

> It was fashionable in the early 1970s to make acquisitions on borrowed money, rationalising the target company, selling off the surplus capacity then using the cash to make further purchases. It was called asset stripping. In Britain, conglomerates following this policy, such as Slater Walker, Jessel Securities and Hanson Trust, achieved a high rate of earning per share and all had a big stock-market following. Then the climate changed as several of the cycles described in Chapter 2 reached their low point; there was a spate of volcanoes, the weather became very dry, crops failed and raw material prices rocketed; this led to a rapid rise in the oil price and inflation was rampant. By 1974, the government was forced to raise interest rates and the highly-borrowed Slater Walker and Jessel Securities collapsed.

> Another spectacular collapse in the early 1970s was the Wall Paper Manufacturing (WPM) group which determined on a strategy for buying their distributors. Unfortunately the market was falling faster than WPM could buy their outlets so that sales actually fell. The manic shopping spree on borrowed money fatally destroyed WPM's balance sheet and the business failed.

It is a truism that when the heavyweights enter the market it is time to sell. When property speculation was fashionable in the early 1970s several fringe banks failed, almost followed by one of the major UK clearing banks. One might have thought that in the 1980s the big institutions' policy makers might have learned the strategic lessons of the previous decade but not a bit of it. Once again real-estate speculation was rampant to the extent that Prudential Insurance and Lloyds Bank decided to invest in estate agents. This was not an unknown market. Both institutions knew the housing market from mortgage operations and believed agency profits could accrue to the new owners. Like most brokers, agencies had contacts and knowledge but no assets – an ideal business during a boom but devastating after the typical end-of-decade Juglar cycle recession clearly marked by the leading indicator in 1986. The housing market and broker-age fees collapsed, and the institutions were left with few disposable assets and huge losses.

In each of these examples, the companies were run by highly intelligent men who could afford the best strategic advice, knew the markets they were entering and had ample resources to make acquisitions. What they lacked was some overall framework in which to make decisions based on a study of cycles. Clearly, there has to be an added ingredient in strategic thinking which takes account of climatic and economic cycles.

Cycles and Business

We can now apply some of these ideas to the nuts and bolts of strategic policies, such as decisions to enter new markets at home or overseas, product design and innovation, marketing, manufacturing and investment, people, organisation and financial control. There is also a section on how housing and political decisions are also conditioned by cycles and their effect on strategic decisions. Each of these factors may be influenced by the 179-year climatic cycles – all of which reach their low point during the 1990s.

In this quite remarkable business climate it is important to review how strategic thinking and management action could be finessed to take account of each nuance of the cyclical influences likely to be encountered.

Shell's Central Planning Group works on the principle that the company should not be surprised by world events impacting on their energy business. After identifying the few scenarios dominating their world, they then look for leading indicators which either modify or confirm their hypotheses. In this way the group is helped to make sound operational decisions. In the 1991 pamphlet 'Challenges and Opportunities in the Petroleum Industry' it suggested there were two overriding influences: the first was growing mercantilism from trading blocs created by a weak international order resulting from the end of the Cold War. The second focused on the influence of the environment on political and economic thinking.

A knowledge of cycles would have helped the planners fine tune and expand their thinking. Firstly they might have concluded that the long wave could be entering the downwave and give rise to the dangers of default and currency collapse from increasing global debt; history shows that this could lead to deflation and the risk of a deep recession. Next they could have reviewed energy prices from the historical implications behind the 179-year sun retrograde cycle. Finally a review of Raymond Wheeler's 500-year cycle might have led them to a contingency plan for considerably reducing the power of central governments.

The start of most external strategic studies is the PEST analysis which considers the environmental factors most likely to impact on policies. PEST stands for Polical, Economic, Socio-cultural and Technological factors which are all affected by cycles described earlier.

Political considerations are highly influenced by the position in the long wave as they impinge on such matters as monopolies legislation, environmental protection, foreign trade and taxation. This is a factor that will be considered in more detail later but environmental legislation provides a good example. Complying with regulations which tightly control emissions can be afforded during the upwave but could place an intolerable cost burden on businesses during the downwave. The political choice is then simple: either reduce the regulatory burden or risk rising unemployment.

Economic factors in one strategic manual mention business cycles without defining what these are and how they work. This is highly surprising for they control such vital factors as interest rates, inflation and unemployment.

Socio-cultural matters cover such areas as demographics, changes in lifestyle, attitudes to work and pleasure, and levels of education – all of which can change dramatically between the upwave and downwave. Rising confidence during the upwave encourages a general rise in living standards, moves to a more pleasant working environment and a rise in leisure activity. This barely alters during the plateau phase but changes radically in a downwave; now people concentrate where the work is, there is less talk about leisure and more about survival, and for most people education is about learning how to earn money, including working for oneself.

Technological intensity is also influenced by cycles. It is usually applied to producing high volume consumer products during the upwave but plays a much more intense role during a downturn because competition forces innovative solutions and short product life cycles. Do not expect help from government spending during the downwave because the cash will not be there; this will disadvantage companies relying on state contracts or technical assistance.

The cost of *entering new markets* will change radically during the long wave; the rising demand during the upwave encourages a spate of new products which may be supplied locally or imported. The pattern changes during a downwave when quite often tariff barriers make doing business in another country expensive. Only large companies are likely to have the resources to set up a manufacturing or development unit overseas, others will have to rely on systems like licensing.

The upwave is normally the time for aggressively minded companies to buy into new products and markets often by making acquisitions using a highly leveraged share price to absorb less forcefully run businesses. This was the route taken by Hanson Trust and other conglomerates in the 1970s and 1980s when financial leverage was all important and synergy almost inconsequential. Sometimes the entry of competitors into a new market through acquisition totally changed the business outlook as when Philip Morris bought Miller Beer, and Proctor & Gamble acquired the Charmin Paper Company. It will be easier to enter overseas markets during an upwave because local suppliers are less likely to call for tariff protection.

The recession during the early part of the plateau gives a warning of what could happen later on but otherwise leads into a more intense version of the upwave in its latter stages – something which happened during the 1980s. The converse is true during the downwave when it is difficult and costly to enter highly competitive recessionary markets. However, particularly innovative new products can be successful as were refrigerators and aircraft during the 1930s. Alfred Sloan in his *My Years with General Motors* describes how his company coped with the Great Depression and the subsequent recovery. In 1929 General Motors bought the Allison aero-engine company and made investments into the Fokker Aviation Corporation of America and the Bendix Corporation for the total cost of $23 million. These investments did spectacularly well during the Second World War.

Another example is how GM bought into the diesel locomotive business. In 1930, Charles Kettering, the development vice-president of General Motors, had been investigating the possibility of adapting two-stroke diesel engine to cars. Although the unit was potentially viable, GM had no production facilities at that time but providentially two existing companies in the diesel engine business, the Winton Engine Company and Electro-Motive Engineering, both of Cleveland, Ohio, were seeking funds. This encouraged GM to buy into the diesel engine business at a relatively cheap price. At an exhibition in Chicago during 1933, Ralph Budd, the president of Burlington railroad, saw the new diesel on display and insisted it be adapted to power his new Zephyr unified train from Denver to Chicago; the train achieved a record-breaking average of 78 mph. Later a Wilton-powered Union Pacific diesel knocked a third off the time from the west coast to Chicago which motivated GM to set up a diesel locomotive plant at La Grange, Illinois.

A climatic change coinciding either with an upwave or downwave may prolong or shorten the influence of either cycle by requiring the introduction of innovations or the possibility of rearmament. For example, if it becomes particularly cool in the latter part of the 1990s then warm clothing and heat-saving equipment and services would be much in demand. Likewise a threat of war later in the 1990s would have the same stimulatory effect as Britain and France re-arming against German and Japanese aggression in the late 1930s.

Product design and innovation are primarily influenced by such things as market research, the appropriate technology, cost, packaging, competition – although a study of cycles suggests there may be some overriding factors. For example, there is no point in introducing an excellent product at the wrong time which only alerts the competition; there is also no merit if the cycle phase is wrong. However, two major factors are likely to be at work in the 1990s: the down phase of the long-term cycle and the likelihood of a climatic change. Often these factors work separately, but most unusually they are due to work together in the 1990s – as they did in the 1930s.

Consumers go for volume during the Kondratieff upwave, buying products that quite suddenly become affordable. Typical was the model T-Ford in the early 1920s before General Motors offered a choice of colour, style and horsepower. And in the 1960s everyone wanted a washing machine or ate cornflakes. Neither of these enthusiasms will repeat themselves during the next upwave because there is now such a choice and spread of products that the market will never return to a single product – each phase creates its own products and competition. During the upwave service tends to be less important than market share; fashions change so that the old is discarded and the new design substituted. The Kondratieff plateau phase can often be taken as a continuation of the upwave, although very careful attention should be paid to the leading indicators signalling a downturn because the next recession could be quite deep.

Matters are reversed in the downwave. Cash is short, products have to last longer and need the support of spares and service. Creating niche markets not market share is the most sensible policy when tough competition is forcing ever-tighter margins which destroy profitability. It was possible for a lead firm to take cost and market leadership in the upwave but this is no longer possible in the downwave for the rate of innovation increases rapidly. Now the customer has a choice: either the product is so good it *must* be bought now or the purchase delayed and bought later – possibly at a reduced price.

This focus in the 1930s forced General Motors to concentrate on the Chevrolet marque at the bottom end of the range, whose share of GM output expanded from around 50% to 70%. Within this tight bracket customers were given the choice on such matters as colour, engine size, accessories and trim. Although brand loyalty is a factor, this tends to be less important where price and product performance are uppermost in people's minds.

A change in climate might moderate the long wave by differentiating a product's attraction. In warm times people tend to follow fashion, wanting to do similar things, look the same, respond to similar influences. Traditionally warm period products are slender, curved and imaginative, almost abstract. When it becomes cooler people seem more individualistic, wanting to be themsleves – not part of a crowd. Their whole approach tends to be practical as befits living in a cooler climate; they demand functional products with the clean natural appearance normally associated with Scandinavia.

Marketing and sales will follow similar principles to product design but there are important differences in the approach to promotion and distribution because of control and cost structures. During the upwave, advertising, promotion and sales policies will be designed to satisfy the need of a rapidly growing consumer market and attempt to improve market share. One technique to exclude competitors and improve margins is to buy distributors, as in the WPM example cited earlier. This should also improve market share, which in the upwave is more important than reducing costs. The plateau is similar to the upwave, although increasing competition may force distributors to be much more direct in their promotion campaigns.

Conversely, the downwave forces a more personal approach for it will be a buyer's market. As price, durability and service will be dominant factors, manufacturing and service industries will attempt to differentiate their products and seek profitable niches within a broad market. For example, in the United States, Porter Paint focuses not on the DIY market but on the professional decorator by offering free paint-matching services and site delivery. During the squeeze on the Japanese Yen in the second quarter of 1995, food margins were so tight that Japanese retailers were forced to cut out the wholesalers and buy directly from suppliers.

During a downwave most businesses will be forced to convert fixed to variable costs by changing their owned distributors to become franchises or appoint commission agencies to handle their selling. These are Third Generation techniques (described in Chapter 7) for keeping legal control of the sales process without the cost of ownership. During a deep recession one can expect much more personal methods of selling, such as the Tupperware or Avon commission agents or direct selling through catalogues. Direct selling is being made more effective through information technology; by analysing credit cards and purchases, it is now possible to pinpoint customer tastes as a base for making attractive offers, so making wider use of a particular store, agent or product range.

A climatic change will probably emphasise the stage in the long wave – a warm phase reinforcing the upwave and a cooler period deepening the downwave. For example, if the downwave of the 1990s is accompanied by an unusually cool period then one might expect marketing to be aimed at the individual. Just as dollar weakness is squeezing Japanese prices, a deep recession would fragment the present retail and distribution system; in addition manufacturing companies could opt for direct selling through specialised agencies able to offer the customer added value and service.

As suggested earlier, *political attitudes* will change during cycles which will affect strategy because often attempts at market regulation will have had the reverse impact of what is intended. In addition, restrictions introduced to deal with quite a different political situation could delay the full benefits when the wave turns. For example, after the Second World War the then Labour government kept many of the wartime restrictions in an attempt to regulate the British economy in the early stages of the upwave. These were removed by the Conservative administration starting in 1951 which accelerated the upswing.

This also happens in reverse. In the years to the early 1990s most European governments imposed considerable social security costs and restrictions on labour mobility in industry in the belief that the upwave would continue. It also had a secondary objective to help governments become re-elected. When the downwave started around 1990 these additional costs and taxes made it impossible for firms to continue to trade profitably; these are now expanding, not in Germany, but in lower cost areas such as Poland and the Czech Republic, creating the reverse response to that indended. For example, the chairman of Daimler Benz reported early in 1995 that his company was becoming less competitive and was planning to relocate operations – probably in Poland. The unemployment position in Germany could become quite serious if the Ifo Research Institute's findings are accurate. It showed that 56% of manufacturers intended to increase their investment abroad compared to only 14% at home. Already 6% of workers lost their jobs in 1994 with a further loss in 1995. Not surprisingly, the Bundesbank is worried about rising unemployment and there are discussions with unions on how to reduce social costs and improve labour flexibilty. The same fate befell Lyndon Johnson's 'Great Society', introduced in America to eliminate poverty which has had quite the opposite impact to that intended. Instead of bringing all up to a minimum level it has created a dependent society supported by an expensive bureaucracy.

The plateau temporarily interrupts the euphoria and often changes the political climate. In the 1980s it introduced leaders like Ronald Reagan and Margaret Thatcher who challenged the existing orthodoxy that had appeared flawed – particularly during the sharp, but temporary, recession at the beginning of this phase. There were similar forces at work in America during the 1920s. Quite the reverse occurs in a downwave, where the earlier added costs can no longer be afforded, but to unwind these is politically highly unpopular, as Germany and France have discovered when state entitlements were trimmed. Keeping the Welfare State running during the 1990s has put western countries increasingly (and dangerously) in debt. Politicians love to feel they are in control of economic events, which is why they have continued state pensions and other entitlement programmes in the belief that the state can end the recession – but in the end these only deepen it. In addition, politicians only make matters worse during a downwave by attempting to regulate markets. One obvious example is the European Commission, which is applying upwave policies in an attempt to produce a 'level playing field' during a downwave which will only create even more irregularities.

Doing business overseas is normally a matter of either exporting, licensing (or franchising) or organising some form of local manufacture. Exporting is often the preferred choice, as the additional volume recovers its share of the overheads but attitudes, opportunities and the competition within the host country – or tariff areas – influence whether a local presence is needed. These decisions are becoming increasingly blurred in the 1990s. Sophisticated manufacturers in high-cost countries now take advantage of low-cost labour regimes in emerging economies which create a network of producers and assemblers to gain the greatest possible competitive advantage. The stage of the cycles will also be influential.

There are several influences during the upwave affecting

strategic decisions. First, there will be little call for import protection from most home industries – governments might actually welcome outside competition for local manufacturers to keep prices down. The complaints, however, will come from older unionised industries already facing increasing competition from substitutes but still powerful because of their political influence. During the Great Depression and after the Second World War, protection was demanded by staple industries; for example, cotton faced competition from synthetic fibres, the steel industry from aluminium, and mined coal from oil and gas. These conditions continued during the plateau phase.

The position reverses during the traditional downwave when there is increasing call from local businesses to reduce foreign competition that not only hurts profits but increases unemployment – a more politically sensitive issue. This is accentuated by the welfare legislation described earlier which creates labour rigidities and is one of the greatest bars to meeting low-cost competition from the Asiatic south-east rim and Eastern Europe. This legislative arthritis makes it increasingly costly to set up a new manufacturing business in a western host country.

So far in the 1990s memories of the 1930s tariff restrictions have encouraged global free trade by the passing of the Uruguay Tariff Round, the creation of free tariff areas such as the North American Free Trade Area (NAFTA) and the extension of the European Union. However, if the financial crisis foreseen by the cycles described in earlier chapters is triggered, then public opinion could force governments to take much stronger action against imports.

> *During the 1930s Depression, powerful lobbies forced President Hoover to pass the Smoot-Hawley Act which applied across-the-board tariffs of around 30%; in addition, the US dollar was devalued nearly 70% against gold, making it virtually impossible for anyone to export to the USA in anything other than specie. By 1940 the US had amassed well over 50% of the world's gold reserves.*

In addition to possible tariff protection, the industrialised west is finding increasing difficulty (even in the mild recession of the early 1990s) to be competitive against the rising low-cost areas of south-east Asia, where over 30 people can be hired for the total costs of one German worker. Already Swissair has saved considerable costs by locating its accounting function in Bombay and repetitive operations such as checking and matching American insurance claims are handled at a fraction of the cost in Ireland. For the first time the power of modern technology is making it increasingly easy to relocate these operations which are completely outside the control of host governments.

Although technology has made it easier for firms to move factories to the lowest cost areas, governments can still influence buying decisions against foreign companies; some like the Japanese have introduced technical difficulties against firms trying to enter home markets. However, important concessions may be negotiated by firms wishing to manufacture among the many competing high unemployment areas; for example, Britain has been particularly successful in attracting Japanese and American companies wishing to be within the European Union tariff area by offering lower costs, tax concessions and incentives unmatched elsewhere.

Attitudes to manufacturing and investment will also change with the phases of the cycle because in the upwave the emphasis will be on volume production to meet the growing need. Companies may also acquire their suppliers through a process of vertical integration which will both safeguard their deliveries and control costs. Adding the supplier's inventory to the parent company will be an additional bonus because when prices are rising, increasing stocks values are a valuable source of profits. Investment in the upwave will be primarily in expanding factories and plant to increase volume. Similar principles apply during the plateau phase although by then manufacturing techniques will have become more sophisticated with plants being able to customise their production.

Everything changes during the downwave; economies of scale that were so important during the upwave now become a liability. As volume falls, high fixed costs have to be trimmed by closing plants and laying off staff – as General Motors did during the 1930s. This whole process is accelerated by the introduction of the Cybernetic Revolution, considered in another chapter, which replaces clerical decisions and human brawn by automatic machines and computers.

Where holding inventory was a source of profit during the upwave, this now ties up cash and is a loss maker in a regime of falling prices. Manufacturers will be forced progressively to adopt Japanese Just in Time (JIT) techniques of integrating independent suppliers into the manufacturing chain; this reduces the inventory carried, applies strict quality controls and requires the vendor to respond rapidly to changes in demand. Investment will be applied not to increasing volume but to reduce costs, enabling single machines to turn out a variety of different products.

Strategy for people changes markedly during the up- and downwave of the Kondratieff cycle and between varying climates as was shown earlier. During the upwave people are taken on full-time because to hire their services under contract or part-time would be too expensive; the tendency will be for most jobs to be undertaken in-house and paid for by increasing business. This is the ideal breeding ground for trade unionism which can be expected to flourish. The new-found security is expressed in casting off 'boring' old morals and principles and 'letting it all hang out' – something quite different from the austerity of the previous downwave.

Union pressure continues during the plateau when, sensing that their power might be waning, the leaders push hard for advantages as they did during the 1960s and later in the 1970s. These privileges became an anathema during the 1980s – as in the 1920s. Both periods saw tougher union policies from the elected leaders in the United States and Britain and union membership declined.

The fall continues during the downwave when opportunities are taken to convert fixed to variable costs, nothing being paid for unless work is completed. The number of full-time staff is reduced and temporary-contract skills are hired as needed. Security and the power of trade unions continue to decline as full-time employment falls but many people, even those whose jobs are apparently secure, feel unsettled about the future – wondering what may happen next.

People could then behave in two distinct ways: first they could rebel against authority by rejecting those who were responsible for their predicament – as did the electorate in the 1994 American elections despite ostensible prosperity. Secondly, there is likely to be a return to previous moral certainties accompanied by a reversion to more basic faiths. It will be interesting to observe the influence of Christian Evangelicals on the new United States Congress in the later 1990s.

The variations occurring during a climatic change are more stark and will need as much thought and care as during the long wave. As suggested in an earlier chapter, there are two primary phases: when it is warm the empirical evidence shows that people cooperate, they are more creative and confident and tend to respect authority. There is a particular condition when it is both warm and dry, as it was in the 1930s, when they accept trade union barons or even dictators in preference to the democratic process.

Quite the reverse happens when it becomes cooler: there is a sense of aggressiveness which makes for difficult relationships unless the difference is recognised. There is also less tolerance for poor decisions when those responsible can expect to be criticised. There will also be a tendency, similar to that during the downwave, to return to more fundamental standards. Each of the major resurgences of Christianity has occurred during cool periods – as did the Islamic holy wars.

Different times call for a change of management style, or expressed in a military sense, different wars need to be fought by different generals. For example, most upwaves encourage aggressive managers who achieve earnings growth through a cascade of acquisitions – just like the conglomerates listed earlier and the large armies discussed by Sun Tzu. They use the power of leverage to increase earnings per share which is intended to bring about a more highly rated share price – and then to make even more acquisitions. This strategy succeeded for a time but then collapsed as it did in the plateau phase of the 1920s and 1970s – and then later in the 1980s.

Then, as we have seen earlier, the large organisations in Britain and the USA made some of the greatest errors of judgment when banks and institutions were obliged to wipe billions off their balance sheets. In Britain, high interest rates in 1989 made borrowing too expensive. It forced highly geared companies either to reduce their debts or call in their creditors which many of them did – such as Colorol or Polly Peck. In America the central government used billions of taxpayers' dollars to bail out defunct Savings and Loans losses in a scandal that forced the government to become the largest house owner in the country.

Now, in the downwave, which probably started in 1990, a different management style is needed – just as it was necessary in the 1930s. Offensive generalship goes out of fashion and the era of the defensive commander begins. The previous heroes of the 1980s, like the junk-bond king Michael Milken and insider dealer Paul Boesky were sent to prison, Robert Maxwell died, and a more sober-suited group of people have taken the helm. In fact, the whole acquisition edifice proved a terrible mistake for the majority of companies; it enriched the acquired company's shareholders, the acquiring board's directors and, of course, their advisers and bankers. However, in most cases it did very little for industrial efficiency when many deals went sour.

In *Thriving on Chaos*, Tom Peters quotes a Harvard study of thirty-three major US companies showing that over 50% of all acquisitions were subsequently sold and that nearly three-quarters of these were in unrelated fields. In other words, the vast number of the acquiring company's managers found they could not profitably manage a business outside their own mainstream of competence. This is hardly surprising because an executive group set up to optimise the running of one business might not work well for another, requiring quite different sorts of decisions.

So if we have the state of affairs described in earlier chapters we need not necessarily adopt an offensive or defensive style of management but one that is highly flexible. We will need someone with the talents of a Sun Tzu, whose ideas later influenced Mao Tse-tung when harrying Chiang Kai-shek's armies. So not only will our new managers be obliged to improve the efficiency and stability of their existing companies but possibly have to steer them through a rapid rise in inflation, followed by a crash and a deep recession lasting for several years.

The downwave may also need a management support team constructed more like a military staff than a conventional board of directors; they should be able to respond rapidly to the vagaries of weather, the competition, the marketplace and economic conditions. Our new chief executive might be surrounded by a full or part-time staff reporting on rapid market or technology changes, competitive intelligence – and the company's proposed response to economic or political events. This will require a team drawn from a wide range of talents and experience and its composition should be kept continually under review.

The military analogy might also continue through to the management thinking about intensity. Just as in war there will be periods of calm, almost boredom, when nothing seems to be happening and it would be prudent to slim a business down to a small nucleus. At other times the team should be on a war footing when everything seems to be changing so rapidly that every opportunity should be seized as if it was the last on offer.

An Industrial Example

It is evident that if the long wave applies to strategies, it also relates to industries – perhaps the most important being housing and construction which account for some 7% of western GDP. Until after the Second World War, housing and real-estate cycles were particularly appropriate to the USA which underwent three distinct waves of expansion and immigration coinciding with the long wave cycles described in Chapter 2. These opportunities in a new country attracted waves of migration initially from Europe but later also from Asia.

The first cycle, K1, started around 1792 at the time of George Washington's second inauguration. It coincided with the frontier territories in the north-east becoming available for settlement around the Great Lakes when the British and their Indian allies retreated to Canada. This allowed settlements into the area now occupied by Michigan, Wisconsin, Illinois, Indiana and Ohio including towns which are now the cities of Detroit, Chicago and Cincinnati.

The drive west became a stampede after the US government negotiated the Louisiana Purchase in 1803 from a bankrupt Napoleon for the equivalent of $15,000,000 in gold. This huge area doubled the land mass of the USA including the states of Arkansas, Missouri, Nebraska, Iowa, South Dakota and parts of other states in the west. Farmers borrowed heavily to purchase the land.

The intermediate *plateau* phase that started in 1817 lasted until 1826 when the economy, over indebted from headlong growth, began to slow down and bankruptcies began. Overextended banks were compelled to foreclose, forcing property prices down until 1837 when the US experienced a severe real-estate crisis which lasted until the bottom of the K1 cycle in 1848. This was a notable year when Britain also experienced a food crisis, leading to a run on her gold reserves. In Ireland the terrible potato famine led to deaths and mass migration reducing the population by more than half. Similar privations triggered rebellions in France, Austria and Germany.

K2 began after the Mexican war of 1846–8 ceded the territories of Texas, New Mexico, Arizona and California to the USA. The move west was accelerated by the discovery of gold and silver in the new territories of northern California and Oregon which acted like a magnet to previously unsuccessful farmers and fortune hunters. Encouraged by the potential for new wealth, over 40,000 people headed west along the Oregon trail in the north and the Gila trail to 20 million acres of farmland. The boom ended with the civil war and in the post-war recession a decline in commodity prices forced down land and farm values. There was a recovery of prices in 1869 before falling again as the accumulated massive debts started to unwind. By the low point in 1896, prices had declined over 70% from their peak.

The exuberance of Theodore Roosevelt, the 26th President of the USA, encouraged the start of K3 after the 1890s recession. But this time the real-estate development was not so much settling agricultural lands but expanding the industrial base of the country in the middle-west and east. Initial developments were slow because distressed properties had flooded the market, but with mortgage rates at around 2% these were soon swallowed up and, as industrial production increased, more housing was needed in the fast expanding industrial towns. By 1915 output was growing rapidly with the demand for the First World War armaments and the nation was in the grip of a real-estate boom fuelled by migrants from war-torn Europe and the Far East.

The boom peaked in 1919, encouraged by the huge amount of war credit injected into the US economy, then fell back in the sharp recession of 1920 to the plateau phase which lasted until the next peak in 1927. By then, new construction had increased by 400% and once again the speculators were rediscovering the joys of highly leveraged deals; land lots in Florida and elsewhere were bought and sold easily. By 1929 construction volume had declined by over 30% and collapsed by a further 50% by 1934 in the vicious early years of the Great Depression.

During the 1930s the slump in US real estate was almost complete despite record low interest rates of below 1%. So serious was the level of repossessions in 1933 that one of the first measures of Franklin Roosevelt's New Deal was to pass an act creating a government-funded agency called the Home Owners Loan Corporation (HOLC). Another federal agency called the Federal Housing Administration (FHA) was set up in 1934 to guarantee the mortgages of a wide variety of qualified *potential* homeowners.

Britain escaped most of the speculative bubble in the 1920s. The country had been in recession since returning to the gold standard in 1925 and the relatively high interest rates had put most people off owning their own homes. However, from the 1990s perspective housing during the 1920s was cheap with the more expensive homes costing £2,000 and smaller ones as little as £600. A highly paid workman (or a couple) earning £5 per week in Britain could save the downpayment of £125 and raise a mortgage for 75% of the purchase price; 5% interest was levied and the loan was repayable over 20 years. By 1931, only 1 in 5 homes was owner occupied, the remaining families living in rented accommodation.

The price of homes actually declined in the 1930s by nearly 20% and the mortgage terms relaxed so that a £500 house could be bought for a down payment of only £25 (5%) enabling those earning £4 per week to afford the deposit and subsequent repayments plus interest. By 1939, the number of owner occupiers in Britain had risen to one quarter. By contrast, in 1940 the US level of house construction had declined by 40% reaching a value of just $12.4 billion (1972 dollars) down from a peak of $20.9 billion in 1926.

The anatomy of construction strategy is best described by following K4 which probably started in the early 1940s. As is usual after a slump, activity barely rose to allow the huge stock of dispossessed homes to be taken up even though interest rates of 2% or 3% were offered. There is a natural suspicion of owning property after a depression for fear of further price falls, which is why the new buyers are mostly the young who have not known the previous slump. This is unfortunate because for many this is the best time to buy a house. The reluctance is, of course, the natural consequence of the Kondratieff cycle which teaches the truism that wisdom often skips a generation!

As the housing recovery picked up, the demand was stimulated by governments offering tax relief on interest payments; housing in the US was further encouraged by the offer of long-term loans at low fixed borrowing costs. In due course the existing housing stock was taken up, new development land was needed and there were growing calls upon the construction industry to produce more private dwellings. As the demand for space continued, wages and prices started to rise as did interest rates.

The results in the United States and Britain were remarkable, with house building rising by 3.7 times in the US and 2.7 times in the UK during the years 1945 to 1972. In the same period, other construction increased 5.3 times in the US and 3.4 times in Britain. By the start of the plateau in the mid-1970s, the construction markets in both countries were euphoric, their expansion fuelled by the large lending institutes such as the banks, insurance companies and pension funds investing heavily in commercial real estate. The price of land had risen 8 times from £10,000 to £80,000 per acre in Britain from 1948 to 1970 with the cost of construction materials, interest rates and labour costs also rising steeply – just as they did in earlier cycles.

The start of the plateau in the mid-1970s was a typical setback previously experienced in the 1820s, 1860s, and in 1920. It was then put down to OPEC increasing their oil prices but their rises had been triggered initially by the surging cost of grains from the main producers – themselves suffering from poor harvests. Initially governments tried to accommodate the increases by holding down interest rates, but then inflation took hold and the authorities were forced to raise the cost of capital sharply. As always, housing reacts very badly to rapidly rising interest and house construction fell about one third from 1972 to 1975 in the US and rather less in Britain.

After the set-back in 1980, house prices then rose to a secondary peak in 1990 after the number of additional mortgages taken out in Britain increased by 50% in the decade when the value of the average standard dwelling (reported by the Halifax Building Society) more than doubled. In the US, the value of outstanding mortgages increased by 2.5 times with house prices increasing nearly twofold in the decade. House prices still rose in the US in the early 1990s although they declined 6% in Britain from the peak in 1990 to 1995 and were recovering slightly in 1996. In a regime of the cycles described, earlier governments in both countries will try to reverse a flagging housing market by lowering interest rates, but this may not be possible in a regime of rocketing commodity prices. The history of housing in previous cycles shows that housing values are likely to decline by at least 50% from 1990s values in a deep recession towards the end of the decade.

Consider the balance sheet: It is curious that books on business policy hardly mention the balance sheet as a strategic factor – as if the strength or weakness of a company's finances was a matter that emerged from other decisions. In fact, a mistake in judging the position in the long wave cycle can either place a company at risk from being plundered by an acquirer or face extinction during a credit crunch. Some of the most important differences in approach are those between the Kondratieff upwave and downwave.

At the beginning of the upwave, the most successful businesses will have strong balance sheets with little borrowings – for without both they would not have survived the earlier recession. However, something always changes this perception; in Britain Charles Clore successfully bid for Watney Mann, the brewers, who had huge undervalued property assets just by Victoria Station. Quite suddenly managers realised that the former downwave rules of prudence and solidarity no longer applied; what were considered virtues now become liabilities. As suggested earlier, sober managers now give way to tigers prepared to sacrifice balance-sheet strength for growth and high earnings. This new breed of managers sees increasing leverage as a means of acquiring companies that have undervalued balance sheets. Making money like that is quite easy; as Charles Clore showed, research pinpoints a target company that has (mainly) undervalued property assets which can be rapidly redeveloped. The business is bought, swapping highly rated paper for solid worth, the property is sold and the next acquisition planned. The masters like Clore were followed by Jim Slater in the late 1960s and a host of other imitators who were successful for a while until the cycle described in Chapter 2 reached its low point in the early 1970s and ended the upwave. There was a quiet period during the early plateau phase before the next wave of corporate gunslingers came on the scene in a frenzy of speculation in the 1980s.

The 1990s downwave combined with a low point in the business cycle initiated a short recession. Almost overnight the culture changed, as illustrated overleaf. Consider what happens when a highly leveraged business making reasonable profits during the latter half of the plateau phase encounters a downwave when there is no time to unwind debts by the sale of assets.

Company X has expanded rapidly on borrowed money during a boom. Let us say the sales had grown to 100,000 units; the profit before interest was 20,000 units less 10,000 for interest, and the pre-tax was 10,000 units. Everyone is happy and the bank will be willing to lend even more.

Sales of Company X	100,000 units
Profit before interest	20,000
Less interest	10,000
Pre-tax profit	10,000

The company meets a recession; sales fall 10%, interest rates are static and the company attempts to negotiate further loans to fund working capital. The position is now:

Sales in recession	90,000
Profit before interest	10,000
Less interest	10,000
Pre-tax profits	00,000

This is what is known as a credit crunch, for X will not be alone in requesting further loans and the competition for cash will drive up the cost (interest rates) of money. If our company had cash there would be no problem in funding the purchase of goods and services while there was time for the management to restore profitability. As it is, Company X is trying to raise even more loans against a background of increasing insolvencies and a banker might well require the loan to be called instead of granting a further advance. This happened quite often in 1991 and is likely to recur later in the decade.

But having cash on deposit may not automatically imply solvency if the currency itself is losing value – just as in Germany during the great inflation of the early 1920s – and as befell sterling and the US dollar in the second quarter of 1995. In Weimar Germany, businesses kept all their liquid funds in sterling, dollars or francs because the mark was collapsing against almost every other currency. If the conditions described in earlier chapters apply, then corporate treasurers will seek to protect their cash balances either by holding them in a stable currency such as the Swiss franc or alternatively hedging sterling or dollar deposits against gold or another valuable commodity.

To be *cash* rich is one essential; other measures protect items of working capital such as the value of inventory or receivables –

something discussed in greater detail in the next chapter.

Inventory is invariably a profit earner when held during inflation but a terrible liability during a recession when its value falls with declining commodity prices. As the earlier example showed, unless the stocks can be turned into cash at the right moment, this might bring a business down. Fortunately techniques such as Just in Time (JIT) exist so that should they choose, companies can increase their inventory of bought-in components and work-in-progress to a maximum during an inflation to take advantage of rising commodity prices. They can then reduce their inventory to a minimum well before another recession is signalled.

Receivables will be relatively easy to collect during an inflation but incredibly difficult during a recession – but there are several ways of easing the position. The first and most obvious is to offer discounts for any accounts settled immediately, or within 30 days; implying that it is more important to convert debts into cash than retaining margins. Alternatively, businesses can insure their debts through companies like Trade Indemnity (TI) in Britain, so that any declared failures are covered up to around 80% of their value; TI do not cover late payments, only defaults.

Debts can also be factored through specialised divisions – usually of banks – whereby 80% of the debts are paid within a few days of a valid invoice being issued and the balance on maturity; factors make their profit from the interest payable for early settlement plus a debt collection fee. The vendor can pay an additional fee for taking out a non-recourse contract where the debt is also protected against failure. Although factoring seems a sensible method of funding working capital and ensuring payment, many customers resent the generally hard-nosed approach adopted by factors and may go elsewhere for their supplies.

Finally, treasurers may consider hedging their debts against a yardstick such as a rise in interest rates that equates with increasing failure rates or lengthening terms of payment. For example, a company might have outstanding debts of £100 million and, having decided that 10% could be at risk, take out an option or futures contract against a rise in short-term rates. Should interest rates rise, the business would receive a sum equivalent to the additional risk.

Cyclical turning points of the long wave and business cycle have been considered in the last chapter – the most important of these being the judgment between the end of the plateau and the downwave, the point of the greatest danger for business.

The end of the previous recession can usually be judged from the turning up of the leading indicators. The first will generally be the money supply figures followed by building permits once the housing overhang starts to fall – encouraged by low interest rates and more stable employment prospects. In addition to increased activity by contractors and building suppliers, the retail trade will be picking up; as their inventories decline, manufacturers will be increasing their schedules.

The end of the upwave and the start of the plateau are usually marked by the bottoming of a cycle such as the Kuznets or Hale cycles; since 1792, they have been accompanied by a war – either a civil or a more general conflict. Higher prices from reduced crop yields are normally responsible for fuelling inflation until governments are obliged to raise interest rates sharply – so quelling the boom.

The end of the plateau and the start of the downwave are usually marked by rapidly rising debt as once again people become euphoric with the discovery of excessive leverage. It often only needs a relatively mild cycle such as the Juglar to tip the scales into the downwave and an increasing level of failures or defaults typical of a credit vortex. The recessions of the business cycle are deeper and the recoveries less pronounced than during the preceding upwave. Figure 6 shows a summary of how management attitudes change during the up- and downwaves and the headings considered earlier. They are an important contribution to strategic thinking.

The Wisdom of Sun Tzu

This is a brief distillation of Sun Tzu's writings which, although expressed in a military context, has wide messages for business, politics and commerce because it focuses on priorities and ideas seldom expressed in business textbooks. Where possible the ideas have been collected under single headings.

Self-knowledge is an essential first step to planning strategic moves for even if little is known about the opposition there is a 50/50 chance of winning a conflict providing one is completely clear about one's own strength and weaknesses – even if this means not engaging the enemy. Sun Tzu urges his readers to study the five factors upon which success depends. These are: understanding the way (the shared objectives between leaders and the led), terrain, weather, leadership and discipline of each combatant. This must be completed before setting foot outside the encampment or engaging the foe – even if these are just spoiling tactics – for men will give willing respect to commanders who have done their homework. When strategic thinking is shallow this is an exercise in futility and the battle is lost before starting out. Conversely, those with foresight and a sound strategy will prevail.

Deception will hide your intentions even to the extent of appearing incompetent when able, and ineffective when potent. Exercise humility to make the opposition arrogant; appear formless to deceive numbers and state of deployment; attack when they are unprepared; act when least expected. Exercise surprise. Never trust an enemy who speaks softly but is building his forces for he will attack shortly; conversely, a show of aggression and bluster is often a prelude to retreat. Interrogating captured scouts can often reveal the state of enemy morale; many punishments indicate the enemy is losing control and is worn out. It is not possible to continue to exercise skill over a long period, and lengthy campaigns exhaust the exchequer and the will to continue the conflict.

Sun Tzu believed it essential for a nation to practise *the arts of warfare* for in this way a nation can be alert to the possibility

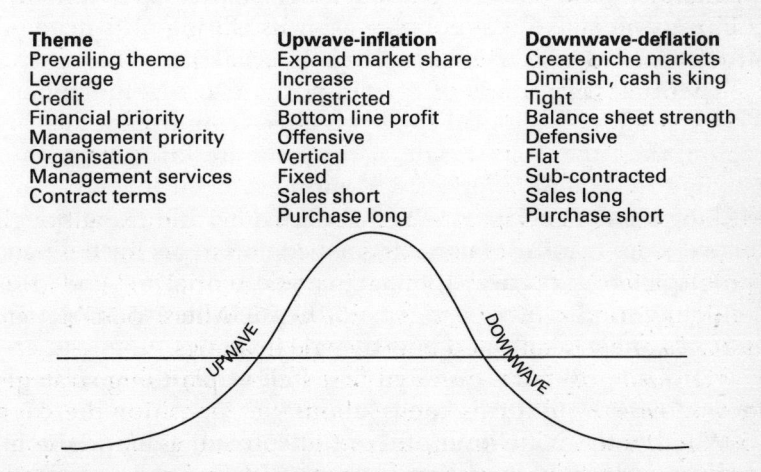

Theme	Upwave-inflation	Downwave-deflation
Prevailing theme	Expand market share	Create niche markets
Leverage	Increase	Diminish, cash is king
Credit	Unrestricted	Tight
Financial priority	Bottom line profit	Balance sheet strength
Management priority	Offensive	Defensive
Organisation	Vertical	Flat
Management services	Fixed	Sub-contracted
Contract terms	Sales short	Sales long
	Purchase long	Purchase short

Figure 6. Summary of management attitudes during the long wave. (Courtesy ESCI.)

of neutralising a potential enemy without firing a shot, by implementing spoiling plans, disrupting supplies or destroying morale. Even though an opponent may be superior in numbers he may be defeated through better discipline, greater alertness, skills in the unorthodox and knowing when to fight.

The wise commander chooses his ground; prepares, positions, feeds and equips his troops and lets the *enemy attack him* – although he should be aware that the foe might also deal in subterfuge, seldom letting true intentions be known. Hence the attacker should advance when there is no defence, never create gaps which the other side can exploit, move swiftly with the required force, then withdraw while there is still confusion; he should also keep his intentions shrouded until the last moment. By the same token try to exploit the enemy's weaknesses and make them declare their intentions. Good militarists create confusion by disrupting enemy communications, weakening his morale and if possible sowing the seeds of dissent within the opposing high command.

There is no such thing as *bad luck*. Misfortune almost invariably happens when generals are weak, lack authority, issue confused commands and have badly-formed strategy; then the forces are disrupted and confused making it easy for the opposition to outflank and harry. However, even a disorganised enemy may be made desperate when cornered with no way out, and it might be prudent to give them an exit. A competent army is like a swift snake that counters with its tail when its head is struck and responds with its head when its tail is attacked.

There are five kinds of *spies* important to a commander. There are first of all local spies recruited from the locality or region; then there are inside agents who are hired from the enemy's ranks and reverse spies who have been turned from working for the enemy. Finally there are dead and living spies: turned spies transmit false information to enemy agents and living spies report back. Intelligence is essential for the able commander, who must understand the identities of opposing generals, their talents and how they relate both to their superiors and subordinates. Sun Tzu concludes that it is unwise to move unless this information is known.

Whether times are bountiful or difficult Sun Tzu's genius is instructive. He adds a wise and exciting dimension to creating business strategies within the discipline of cycles.

CHAPTER 5

COMPETITIVE TACTICS DURING THE BUSINESS CYCLE

If the long wave cycle is one of the deciding factors determining business strategy, then the four to five-year business cycle decides tactics. The words strategy and tactics started life in a military context to distinguish between long-range planning and manoeuvres during combat; they also accurately describe, in a business sense, the difference between the long-term direction of an enterprise and the shorter-term changes needed to ride the vagaries of the business cycle.

This means that within the overall strategic framework we can fine tune management, marketing, inventory and production decisions not only to remain solvent but to make the most of a competitive situation. Although these shorter-term management decisions are largely independent of the position within the long wave, it is clear that the seriousness of these judgments will depend very much on the phase of the cycle. For example:

> Recession during an upwave will be relatively shallow and recoveries rapid. Conversely, a recession during a downwave will be unusually deep and the recoveries anaemic.

We know from Figure 5 that the shape of the business cycle will be anything but the smooth sine wave shown in Figure 2, but this is less important than our ability to define the four stages of the cycle. We also need to be able to read the turning points in the leading, coincident and lagging indicators, for these will determine the correct cyclical phase – in other words whether we are approaching a peak or trough. Just because the leading indicator has turned upwards from a trough does not mean an upturn is imminent because there may be a lag of over a year. However, it does mean that plans for a trend change should be drawn up – to be implemented when confirmed by the coincident or even the lagging indicator.

There are four phases of the business cycle starting from a previous trough as defined by the leading indicator:

Phase A – emerging from recession which anticipates that sales volumes are likely to recover within a short time. Take advantage of low interest rates to negotiate a term loan and extended purchase contracts.

Phase B – evidence for the upturn is well underway; prices can be raised and inventory increased. It is now safe to exploit the recovery.

Phase C – indicates the beginning of the slowdown although sales volumes are unlikely to fall immediately. Commitments should be shortened and cutbacks planned.

Phase D – volume is declining; cutbacks should be implemented and borrowings reduced.

Having identified each phase of the cycle and the broad management stance, we can now expand each of the management actions in more detail:

Phase A. This could be a major opportunity to plan a rights issue for when the stock market catches up with the real possibility of at least two years expansion ahead. It would also be timely to negotiate a low-interest term loan to finance a sustained business upturn. The time would also be opportune to review productive facilities and decide whether it would be more expeditious for work to be done within the business or outside – depending upon the position within the long wave.

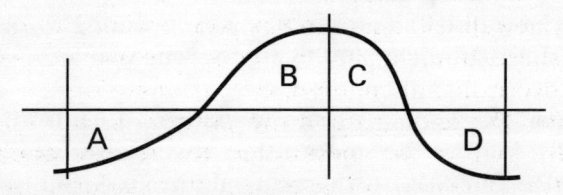

Figure 7. Phases of the business cycle.

These are some of the detailed matters that should appear on the agenda:

Management: Additional people will be needed for the increase in business, either hired as permanent staff or under contract. Although the expected upturn is several months away, this would be a good opportunity to prepare contingency plans and watch the indicators very closely.

Marketing: Decisions will soon be required on such matters as new product introduction, increased sales representation, new promotion campaigns, terms of payment, pricing policy, increasing inventories and widening distribution.

Production: Firms will need to review the adequacy of supplies for the likely volume rise, secure longer than normal supply contracts, consider the need to hire and train new operatives and plan for any capital equipment purchases or tooling.

Phase B. This comes at the point where the coincident and lagging indicators have now confirmed the recovery and the leading items are all still positive. This is a period when a stock offering or rights issue can be made and a higher share price will be justified by rising profits and distributed dividends. The more specific management actions confirm the decisions already taken.

Management: May be strengthened either through improved information or research systems, hiring additional staff or introducing incentive and training programmes to retain the existing team. It might also be appropriate to strengthen the board with additional outside directors or others who can provide intelligence on new product or market sectors. This would be a good time to review investments as part of the overall long wave strategy: holdings may be made in new products or markets during the upwave, possibly for culling during the downwave.

Marketing: Consider increasing volume through the appointment of new distributors or sales people aimed to increase market share. It might also be appropriate to add incentives such as overriding discounts or sales commissions.

Production: Depending upon the position within the long wave, this will be the time either to increase one's own productive facilities or strengthen relationships with suppliers. During the upwave the balance sheet would be strengthened by adding to the property portfolio while, conversely, any business cycle upturn during the downwave should be balanced by converting real estate into cash.

Phase C. The signal that the peak has been reached will be the weakening of the leading indicators described in Chapter 3; usually the money supply M1 and M2 will be the first to turn, probably followed by an item like housing permits. Although sales will still be rising, it will be the time to prepare contingency plans for the expected downturn involving cost and inventory reduction and debt repayment.

Management: This should be concerned with plans to convert fixed to variable costs, probably by transferring previously full-time staff either to part-time or on sub-contract. Managers should also start to shorten purchase contracts, pay off debt, reduce inventories, tighten working capital and review forthcoming budgets.

Marketing: This would be the opportunity to review the pattern of sales and distribution in preparation for weeding out the marginal areas and concentrating on the most important accounts; what the strategists call differentiating products and seeking niches. The review should also take into account the inventory carried by distributors, and plans for varying the terms of payment depending upon the account reliability. Review advertising and the promotion budget to flagging sales or product areas and where possible negotiate long-term sales contracts.

Production: Review make or buy/bought-in decisions in relation to marginal plants. This would be the time either for trimming during an upwave or making more radical cuts during the downwave. Purchase contracts should also be reviewed in anticipation of lower demand.

Phase D. The turn of the leading indicators will have been confirmed by the coincident and lagging statistics, volume will be falling and the contingency plans should now be fully implemented. By now, competitors who were not following the business cycle could be in trouble and it might be possible to buy them up either in whole or in part. This would be an excellent time to concentrate on new product development or negotiating licences to prepare for the next upturn.

Management: Should be battenning down the financial

hatches, conserving cash, protecting vital markets and redoubling customer services. It is also the time to plan ahead for the forthcoming upturn when the next stage of the overall strategy can be implemented.

Marketing: With all the contingency plans implemented, it would be beneficial to plan and implement missionary work with new products and markets and forthcoming sales campaigns. Quite often companies overtrade during the business cycle upturn so special attention should be paid to credit control and to avoid quoting low prices for long-term contracts.

Production: Maintain very tight control of inventory and quality; investment in new plant should concentrate on improving quality, flexibility and cost reduction.

CHAPTER 6

THE CYCLES OF FAILURE AND ACTION TO ACCELERATE RECOVERY

Just as the various cycles described earlier improve the timing of implementing strategy – so conversely they reveal the flaws of weak management and highlight stupid decisions when a business is at its most vulnerable. It is not unlike navigating a vessel close to a rocky shore: a prudent mariner may possibly take risks at high tide when he knows there is adequate water under the keel; only a stupid sailor would take the chance at low tide.

Obviously the best time to start a business is when the Kondratieff upwave and business cycle coincide, although even in boom times a start-up almost invariably takes much longer than the original estimate and quite often runs out of money. The percentage of insolvencies from start-up is appalling: in 1990, nearly one third of all US companies had failed after 3 years, 50% were still going after 5 years and only a quarter made the decade. The record in Britain is similar. There is much less excuse for a mature business to fail during an upwave although some do from granting a credit to a poor risk or placing too great a dependence on one customer – see the section at the end of the chapter. Bill Mackie, a veteran British insolvency expert, created a telling list for assessing potential failure. He believed the critical signals included:

- The erection of a new office block by a company which could not afford it. Insolvency is more likely if the building has a goldfish bowl inside and a flagstaff outside.

- The chairman takes a pride in his new car and personalised number-plate.
- The chairman or chief executive have a vigorous out-of-hours relationship with their secretary.
- The company receives a performance award.
- The chairman's statement listing the good works and accolades given to himself.

The more cynical need not stir from their chair, they just have to read a company's statements and reports to know what is happening:

'The company is well placed to take maximum advantage of an early improvement in business conditions' means 'their fingers are crossed that things will get better'.
'The directors know of no good reason for the sudden drop in the share price.' Interpreted this means that the directors know perfectly well why the stock has crashed.
'The company has the facilities to respond to the market demands' – they are on a three-day week.
'The dividend has been adjusted to a level from which it can be raised in the future' means it has been cut.

The danger of insolvency from misjudging the phases of the cycle are evident from Edward Altman's books, *Corporate Bankruptcy in America* and *Corporate Financial Distress and Bankruptcy*. The later book lists American company failures from 1970 to 1992, which fit well with the business cycle described in Chapter 3. However, the greatest number of companies fail when the business cycle low point coincides with the Kondratieff downwave.

There were massive farm bankruptcies in the latter part of Kondratieff 1 (K1). Farms also failed at the end of K2 but this time the greatest defaults were from railroads and banks including Barings in 1891 – but this was baled out by the Bank of England. The end of K3 was accompanied by the failure of real estate, hundreds of banks and industrial companies like the empire of the Van Sweringen brothers.

The downwave of the early 1990s has again been dominated by massive failures. The largest was probably Olympia and York which filed for bankruptcy with debts of nearly $20 billion; others were First Capital Holdings which owed $14.5

billion, Continental Airlines (over $6 billion), Macy's (over $5 billion), Maxwell Communications (over $4 billion) and a further seventy American companies with liabilities in excess of $100 million. In Britain the most spectacular failure was Polly Peck – one of the shooting stars of the 1980s, the Arab-owned bank BCCI, and other leveraged companies such as Colorol, and British and Commonwealth.

From 1970 on, there were also failures coinciding with the 8 to 11-year Juglar cycle: one of the largest was Penn Central in 1970 owing $3.3 billion, then in the early 1980s Wicks, Braniff Airlines, Manville and Itel – each with liabilities of over $1 billion; there were a further sixteen insolvencies with debts of over $100 billion. One of the largest potential failures was the Chrysler Corporation which nearly went bust with liabilities of $12 billion but was bailed out by the federal government in 1981. In Britain the industrial conglomerate Acrow failed in the early 1980s as did Airfix, John Brown Holdings and Fobel International.

The 22.4-year Hale cycle and the accompanying inflationary crises were also the causes for failures when governments felt obliged to raise interest rates to quell rising prices. Altman reports that WT Grant failed at the last low of the cycle around 1973 with debts of $1 billion plus a further seven companies with debts of over $100 million. Several British conglomerates also failed such as Slater Walker Securities, Jessel Securities, some fringe banks and one of the major clearing banks nearly became a victim. Several industrial companies went bust including Staflex International which collapsed straight into liquidation.

It is interesting to compare the number of failures experienced in America with the business cycle; one would expect insolvencies to be low at the top of the cycle with a rising trend towards recession. Taking a relatively short time scale since 1970, there is generally a lag of over a year from the low point in the cycle to the maximum level of failures; conversely, there is a similar delay from cyclical highs to when insolvencies start to decline.

The earlier examples were applied to manufacturing and trading companies, but like the 1920s there were a rising number of bank and insurance company failures in the 1980s. The number of failed banks increased from a low of 79 in 1984 rising to over 200 in 1989. These were as nothing to the huge losses of $120 billion (partly paid out by the US taxpayer) to bail out the crashed Savings & Loans sector through the Resolution Trust Company. The collapse of the so-called 'thrifts' carried with it losses of $500 million from property related insurance.

Unfortunately there could be a much worse recession in 1998 than in 1992 when the business cycle is due to make another low point superimposed on a declining downwave. This convergence could be more severe due to the rising price of grain from the continuing cool/dry weather of the 179-year rhythm. This conjunction is known to economists as stagflation, i.e. that business will be subjected simultaneously to rising real interest rates and falling sales – a disastrous combination for highly leveraged businesses.

How then are those people associated with investing in business to cope with a rising tide of insolvencies and who, if any, will benefit? This chapter is concerned with some of the sophisticated means of measuring solvency and the type of management action that would lead to a reduction of bankruptcies; conversely, boards can adopt policies that will make failure more likely. The next two chapters introduce tried methods of helping companies prepare for the next century.

Measuring Potential Failures or Recoveries

Traditionally banks and credit agencies have used a series of spreadsheet ratios to measure their customers' performance. Once the significant revenue and balance sheet items had been entered, calculations then generated important indicators such as profit related to sales, current assets to current liabilities and total borrowings to net worth. The analyst then adds these details to those already recorded for earlier periods and analyses the trend. Bankers often require their customers to produce monthly data as a loan condition, which gives them considerable advantages over credit agencies who only receive annual data with the report and accounts.

Difficulties with traditional methods arose from the selection of the critical ratios that would provide a trend. For example, profitability could be massaged to appear to be healthy despite a deterioration in the current assets/liabilities ratio. Credit ratios are used by international agencies such as Dun and Bradstreet who keep global records of over 16 million companies – most of these in the USA and Europe; in addition they receive details of payment records from a number of top companies which they then score and report to their clients.

It was only in 1971 that Professor Edward Altman of New York University applied modern statistical techniques to deduce what he called a 'holistic' approach towards measuring solvency. This he achieved by taking data equally from a random number of failed and solvent companies; then, using a sophisticated programme called 'multiple discriminate analysis', he narrowed down a large number of ratios to those that best represented the failed and solvent samples. The result of his work was the following formula whereby the Z-score represented the solvency in a single figure:

$$Z = C1 \cdot \frac{\text{Working Capital}}{\text{Total assets}} + C2 \cdot \frac{\text{Retained Earning}}{\text{Total assets}} + C3 \cdot \frac{\text{EBIT}}{\text{Total assets}} + C4 \cdot \frac{\text{Market Value}}{\text{Total debt}} + C5 \cdot \frac{\text{Sales}}{\text{Total assets}}$$

Where C1 to 5 are coefficient weightings for each ratio, C5 represented nearly 94% of the total.
* Earnings before interest and taxes.

Altman's formula then uses four ratios which address working capital, retained earnings and earnings before interest and taxes and sales – all related to total assets. The fifth ratio divides the company's stock-market value to total debt. Before the model can be considered to be predictive, Altman then applied the formula to other failed and solvent companies outside the original sample to test its robustness.

In Britain similar work was undertaken in the early 1970s by Richard Taffler, now Professor of Accounting and Finance at the City University Business School. Taffler used similar analytical techniques to Altman but discovered that a single formula could not be used for different types of companies (industrial, distribution and service) for their profile would be different; he also excluded the stock-market rating for, although a significant factor, it was dependent on factors external to the company. Taffler's industrial quoted formula has the following profile.

$$Z = C1 \cdot \frac{\text{Profit before tax}}{\text{Current liabilities}} + C2 \cdot \frac{\text{Current assets}}{\text{Total liabilities}} + C3 \cdot \frac{\text{Current liabilities}}{\text{Total assets}} + C4 \cdot \text{No credit interval*}$$

C1 to 4 are coefficients, the maximum contribution is for C1 at around 50%.
* No credit interval is an Americal measure. It represents the number of days a business could survive from current liquid resources after all the current commitments had been met.

Note. There are two other models for listed distribution and service companies plus a further three for non-listed businesses.

Taffler's models have now been incorporated into Syspas Ltd, a company that supplies a comprehensive risk-management service to clearing banks, accountants, lessors, local authority and fund managers from an office in the City of London. Financial information from the databank of 3,000 listed and unlisted companies is extracted from company accounts and entered in the firm's computer in a standardised form. Clients then receive a comprehensive service of the six solvency and other statistical models – sent via a three and a half inch floppy disk – every week with updated information, which is then entered into their own machines; clients can now conduct solvency analyses on the 3,000 companies supplied by Syspas plus other data entered by themselves. The company also supplies regular solvency overviews to their clients and special reports on the companies they follow.

The results are remarkable when placed alongside the business cycles described earlier. The chart confirms the lag of up to two years with the business cycle and the impact of the downwave. Until 1990, the percentage at risk during the 1981 crisis rose to 23%; it then made a record high in 1993 when nearly 30% were at risk of financial distress. The outcome is shown in the next figure over the same period. The numbers of insolvencies dropped from a high in 1984 but then reached an all-time high of around 7% in 1993. These were far outdone by the number of reconstructions which reached 25% in 1994 showing that banks and shareholders were cooperating to correct balance-sheet weaknesses.

Undercapitalised companies fail due to overtrading (trying to expand on too narrow a financial base) at any time but particularly when emerging from a recession. This is because they may take on contracts at too low a price and run out of cash. The tell-tale signs will be weakening sales margins and a deteriorating current asset position as the business struggles to grow with extended borrowings. The Syspas service is ideally suited to reporting on potential overtrading from the choice of ratios.

Syspas's record of predicting insolvencies has been impressive – particularly in the critical years of the early 1990s. Normally a company showing signs of stress does not fail when

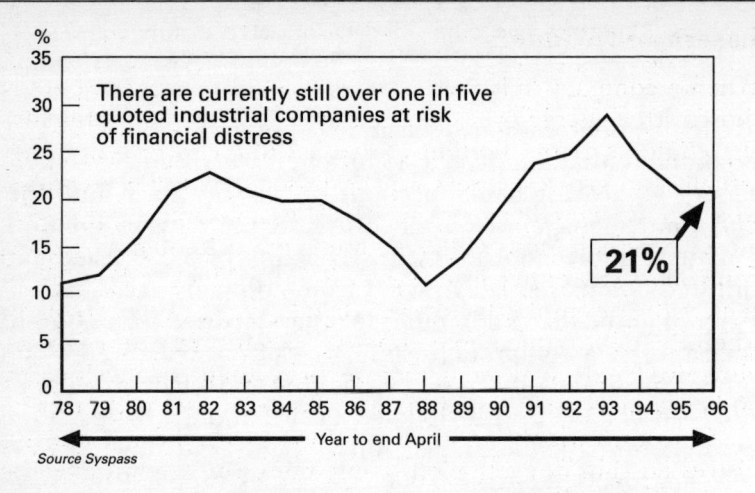

Figure 8. Percentage of listed UK industrial companies at risk of financial distress from 1978 to 1996. (Courtesy Syspas Ltd.)

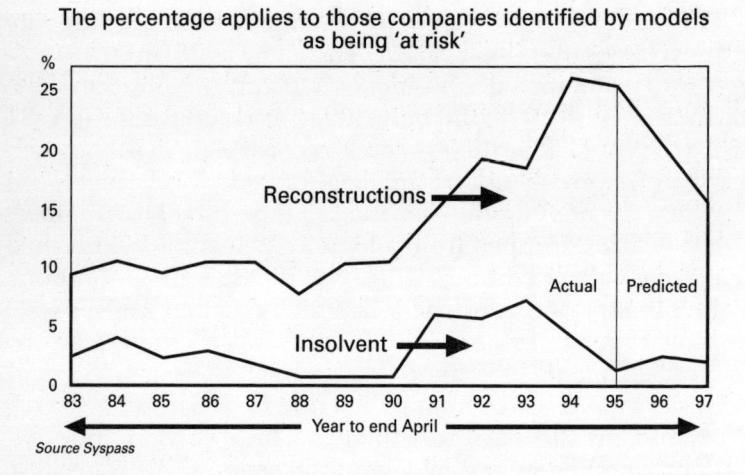

Figure 9. Number of insolvencies and reconstructions from 1983 to 1995 with a forecast through to 1997. (Courtesy Syspas Ltd.)

entering the danger region, but if remedies are not applied the risk of failure increases. Syspas have refined their prediction by combining the number of years a company has been at risk of financial distress with the anticipated growth or decline of the economy. This formula correctly forecast 101 out of 103 failures in the period from 1990 to 1994.

Losers and Winners

When a company fails there is a legal set of priorities whereby those with a charge over the assets are usually repaid, while the shareholders at the bottom of the list often receive nothing. Usually the greatest losers will be unsecured trade creditors, who can use a credit agency such as Dun and Bradstreet to give advice on credit limits. If they require greater protection, credit controllers can either insure their debts up to around 80% of their value or employ factors who can both guarantee payment when the debt is due and compensate against failure. However attractive factors may seem, their services can be relatively costly and customers are often upset by hard-nosed debt collectors.

Almost invariably, another set of losers are those acquiring distressed (but not yet failed) companies who are attracted by a low share level following a price collapse. Unless the acquirer has a particularly strong balance sheet, its own assets can often be placed at risk in the rescue attempt of cleaning up poor contracts and disposing of unwanted assets. Unfortunately those usually attracted to this sort of deal are weak managements trying to be macho. Observers of the company will note the triumphant tone of the directors when they first make such a deal, which becomes more strident as the acquisition goes sour and their own business is pulled down – until both collapse together.

The clear winners are the insolvency professionals. The lawyers and insolvency specialists, paid by the hour, have first call on any cash raised from disposals. Others to benefit are often the purchasers of sound businesses from the receiver when there is otherwise a poor market for near-insolvent companies. In the economic conditions explained earlier, the levels of bankruptcies will rise alarmingly, putting off most potential buyers. Agencies investigating possible failed companies will be able to generate excellent business prospects from those wanting to buy parts of dead firms who also need help with finding cash.

Management Action to Help Avoid Insolvency

To be successful any rescue attempt must take a company out of risk by achieving a positive Z-score. By definition this means taking action that improves critical ratios which, for a listed industrial company, means strengthening the numerators of positive ratios in the Altman or Syspas equation and reducing the denominators. In practical terms this means increasing profitability and reducing current liabilities. It also means increasing current assets in relation to total liabilities and improving the quality of the quick assets.

It is no accident that company rescues require the rapid phased actions which improve the ratios making up the Z-score. This is how a rescue operation might be mounted – usually from someone coming in from outside – for they are not committed to previously failed policies:

Phase 1   Preliminary analysis

A considerable amount of information can be gleaned from published data to show the trend in sales, margins, borrowings, etc., to spot, if possible, when and how the deterioration started. The analysis would be greatly assisted by having access to Z-score data. The analysis will be considerably helped by comparing these results with reports and statements made by the directors, noting any of the hackneyed excuses listed earlier in the chapter.

At this stage it is possible to achieve at least three objectives: the first is to judge whether the business can be saved, for sometimes the assets have been so pledged it is impossible to raise cash to pay-off creditors. The second is to assess what line of enquiry should be pursued. For example, a company engaged in construction work might have encountered a difficult contract that was pulling down the business; another might be a diversification that had soured – often accompanied by an acquisition, as suggested earlier. Finally, to determine who are the major shareholders and secured creditors.

Phase 2   Stop the cash haemorrhage

No recovery can take place unless asset disposals reduce debt and costs are covered; it is a fallacy that companies can trade out of trouble unless they have strong balance sheets. For this reason an action must include the following:

- A decline in sales as unprofitable lines, or contracts, are weeded-out and the redundant assets are sold.

- By definition the remaining activities will generate less costs – hence the output per employee is increased.
- The sale of the redundant fixed and current assets is used to pay off debts. Unfortunately the value realised from these assets seldom reaches book value which is why rescued companies need to write off the difference against reserves.

Most accounting systems are able to produce the direct cost of each product or service but this information will be inadequate for determining overall profitability, including overheads. In consequence small confidential working groups from each department need to be assembled, not unlike the process teams advocated by Hammer and Champy in *Re-engineering the Corporation*. Their tasks in order of importance are:

- Stop the cash haemorrhage by prohibiting all cheques above a certain level (say $5,000 or £3,500) unless these have been personally approved by the group. Also stop all recruitment, overseas trips, entertaining above a certain level, new liabilities or other commitments. This is a highly unpopular programme and the group may wish to nominate a hard money-person to hold the purse strings.
- Cash may also be generated from chasing up overdue accounts which could be held up awaiting credit notes. These should be agreed within reason; at this stage, collecting cash is more important than earning profit margins.
- There is also likely to be an out-of-balance inventory with some high-value slow-moving stocks. Experience shows that quite often these may be assembled and sold cheaply to markets not normally entered by the business.

These remedial actions should be enough to stabilise the cash flow and to convince bankers and creditors that the business is taking serious action to return the company to viability; they may also be asked to accept interim interest and payments for receivables outstanding to help the firm's cash flow. If there is no 'light at the end of the tunnel', the firm is in danger of unlawful trading and the creditors should be informed immediately.

At present it is unlikely that the shareholders would want

to be told the true position of the company for this would mean they could not deal in the stock. However, the rescue attempt might have been initiated by a group of the owners, in which case a few may have been elected as insiders and no longer able to buy or sell shares.

Phase 3   Work out a recovery plan

The team assembled for Phase 2 can now be put to work creating, then later implementing the recovery plan. In stockmarket jargon this means identifying the 'holds' from the 'sells'; those lines or activities that are holds are to be nurtured and expanded, those losing money are either sold, liquidated or closed down. This is the most painstaking part of the rescue, for those involved it often requires a re-orientation of the firm.

Chapter 3 of *Avoiding Adversity* considers five stages for analysing and preparing a recovery plan which will, at the same time, identify the initial misjudgment that triggered the downfall. The book suggests the following procedure:

Stage 1. Sort out the obvious holds and sells which are evident either by the people involved or their location. The working group may then take immediate action to redouble promotion effort on the profitable activities and jettison by any means the obvious 'dogs'. Experienced company doctors develop a particular skill in packaging and selling loss-making divisions. They have the advantage of being totally unsentimental about either the history of the loss-makers or the outcome of the transaction. All that matters is converting loss-makers into cash. One particular business was the subsidiary of a foundry group. It had undergone a relocation from London to North-East England and the losses were in danger of destroying the parent company. The new group chief executive saw no hope of a recovery and offered to sell the subsidiary to the general manager for one pound sterling. There were conditions, however: some of the activities and their associated machines would be transferred to the parent business plus the cash for liquidating the associated work in progress. The story had a happy ending since the new owner was able to procure local assistance for refurbishing the foundry and the parent business was invigorated by new and profitable machines and sales.

As buy-outs are potentially an important part of disposals it is worth considering how a group of employees, with or without outside shareholders, can purchase their own company – or a section of it – from the parent company. Managers have bought out their own businesses for many years but the process became particularly popular in the 1980s when groups of managers made a bid for their own business; they put up some of the capital themselves then raised the balance through loans and equity, often provided by venture capitalists (VCs).

For many situations the game plan was simple. All that the shareholder/directors now had to do was to improve the performance of their company (not difficult in a rising market) and pay off much of the debt; then they could either sell the business to a larger company or float it on one of the new exchanges that blossomed during the decade. Within the context of this chapter, buyers of distressed parts of companies will be obliged to stay with their gamble and turn it round; as in the above example, the foundry owner was prepared to sell it at any price.

Stage 2. The same team involved in Phase 1 can now be involved in the analysis of the lines that came between the obvious holds and sells. *Avoiding Adversity* describes the process of first defining the activities that needed analysing in detail then allocating *all* associated costs and assets according to criteria suggested in the book. One of the recurring relationships in this sort of exercise is the Pareto Rule which states that 80% of the profits come from 20% of the lines – or something very near this pattern.

Stage 3. This requires the findings to be tested for obvious anomalies or disagreements among members of the team that need arbitration from the team leader. *Avoiding Adversity* recommends that the findings are sorted out and agreed before proceeding to the next stage – which is to work out an action plan and a new organisation. At this stage banks and selected shareholders may be told of the findings as a progress report; but they are unlikely to be told of their part in the rescue.

Stage 4. Dump the loss-makers either by sale or some other disposal. This is best achieved by forming small disposal teams, whose redundancy terms have been previously agreed, to negotiate and dispose of the surplus buildings, plant, assets and any residual goodwill. Timing for this stage is critical. It is most unwise to announce closures or other changes piecemeal; more sensible all together so there are no lingering doubts in the medium term for those who are staying. Most specialists arrange a coordinated series of meetings with unions, the employees themselves and then local newspapers and radio stations to minimise the distress and reduce unfounded rumours to the minimum.

Stage 5. Create a new organisation. Since writing *Avoiding Adversity*, those in charge of recovery plans have been considerably helped by the ideas of Michael Hammer and James Champy in *Re-engineering the Corporation*. While believing their work is useful to business recovery, the two writers concentrated on improving the efficiency of mainly viable businesses through setting up similar groups to those described earlier. They also showed how information technology should be incorporated into any plan that recreates an organisation from the bottom up which, after all, is what happens during a company rescue. *Avoiding Adversity* recommends several principles which can be considered with those of *Re-engineering*:

- Reconstruct a business from the bottom up so that as many tiers of management as possible are removed between the general manager and individual operatives. *Re-engineering* goes further by urging that those at the 'sharp end' should be given all the information they need for making decisions about their work. Instead of handing down management decisions, a supervisor's job is to act as a mentor for the new quality-conscious groups that now form the core of modern organisations.
- Although this may not be immediately affordable, plan to use technology for regular communication between head offices, plants, sales and distribution centres to ensure that all have current data on such matters as pricing information, progress with orders, inventory levels, progress with developments, financial information and the like. In this way salesmen can provide customers with information within hours that previously might have taken weeks.

- As a further refinement, technology can be used to avoid paperwork. For example, firms like Otis and Avis car hire have taken this principle a stage further by using portable computer terminals. Those of Otis update central office machines of any service work carried out; car company stewards use mobile computers to produce immediate customer statements when cars are returned.
- Larger groups can use rapid transfer of information to save costs. As a matter of principle, Hewlett Packard decentralise purchasing decisions to individual plants but use the combined power of the group to negotiate overriding discount on bulk items. The company reports it could save upwards of $50 million annually with this system.
- Make use of benchmarking to bring the business up to an international standard. Again this may require more resources than the rescued company possesses at an early stage of recovery; for an example consider the techniques adopted by Frank Ruhermann at Raleigh Cycles described in Chapter 8.
- Wherever possible promote from within and train the new supervisors not only in fresh technology but also in the group approach.
- Use re-engineering ideas to avoid specialist operations. As the Pareto analysis showed, most work falls into the 80/20 relationship. Hence a customer request that used to be handled sequentially involving several departments can now be dealt with almost simultaneously by one or more persons using information stored and distributed electronically.
- As Hammer and Champy point out, consider how best to orientate the commercial profile of the business as sick companies tend to neglect their core accounts and pursue either different customers to diversify, or accept many small orders on the misguided principle that they are more profitable. Both problems are relatively easy to overcome by scanning past sales ledgers to understand the historic profile and to consider distributors for small-value business.
- At this stage it will be possible to foresee the future trading 'shape' of the company and determine how the

balance sheet may be strengthened. An asset write-down is almost inevitable following disposals and a conversion of short- to long-term debt can usually be negotiated with bankers; if there has been a gross debt distortion, debt can also be turned into equity with the agreement of the shareholders.

Once a company is on the path to recovery it will become free of the tensions associated with incipient failure, morale increases and there is greater confidence among customers and suppliers. There is, however, a downside to most turn-round action, for the situation almost invariably attracts predators. In many ways this is an ideal timing for the buyers for the difficult part of the recovery is over and the share price is unlikely to have risen strongly enough to represent the full value of a now viable business.

Examples of Rescue Operations

Here are three examples of successful profit improvement programmes. The first is of a nearly bankrupt foundry group based in England – we have already seen how one of the disposals was negotiated. The second is an American-based hose and fitting business that, to become viable, needed to hive off a major part of its manufacturing capacity. The third is a radical profit improvement programme for an American-based hi-tech glass business.

Example 1. Rescue of a near terminal foundry group

This business, once the leader in its technology, had relied on a major account which had since failed. In consequence it attempted to replace the lost work by taking on business at too low a margin and profits had declined. The group chief executive, instead of concentrating on tackling the main business, had attempted a diversification which had starved the business of cash. The board decided to appoint a new chief executive who carried out the sort of programme outlined earlier. The results are shown in the abbreviated accounts.

Rescue operation on a foundry group

(Balance sheet in £ million)

	Sept 30 1992	Sept 30 1993	Difference	Ref.
Fixed Assets	14	11	(3)	1
Current Assets				
Inventory	5	4	(1)	2
Receivables	12	10	(2)	3
Cash	1	1		
Less liabilities				
Bank overdraft	(6)	(4)	2	4
Creditors	(8)	(6)	2	5
Net current worth	4	5		
Net worth	18	16		

Operating statement

Sales	46	35	(9)	6
Less costs	47	33		7
Profit before tax	(1)	2		
Employees	1,200	800		
Sales per employee	38K	43K		8

Explanation of references:
Ref 1. Fixed Assets: this included a property realised at book value plus a loss on the written-down value of plant.
Ref 2. Inventory reduced by running down production on the disposed lines and sales of redundant stock.
Ref 3. Receivables based on reduced sales.
Ref 4. Overdraft reduced by cash received.
Ref 5. Creditors as for overdraft.
Ref 6. Sales reduced by concentrating on more profitable contracts.
Ref 7. Costs considerably down by concentrating on major site and on the most profitable work.
Ref 8. The first year showed a small improvement in output per employee

The results at the end of the first year showed a return to a modest profitability and a positive cash flow which the group used to invest in automated equipment which reduced cost still further. As often happens in recovery situations, the company was taken over and absorbed into a larger group.

Example 2. Rescue of a pressure hose and fitting manufacturer

Company A was a subsidiary of an American group engaged in the manufacture of hydraulic hose assemblies in Chicago. The customers were mainly involved in hydraulically-operated earth-moving machines, machine tools, agricultural equipment and cranes; they also supplied hoses for the replacement market through distributors. The company manufactured its hose and fittings on the premises using extrusion and multi-spindle automatic lathes; it also had a tool room to back up the machinery. However, the profit record of the business had declined over two years as shown in the abbreviated table:

Year	1	2
Sales	11.0	11.5
Profit after taxes $,000	500	(100)

Following the loss in the second year it was decided to set up a team similar to the one outlined earlier in the chapter consisting of head office specialists and the local management. Their task was to analyse the product line profitability of each of the main groups – pressure hose, fittings and attachments. Unlike previous investigations it was decided to allocate all the overheads in the three categories by actual usage, not just according to sales volume. This was the result:

Product groups	Pressure Hose	Fittings	Attachments	Total
Sales $m	3.5	7.0	1.0	11.5
Less direct costs	0.7	3.5	0.4	4.6
Less overheads and taxes	2.1	4.5	0.4	7.0
Profit after taxes	0.7	(1.0)	0.2	(0.1)

The results put Company A's general manager into a dilemma for he had risen in the company via the tool room and regarded his machine shop as the mainstay of the business. However, he could not discount the analysis and the team now set about finding a solution. They could try to sell the business outright but the market was thin and the group was reluctant to take a major asset write-down. The second alternative was a shut down but again the costs were not acceptable to the group executives. Faced with unpalatable choices, the general manager devised a plan to sell the plant and tooling to a local subcontractor with a guarantee to buy back components at an agreed price over a three-year period; after that he would be free to buy from any source. None of the firms contacted could afford to buy the plant outright, hence a deal was struck whereby the outside machine shop would supply the fittings at cost until the cumulative overheads saved would equal the plant cost. Naturally the machinery remained the property of Company A until its sales price was paid off.

This was a neat arrangement for converting fixed to variable costs. Company A benefited by receiving cheaper fittings, a dedicated source and the opportunity to move into smaller premises; in turn, the subcontractor was able to expand his plant with the minimum of added overheads. Finally the majority of the tool-room fitters and operatives were able to keep their jobs – even though they worked for a different firm.

Example 3. High-tech company preparing for a business cycle recession

This is an example of an American specialist glass company supplying hi-tech products to science-based manufacturers and to the trade. The company had a good solid record but investors had not given the business a good rating because of its unpredictable performance. The record over a 4-year period was as follows:

Specialist glass company

($ million)

Year	1	2	3	4
Sales	18	22	24	20
Post-tax profits	1.7	1.9	2.8	2

Fearing the onset of a recession a small group of shareholders encouraged the company to enroll a non-executive director who had experience with profit improvement programmes. It was proposed that he would work with the executives with the aim of improving the uneven profit record and strengthening the balance sheet. With some reluctance the board accepted the newcomer; after all, the company was profitable and how could an outsider possibly understand a business that the directors had taken decades to master? The view of the chairman eventually prevailed; he was a sizeable shareholder in his own right and had been concerned about the lack of stock-market acceptance.

The new director recommended a 6-step programme for discovering the trading strengths and weaknesses of the company. He insisted that the work should be done by executives on the principle that they would believe and implement the results if they did the analysis themselves. The auditors could provide financial help.

Stage 1 Product profitability programme

Step 1. The products were divided into five groups recognised at all levels of the business. There were complaints by the previous president that some of his pet ideas had been put into the 'others' category but the final outcome was, as shown below: Rods and Tubes, Fabrications, Special Projects, Moulded Products and Others.

Step 2. The direct costs of material and labour were allocated to the products for the last financial year; despite changes in current expense levels it was deemed better to use actual, not projected figures. Any adjustments for current trading could be made subsequently. The accountants were able to produce these accurately so the allocation was no problem. As will be seen from the table, this was a high margin business with a 72% gross contribution on sales.

Step 3. The allocation of production overheads of $5 million was a problem because it had always been assumed that costs were pro-rata with labour. It was decided to allocate expenses initially by major cost centres and then by cost concentration. The plant consisted of several high-cost furnaces (with their associated handling arrangements) and there was other moulding and processing machinery. It surprised the team that Fabrication, regarded as a high-skill operation, attracted so much cost. The results are shown in the table.

Step 4. Development overheads of $2.4 million were allocated by asking the head of the department and his section leaders; unfortunately, no cost record was kept of individual projects and this was deemed the most accurate method. The allocation surprised no one; it was known that a particular section spent a great deal of time with customers on special projects which was entirely justified by the excellent margins.

Step 5. There were sales and administrative expenses of $3 million and $2 million respectively. Many of the costs in both departments were incurred in handling a large number of small orders. There was an efficient internal system which acknowledged, ordered, handled, shipped, invoiced and collected. However, it was expensive and most of the items could be allocated to transactions. Other sales costs could be associated with specialised customer groups. Most of the remaining were divided by sales volume.

The completed table for year 4

($m)

Products	Total	Rods	Fabrication	Special	Moulded	Others
Sales	20	6	2	5	6	1
Materials	3.2	1.2	0.4	0.5	0.9	0.2
Labour	2.4	0.6	0.5	0.5	0.6	0.2
Total	5.6	1.8	0.9	1	1.5	0.4
Contribution	14.4	4.2	1.1	4	4.5	0.6
Less overheads						
Production	5	1.0	1.5	1.0	1.2	0.3
Dev	2.4	0.8	0.2	1.0	0.2	0.2
Sales	3	1.0	0.1	0.2	1.5	0.2
Admin	2	0.4	0.1	0.1	1.0	0.4
Total	12.4	3.2	1.9	2.3	3.9	1.1
Profits	2.0	1.0	(0.8)	1.7	0.6	(0.5)

Step 6. Agree on the conclusions. This was much the hardest part because special interest lobbying was at its strongest, each group trying to retain relics and the principle of 'we have always done it this way'. It fell to the outside director to be a third-party adjudicator; he knew that he could afford to be tough.

The study group's recommendation to the board. The erratic profit record was caused almost entirely by uneven off-take of Special Projects by very few customers. The work was so profitable that when demand was good overall performance was excellent; when it was poor, the losses from Fabrications and Others pulled the company down and made it vulnerable to a takeover.

- Rods and Tubes: Little change was needed except that a minimum order size was recommended and sales to small customers should be passed to distributors. There would also be some administrative saving.
- Fabrications: This was an excellent franchise opportunity to be handled like a *Stage 2* cost-reduction exercise. Reluctantly, the production director agreed that the skills could be mastered by franchisees in a few weeks after instruction by his specialised team; he also agreed that some of his plant could be sold to the franchisees, providing some skills were kept within the company. There were overhead savings to be made but many of the skilled men were re-deployed as franchisees or trainers.
- Special Projects: No change except that the performance encouraged the sales director to find other accounts overseas.
- Moulded Products: These were good lines which were packaged and sold through distributors.
- Others: Despite the outcry from the 'special interests', most of these lines were dropped.

It was estimated that Year 4 profits could have been boosted by around 50% if the programme had been implemented from day one of that year. This took into account the loss of contribution by 'others' and an 18-month gestation period for franchising fabrication. In the longer term, franchising fabrication would add at least a further 25% to profits.

Wrecking Management Action

Just as beneficial action improves a business, so do wrecking policies destroy it. A story is told of a leading firm of insolvency practitioners who kept a list of chief executives and chairmen who were almost guaranteed to ruin any business they headed.

It may seem bizarre to list bad practices but they should serve as an early warning for shareholders, customers, suppliers and all those associated with the business.

Anybody visiting a company should remember the observations of Bill Mackie and the other tell-tale signs listed earlier in the chapter. Any meeting will be able to establish whether the business places too great a reliance on one customer or how the managing director spends his time. We saw earlier how the managing director of the foundry company spent more time working with diversifications than on the core activity.

More of the larger listed companies have failed from making an unwise acquisition than from any other cause. It is often the sign of weak managements that they buy a company near to failure. The decline will be accelerated if the purchase is made on borrowed money.

Another sign of desperation is when the board disposes of a profitable part of the company to pay off debts. The board will hail this as a decisive step towards solvency, but the most competent people are either fired or leave. Unfortunately, this action is often at the request of a bank whose managers are reluctant to change the real cause of the weakness – that being the chief executive or chairman.

CHAPTER 7

THIRD-GENERATION TECHNIQUES FOR 'FLATTENING' THE ORGANISATION

The last chapter provided a grim reminder that companies go bust even in good times, but as the evidence from Syspas shows they are much more likely to fail during low points in a cycle. Over the 25 years covered by the report, several cycles were at work. The first was the rhythm associated with the 22.4-year Hale cycle, the second the 10-year Juglar and then in the early 1990s, the start of the Kondratieff downwave. Each of these rhythms triggered several failures; but these could be accelerated in the second half of the 1990s, as the long wave is felt by business.

The most important component in the Taffler solvency models is profitability. While it is true that a really strong business can weather losses, possibly for several years, most companies can only withstand the cash haemorrhage for a short time before it becomes impossible to pay creditors and there is no alternative but to call in the receiver. Companies can, of course, fail at any time but their real problems arise during a deflation when volume actually falls and the margin on revenue is insufficient to cover fixed costs.

Consider the case of two companies, both having sales of 100 units. Company A is a conventional business with a gross margin (after direct cost of materials and labour) of 50% which, after overheads of 40 units, leaves a profit of 10; sales can fall by 20% before A is marginal. By contrast B has the same sales as A, but because at least 20 of the fixed costs are now made variable, the profit is still 10 but the break-even point is now 66.6 – or a third less than current levels.

	Company A units	Company B units
Sales	100	100
Less variable costs	50	70
Gross profit	50 50%	30 30%
Less overheads	40	20
Pre-tax profit	10	10
Break-even point	40/0.5 = 80	20/0.3 = 66.6

Both companies are profitable but A is obviously more vulnerable to a severe downturn than B because it has converted fixed to variable costs as a deliberate act of policy. Part of the answer for this decision was described in the previous chapter. For although not a rescue operation, the third example showed how profitability could be improved by analysing the product lines, then making different plans for each group to improve the margins. One of these was to franchise or license a product to reduce the break-even point. There are other techniques such as remote working, using agencies and an extension of re-engineering described earlier which are the subjects of this chapter.

About Franchising

Most people are familiar with firms like McDonald's, Kentucky Fried Chicken or Tie Rack; they know they are franchises but are not concerned with how the idea works. Basically franchising is a marketing concept: a franchisor has a branded product or service which he licenses to an independently owned unit called a franchisee who has no capital ties with the originator. The relationship is governed by a format which defines precisely how the business will be managed. Most of the famous names mentioned earlier will be privately owned and their people will be employed by the franchisee to standards defined by the franchisor.

Most of the modern franchises have been made possible by an innovator who has made a traditional craft, skill or service into a business. Some years ago printing was a skilled trade requiring an apprenticeship; no longer. Desk-top publishing and modern offset-litho machines have made it possible for someone entering the trade to produce good quality reports, manuals, sales aids or letterheads cheaply and efficiently. The same techniques can be applied to many different trades – even professions.

In America there were more than 550,000 franchised businesses generating sales of more than $800 billion in 1994; assuming that every person employed could generate $50,000 sales a year then the total numbers employed would be in the order of 16 million people. At a time when many large companies are laying off thousands of people, franchisees have absorbed a great many of those made redundant which is one of the reasons unemployment in America has remained consistently below European levels. For more information about franchising in general, readers should consult the franchise associations listed under the heading of Further Reading.

The franchisor offers a proven business method that has been tried and tested in pilot schemes. The system is called a format which often includes a nationally known and protected brand-name that is supported by promotion. The format also includes complete operating procedures and an initial training course for operating an independent business. When starting, help is given in finding premises (if needed) in the best positions, the necessary tools, sales materials, accounting system, documentation, etc. The franchisor supplies all the initial set-up and training for a franchise fee which may run into hundreds of thousands for a McDonald's down to a few thousand for a simple one-person franchise. There will also usually be a royalty payable on sales volume.

In turn, franchisees have a unique opportunity for independent working within a tried system and requiring little prior experience; they will, however, need determination and persistence to succeed. This is why many franchisors insist that those who want to take a licence first work for some time with an existing franchisee. Franchisees will be required to sign a contract agreeing to work within the terms of the format. These are the headings usually found in a licence agreement:

- The franchisor has the name, idea, process, business method or specialised equipment that is licensed to the franchisee.

- The agreement obliges the franchisor to provide the franchisee with a blueprint for starting up and staying in business through initial training, the provision of manuals and follow-up support.
- The franchisee owns his business, provides the funds and is responsible for management and recruitment. The concern is run according to the standards set out in the licence agreement and operations manual.
- Payment for granting the franchise is usually a down payment for the business format and a management service fee for continued support.
- The agreement includes a termination date and an option to renegotiate the contract.

However, this chapter is not concerned about *starting* a franchise but using the technique for *converting* what was a wholly owned store, depot or service station into an independently owned unit. In this way the fixed costs of each unit then becomes a variable cost of sales – so achieving the primary aim of reducing the break-even point. To convert an existing outlet such as a shop is generally an easier proposition for both parties than to start up a new outlet. Instead of beginning a new venture the potential franchisee already knows the business; the manager buys the store and is responsible for all the administration including hiring employees, accounting, promotion, insurances and the like. These are the relative changes in responsibilities:

- The franchisor exchanges direct sales for a royalty but at the same time loses the responsibility for the fixed costs associated with running the store plus the associated head office expenses. In return the new franchisor receives a down payment for the business plus an improved cash flow when the newly independent unit pays for any merchandise or service received. This neatly fills the objective of converting fixed to variable costs and turning assets into cash.
- In turn the franchisee becomes self-employed and owns a capital asset that could some day be worth much more than the initial valuation. He has an existing customer base, is familiar with the product, understands the

systems and is used to dealing with staff. While he will be required to pay a royalty on sales, this should not be onerous for there is usually a 20% increase in sales volume when an owned outlet goes into private hands.

Franchising also reduces the problem of the high failure rates associated with new business start-ups because, by definition, the franchisee is working to a tried and tested format; in practice the level of bankruptcies is less than 5% compared with around 50% for the first two or three years operation. In addition, the franchisor provides a specialised back-up, seldom available for new businesses.

Licensing

Although franchising is a form of licensing, the technique can be used in its own right either for individuals or for groups of people such as a sales force. The principle rests on the licensor granting a licence, probably to a specialist, for operating under the brand-name of the parent. Business is passed to the licensee who has the necessary equipment to carry out the work. This idea is applicable to people such as aerial erectors or to service engineers.

One very successful example of converting paid employees to, in this case, licensees was in NSI Ltd, a subsidiary of Thorn EMI which erected satellite antennae. The company, based at Harpenden in Hertfordshire, used to employ 130 installers whose assignments were managed by a despatcher at head office. That office obtained the business which was passed to regional managers who then organised the installers and there was little incentive for those in the field to increase either their productivity or customer service. The managing director decided to create a 'flatter' organisation by licensing independent erectors whose work would be generated through several regional centres.

An outside firm of consultants conducted a feasibility study headed by Michael Way of the Centre for Franchise Marketing (CFM) Consulting. The analysis showed that if the erectors worked for a fixed sum per aerial, all the responsibility for managing the erectors, their vehicles, expenses, pension plans, etc., could be devolved to individuals, thereby reducing much of the head-office costs.

The marketing was devolved to nine regional centres so bringing the activity closer to the customer. The erection was handled by licensees who worked to a fixed formula after a successful pilot study in North-East England. This was carried out by two ex-employees plus one outsider called David Hood who had agreed to act as 'guinea pigs'. Within two weeks Hood was generating enough income to take on two assistants during busy times.

Although applicants for licences were invited from current employees, only a few of the original NSI erectors applied. Instead 'outsiders' were recruited and, despite a high management fee of between 20% to 30% of sales, productivity doubled and individuals could earn around £40,000 after their costs of providing the van, consumable materials and paying insurances and pension schemes. When the licensee realised he could make a direct contribution to productivity, sales increased by 20% and individuals helped market the service through the radio outlets.

The company results were equally astonishing; the break-even point was reduced by 70%. Departments that previously had run personnel, motor vehicles, supervision, stores, salaries and pensions were disbanded. Instead of the fixed cost of running installers at over £1,500 per month, the cash saved could be applied to marketing, new product research and diversification to ensure business continuity.

Make Professional People Outworkers

Another method to convert fixed into variable costs is to change the contractual relationships of full-time staff appointments into independent professionals then to hire back their skills. In the early part of the 1980s Rank Xerox photocopiers were subjected to ferocious competition from the Japanese, in particular Canon. In a most unusual move to reduce fixed expenses but retain skills, the company experimented with making professionals – such as personnel selectors, trainers, public relations practitioners, marketeers, internal auditors, health and safety specialists – into self-employed individuals who would subcontract their services back to the parent.

The plan, which is described in more detail in *Avoiding Adversity*, followed a similar programme to franchising. Once a business idea had been formed it was pilot tested and then modified in the light of experience. In the Xerox case the 'guinea pig' was Roger Walker who set up his own business as a personnel consultant and trainer in Stony Stratford near Milton Keynes. Initially his first-year salary was guaranteed but then he was required to quote for every job undertaken. The test was successful and up to sixty people became self-employed. This experiment had a number of interesting results:

Efficiency went up by 100%. When people could carry out their tasks without the interruption of telephone calls, impromptu meetings and the usual social life of a business, efficiency went up. One of the most significant changes was the role of secretaries who became the link between the managers and outworkers.

Cost savings. The company eventually saved £3 million in fixed costs from the professionals who had set up their own businesses and subcontracted their expertise to their previous parent. When analysed, each outworker had saved the company three times their salary from the various oncosts of office space, pensions, paid holidays, cars, social security costs, secretaries, office service and the like.

New independent professionals. These were able to contract their expertise to other clients who were not competitive with Xerox. Not only did the company retain skills and experience but it was enriched with knowledge gained elsewhere.

Office space was shrunk. When the newly independent professionals visited the company they used any room that was available. This idea called 'hot desking' has been used by other companies where employees work from any free desk in a building rather than occupying a fixed space. For example, IBM's sales and marketing team used to occupy about 230 square feet of office space; now this has reduced to 180 square feet. People work from home or use any desk available in the company building. Many companies now estimate that their demand for space will decline by 25% over the next few years causing a serious dent in the need for commercial office accommodation.

Although by 1995 the number of people employed

full-time from their own homes is still only 5% of the working population in Britain, in the United States some 40% work at least some of their time at home considerably reducing the need for public transport. The numbers are bound to increase because technology makes it relatively simple for an individual to work in the country and tax regime of their choice.

Agency Working

As suggested earlier, the franchising route to cost reduction and improved individual performance is open to any operation providing a regular customer service, such as a shop, a distribution depot, or a support operation. The United States has taken this a stage further in several ways. Apart from making a wider use of franchising, there are numerous examples of companies either converting their sales operations into agencies handling several non-competing lines or alternatively encouraging their representatives to join existing agencies. The results of both are the same. The fixed cost of running a sales or service operation is converted to the variable cost of paying a commission.

Agencies provide a relatively low-cost entry into sales territories that otherwise would be expensive to serve through direct sales. One estimate showed that a manufacturer's sales strength was expanded sixfold by deploying the same expense into servicing agents. There were some 30,000 agencies available in the United States during the late 1980s offering a wide range of expertise from hi-tech to toys; the Manufacturers' Agents National Association listed over ninety specialisations. A survey found that on average 50% of manufacturers used agencies; they are also used for missionary work supporting distributors.

Catalogue selling from several different principals is common in most countries but the size of the United States and the wide range of merchandise encouraged growth among the main population areas. In more recent times, specialist salesmen who have cultivated a number of accounts either leave their company to start up on their own or negotiate an agency deal for their territory. In some cases a company wishing to save direct expenses has encouraged their whole sales force to become independent, offering them non-competitive lines to make up the revenue.

Re-engineering Helps to Create a 'Flatter Organisation'

Hammer and Champy describe how re-engineering has a part to play in improving linkages by converting what were once sequential operations into a process. For example, the Ford Motor Company (FMC) in North America employed 500 people to manually check purchase orders with goods inwards notes before payment could be authorised. They compared the same function with Mazda (in whom they had an equity stake) and found only five people in the equivalent department.

Using the Pareto principle that 80% of the problems (in this case) came from 20% of the notes, the investigators came to the conclusion that by far the majority of purchase orders could be checked in the goods inwards system directly on to a terminal to which the orders were recalled. Once the material had been checked for quantity and quality, an entry into the system immediately authorised a cheque to be raised in payment. One further refinement defined payment to be initiated when ownership passed to FMC; i.e. when the component was *fitted*, not received.

Franchising Manufacturing

The franchising ideas described earlier can also be applied to manufacturing. There may be certain bespoke finishing operations, not unlike the fabrication described in example 3 of the earlier chapter that can be sensibly subcontracted to independent units with a considerable saving in order handling and other overheads. Where operations can be brought close to a customer, there is an increase in sales, a better customer relationship and the parent company's expertise is there for support.

An example of this concept in operation is a tile company that was losing money on finishing operations and was able to franchise its speciality – personalised tiles – to independent glaziers; these became franchisees and had either direct contact with customers or contact through retail outlets. The innovation allowed the parent company to reduce considerably the amount of finished inventory (and the probability of dead stock). It also allowed ordering procedures to be simplified and the number of those employed handling small batches to be almost eliminated. Several of these specialists took the offer of becoming franchisees and gained particularly favourable terms when negotiating raw materials and the price of second-hand plant such as kilns.

The tile manufacturer's (TM) products are decorated tiles for interior walls, floors and patios sold mainly to builders' merchants and also directly to specialist shops and larger stores. The clay is bought in, fired into tiles then decorated with transfers before being glazed, packed and shipped to distributors. Business had been excellent but there was increasing competition from specialists selling personalised tiles at a considerable premium. The senior management decided action should be taken. An analysis of the business showed that the number of products and their decoration had become extended during the boom years but their *lack of profitability* was masked by good margins on the major lines. A further analysis showed that many direct small accounts had been opened which were *costly to service* despite the higher margins and the *overheads* were being skewed towards the specialist business. It was estimated that a volume/price decline of some 30% was quite possible in the event of a downturn in the latter part of the 1990s. This would push the business firmly into *loss*.

Proposed Solution

A small management group was set up to consider alternatives to the specialist work; it was a growth business requiring small production teams working with a plethora of uneconomical batches. In addition, it was difficult to forecast individual demand so the inventory of specialist tiles was expanding and it was increasingly expensive to ship small quanitities. The working party came up with the following proposition that was duly costed in the feasibility study shown below.

It was suggested that the finishing operation could be undertaken by franchisees. Unfinished blanks would be supplied, together with a large selection of transfers. On receiving an order, a small batch would be made up and shipped, so keeping the specialised inventory at a minimum. TM would receive a royalty of 10% on sales. The franchise fee would cover the cost of the small-batch kilns, an initial inventory, transfers and the necessary kit and training to run a business. Where TM had surplus kilns, these would be sold at book value.

Feasibility study on franchising specialist finishing operations of TM

Balance Sheet (£ million)

	June 30 1993	Proposed plan	Difference	Ref.
Fixed assets	32	28	(4)	1
Current assets				
Inventory	22	17	(5)	2
Receivables	15	11	(4)	3
Cash	1	1		
Less liabilities				
Bank overdraft	(16)	(3)	13	4
Creditors	(14)	(14)		5
Net current assets	8	12		
Term loans	(14)	(14)		
Net worth	26	26	0	

Operating statement

	Present	Proposed	Reference
Sales	90	68	6
Indirect		16	7
Royalty		3	8
Total		87	
Less direct costs	54	24	9
Labour		26	10
Gross contribution	36	37	
Less overheads			
Marketing	14	10	11
Administration	9	5	12
Development	1	3	13
Interest payable	4	2	14
Total	28	19	
Profit before tax	8	18	15
Employees	2200	1750	
Sales per employee	£41K	£50	
Profit per employee	3.6K	£10.3K	

Reference notes to TM programme
1 Fixed assets. Items of production, transport and distribution sold for cash at WDV.

2. Inventory down by around 25%. Franchisees carrying finished and unfinished tiles.
3. Receivables, as for inventory.
4. Bank overdraft reduced from cash realised.
5. Creditors, no change.
6. Sales. Direct sales reduced by 25%.
7. Sales. Indirect through franchisees. Unfinished tiles sales up 50% on previous sales 22 (less 50% margin).
8. Royalty assumed at 10% on 33.
9. Materials unchanged at 27%.
10. Direct labour reduced by 15% from 30%.
11. Marketing reduced by 4, the cost of distribution and sales to smaller accounts.
12. Administration reduced by 4; fewer people, reduced accounts, less administration.
13. Development activity trebled.
14. Interest payable on bank borrowings halved.

The results of the feasibility study showed direct costs fell faster than sales; other savings were in marketing, and administration. Some overhead costs saved were transferred to development for generating new products; however, the main benefit was the bottom line where profit on sales had increased 100% and sales per employee was up by 22%. The balance sheet was stronger with reduced short-term borrowings from the sale of assets. Finally, the break-even point had been reduced over two thirds from sales of £70 million to £45 million.

This was also a good deal for the franchisees. They were able to set up their own businesses, serving largely the retail trade where the brand-name was well received. In addition, they were able to create new markets using a wide range of transfers to personalise kitchen and bathroom ranges where the product could stand higher margins.

Example of a Third Generation Downsizing Operation

System Resources Inc (SRI) is an office furniture and machinery distributor carrying mostly middle-range lines with a selection of luxury items and some cheaper imported lines from the Pacific east rim; the electronic kit is maintained by the business. Most sales are made on credit although there is a growing leasing business handled through a finance house. There is one showroom at head office and two more in local towns. The business has shown a good growth over the last four years.

Profit Record of SRI over 4 years

Year	1	2	3	4
Sales $ million	12	15	18	21
Pre-tax profits $ million	1.2	1.4	1.8	2

This performance was sound but the private shareholders, fearing a decline in business during a Kondratieff downwave, decided to look more closely at product line profitability with the cooperation of the management. A team was set up similar to that described earlier in the chapter. It was decided to analyse the business under the headings of standard products, other products, leasing and electronics. The gross margin was known but the overheads had always been allocated pro rata with sales volume; it was decided to distribute these according to activity.

Product line profitability of SRI
($ million)

Products	Total	Standard products	Other products	Leasing	Electronic
Sales	21	10	3	4	4
Contribution	8.7	4	1.4	1.8	1.5
Less overheads					
Selling	3.2	1.4	0.5	0.5	0.8
Technical	1.2	0.2	0.1		0.9
Admin	1.5	0.7	0.2	0.3	0.3
Interest	0.8	0.4	0.1	0.1	0.2
Total overheads	6.7	2.7	0.9	0.9	2.2
profits	2.0	1.3	0.5	0.9	(0.7)

The analysis showed that while SRI as a whole was profitable, the electronic side was losing money but closing it down was no answer; the management believed that sales of other products would be damaged if the company could not offer a complete office package. The team suggested several alternatives for board consideration:

1. Retain electronic sales but close down the equipment servicing unit and subcontract the work elsewhere. This

is often a sound option, particularly if some of the technicians can be taken on by the subcontractor. However, it was discarded in favour of the buy-out option – see below.

2. Increase sales to achieve greater recovery of overheads for every unit sold. This could be an excellent policy early in a business cycle when costs need not rise as fast as sales; it could be a disaster in a downwave when the costs of borrowing would more than extinguish any rise in margins and when additional sales could only be 'bought' with tight margins against tough competition.

3. Increase prices to raise margins. This could be a good policy for selected products but might be difficult in a distribution business where branded products are being sold.

4. Prune the overheads to reduce costs and close the loss-makers. This is a bludgeon-like First Generation remedy where costs are pruned irrespective of their impact on the company. In any case it is unlikely to work with a firm like SRI which is well run and has a high turnover per individual. In addition, SRI is not a hire and fire company.

As none of these remedies were acceptable to the board, it was decided to apply either 'Third Generation' or 'Shamrock' ideas explained on page 116. Third Generation techniques operate at the cutting edge of a company by creating separately financed units from what were sales and service units. Shamrock ideas separate the activities at the 'core' of a business from those that might be subcontracted. Both ideas enable an organisation to run at a much lower level of fixed costs.

In the case of SRI, the team recommended to sell the electronic repair and maintenance unit to the management and staff then contract back services from the independent unit. The arrangement could make sense; SRI had the benefit of buying the services when needed, the unit the opportunity of winning new non-competitive business elsewhere.

In addition, the team recommended that to reduce the

break-even point still further it would be possible to franchise the two outside sales branches and use the same format to open outlets in other areas.

Organising the management buy-out (MBO) of the electronic servicing division

MBO techniques were described briefly in Chapter 6. Although the process was well tried in the years after the Second World War, it became quite a vogue in the 1980s to give managers and employees an opportunity to buy a business and run it independently of the original owner. Venture capital specialists would help the new shareholders with presenting the case to the vendors, arranging loans and assisting in the negotiations. Once independent, a new company can often achieve better operational efficiencies than when a division of a larger business; ownership almost invariably gives the management an additional incentive to perform well and very strict cash-flow policies can be applied to pay off loans. After a few years of independence the new shareholders can expect a profitable flotation on one of the emerging stock markets.

For the original shareholder, MBOs are seen as a way for a parent company to prune subsidiaries it no longer wants in exchange for cash. This not only applies to divisions but sections of a business as well. For example, there is nothing to stop SRI forming the electronic servicing unit into a company and selling it to the general manager and his team; one name for it could be System Resources Electronics Inc (SREI), although the name might need changing later.

This is how the arrangement might work: SREI had assets of 10 vehicles worth $80,000 and test equipment and other kit worth $45,000; they also held spares with a stock of $25,000 – total $150,000. On the liability side, they had creditors of $25,000 and bank borrowings of $40,000. Net worth of $85,000. A majority stake of say 60% of the overall value could be sold to the managers and employees. This would cost them $51,000 (60% of $85,000). The remaining 40% stake could remain with SRI to be purchased by the SREI team later on.

Redundancy pay would be due for the people leaving SRI which would help to meet the offered shareholding. In addition, the deal guaranteed 75% of SREI's previous income for the first year; This would give them time to establish other customers; the remainder would come from new service contracts. SREI was also encouraged to sell consumable stores previously supplied by SRI which would reduce some of the parent's low value invoicing costs. Assuming sales of $500,000 a year, and a gross margin of 33%, SREI would have an income of $165,000. The cost of the new operation was further reduced by moving to smaller premises with a few of the engineers working directly from home. Initially SREI did not handle their own accounting which was subcontracted to SRI.

Summary: The new company would be formed with assets of some $85,000, 60% to be owned by the management team, the balance by SRI. It would operate separately from the parent company but have contractual links to handle electronic equipment servicing. There would be a transitional guaranteed payment for the first year, the rest to be on contract. The new company would be free to win servicing business for SRI's customers and non-competing principals. They would also become distributors for other equipment providing it caused no conflict of interest.

SRI now retains a 40% shareholding in the new company and receives $51,000 in cash. Operationally it means that the company has converted the fixed cost of a service department to the variable cost of a subcontractor; there will also be some administrative saving. Clearly there was a risk of SRI losing control of servicing but in a downwave most competitors would have to take similar action to reduce costs. As suggested earlier, independence concentrates the mind wonderfully; people working for themselves put in at least 20% more effort than when working for someone else.

Franchising the sales outlets would be tackled in just the same way as other franchises. In this case, the franchisor, SRI, possessed a well-known trade name which it licensed to independently owned branches, which operated under a procedure or format determined by the parent. In practical terms SRI's branches would be sold to the managers and staff but run on procedures determined by the franchisor. The franchisees were supplied with equipment at an agreed discount and with all the material needed to run and service an independent business. SRI was paid for supplies and received an agreed royalty on sales. This is how the sales branches were franchised:

Assuming that each branch has sales of $3 million, the assets looked like this:

SRI Branch Balance Sheet ($ thousand)

Fixed assets, vehicles, etc.	30
Inventory (turned over 9 times/year)	333
Debtors (paid in 60 days)	500
Less	
Creditors (inventory paid in 60 days)	(512)
Bank borrowings	(250)
Net current assets	71
Net assets	101

Part of the agreed consideration were the redundancy payments due to the new owners; the remainder was provided by banks given confidence by SRI's continued relationship with the new business. If the gross margin on sales was one third, each franchised branch received a contribution of about $1 million on sales of $3 million before expenses and SRI's 10% royalty. However, as sales invariably increase once the owner is running the business, even a net 10% extra volume would raise the gross margin by nearly $90,000.

There were inevitable problems when it came to negotiating the transfer of accounts from SRI's control to those of the franchisee. Generally the franchisor tried to keep national accounts while passing the smaller customers to the franchisees. Initially SRI kept the special products and the leasing business, passing most of the general accounts to the franchisee.

Impact on SRI's balance sheet. By selling each of the two branches to a franchisor and assuming the assets are valued as before, SRI's assets and liabilities would be reduced by the same amount. This means that the company's own borrowings would be reduced by $500,000 quite apart from any cash received. This is how SRI's activity analysis looked after the buy-out and branch franchise:

($ million)

Categories	Total	Standard products Direct	Standard products Franch.	Special products	Leased contracts	Business machines	Reference
Sales	18.8	4	4	3	4	3.8	1
Less costs	12.2	2.4	3.6	1.6	2.2	2.4	2
service	0.9					0.9	3
Contribution	5.7	1.6	0.4	1.4	1.8	0.5	
Plus royalty	0.6		0.6				4
Total income	6.3	1.6	1.0	1.4	1.8	0.5	
Less costs							
Sales	2.1	0.4	0.1	0.5	0.5	0.6	5
Technical	0.2	0.1		0.1			
Admin	1.1	0.3	0.1	0.2	0.3	0.2	6
Interest	0.5	0.3		0.1	0.1		7
Total overhead	3.9	1.1	0.2	0.9	0.9	0.8	
Profit	2.4	0.5	0.8	0.5	0.9	(0.3)	

Notes: There are differences compared to the table in Stage 1.

Ref 1. The standard products are divided $4 million direct sales and a further $6m between the two franchisees at list price less one third. Small value orders transferred to SREI $0.2 million.

Ref 2. There is a gross profit of 40% on direct sales of standard products, franchisees have a resale margin of one third.

Ref 3. The cost of servicing the electronic machines has been included in direct costs.

Ref 4. There is a royalty of 10% on the franchisee sales of $6 million.

Ref 5. The sales cost is reduced by $1.1 million after transferring expenses to the franchisees and SREI.

Ref 6. Administrative costs have also been reduced to reflect the lower number of transactions and personnel.

Ref 7. Interest rates have been reduced to reflect the lower level of borrowings.

Overall, profits have been increased (without taking into account redundancy costs) by 20%. But even more important, the break-even point is now $11.6 million compared with $16.1 million previously, lowering the margin of safety nearly 30% below the sales level of year 4. This was estimated to be enough to meet the expected downturn. In addition, the numbers employed were reduced by about 70, or 40% from the previous level of 175. This increased sales per employee to nearly $180,000 represented a rise of 50%. These changes have occurred with the minimum number of people put out of work because over 60 of the 70 will have been found new employment in the bought-out businesses where they have more control over their own fortunes. The reconstruction will have caused only 10 to lose their jobs. The proposals assumed that both branches are franchised at once, taking no account of opening new franchises. In practice, one branch was run as a pilot scheme to test the format before extending the programme.

With fewer people, there will be less need for staff functions. For example, the company would no longer need the full-time personnel and training manager who might be able to set up on their own as a remote worker. Redundancy pay would be offered and probably two thirds of the previous salary in return for 3 days work a week for the first year. The redundancy could be set against a car and other kit such as a word processor and perhaps office furniture. The pension and other financial affairs would have to be handled independently and the ex-manager would be free to work for other non-competing firms – with SRI possibly helping with introductions.

CHAPTER 8

POLICIES FOR THE DOWNWAVE

Managing a business in the latter half of the 1990s and into the new century could be very testing. It could also be quite different from previous decades – a time where discontinuity replaces convention and the unusual becomes normal. There are historical similarities but this time they will not come singly. One could be the German Inflation of the early 1920s, another the Depression of the 1930s. In modern times the nearest parallel could be the early 1970s, with rampant inflation followed by a deep recession. The good news is that in the past, despite considerable difficulties, the majority of enterprises not only survived but thrived. We should aim to learn from them.

Another parallel could be the Industrial Revolution where fabrication underwent a profound change. Originally a man's craft dominated his machine but during the industrial revolution the spinning jenny and loom became the master. Now in the coming knowlege-based society we have what international consultant Michael White calls the Cybernetic Revolution; what Alvin Toffler calls the Third Wave. Over two hundred years ago entrepreneurs learned how to bring together machines, the people and the power to run them. Individual productivity, formerly craft-based, rocketed; in the course of decades many fresh industries were created and new towns were built to house the workers. Interestingly enough, land productivity also rose – enough to supply the wheat-bread to nourish the industrial workers.

Now in the latter decades of the 20th century, plant can be sited far away from power sources and many can run without any operators. Information technology also enables machines to do the work of the white-collar managers and clerks, formerly needed to monitor and control factories and service industries. Michael White estimates that IT and automation will advance so quickly in the decades straddling the millenium that by 2005 only some 40% of the US working population will have full-time employment: 2% in agriculture, 8% in manufacturing and 30% in service industries. The remainder can look forward to only intermittent work – something that will cause apalling political problems – to be discussed in greater detail in Chapter 10.

Business management is also undergoing dramatic changes through the ability to outsource not only manufacturing but also services. Moving production to the cheapest areas has a long history. The British North American colonies provided cheap labour before the revolution and the Far East was traditionally the source of cheap manufactured goods and components for the West until the Second World War. With the industrialisation of the Pacific rim, many Western companies are now outsourcing production to countries such as Vietnam where over 40 energetic people can be hired for the cost of one German worker.

The choice is so considerable that companies purchase from areas with the appropriate skills. For example, when the Boeing 747 was first launched in 1970 it had 97% American parts; by 1994, specialisation has reduced the American content to 67%. Now American firms produce about 14% of the world's manufactured products but these are spread around the globe employing 8.5 million people and most of the products exchanged are between divisions of multinational companies. Mitsubishi, for example, makes most of Intel's chips under licence and Texas Instruments makes some of the D-RAM chips available in Japan's most efficient factories. These chips are then shipped to Singapore for finishing before returning to the United States to be incorporated in American products.

The interchange does not only concern manufacturing. Swissair's accounting is located in Bombay where well-qualified staff can do the job at a fraction of the Swiss cost. The same is true of processing paper work. American insurance companies have located a large office in the Carribean and a Canadian agency uses an Irish office to handle travel arrangements. Also in Ireland, the American Cigma healthcare company have set up a remote station to filter insurance claims;

about 5,000 forms and documents (about 20% of Cigma's business) are received daily by plane and courier, which are then processed, entered on to computers and transmitted back via dedicated optic fibre cables to Delaware in time for the following day's business.

Managers have had to learn new techniques throughout time but now the sheer speed of applying new ideas will accelerate. Probably the nearest parallel is a country attacked in wartime. Not only has it to resist a foe but embark on a very rapid learning curve. Most peacetime leaders cannot make the adjustment. This is why many of the leading politicians, generals, admirals and air marshals have had to be removed within the first few weeks of hostilities. Luckily there will usually be able people to take their place.

That businesses have to adapt is nothing new as has been proved by their response to the upwave and downwave of the Kondratieff long wave. As the downwave started almost certainly in 1990, this will dominate management thinking well into the early years of the 21st century.

As we saw in Chapter 7, a business can work on a much lower break-even point if as many costs as possible are variable – in that they are only incurred when they arise, usually with volume. This has two primary effects: the first is that the break-even point is reduced so enabling the business to be profitable at a lower sales volume. Secondly, this is only possible if managers learn contracting skills; in other words many professional abilities are purchased from outside the business. The most successful ways of converting fixed to variable costs and at the same time making individuals autonomous are out-working, franchising and agency working.

Another way of 'flattening an organisation' is what Charles Handy in the *Age of Unreason* describes as 'federal'. This consists of a small central office and dispersed self-contained units. The centre should provide the basic direction and monitoring of a business while the individual parts have the flexibility to move and adapt to their given role. In fact many organisations have now adopted this approach with the giant Swedish-Swiss ABB run by 100 people at the centre and BP with 200. Others such as Richard Branson's Virgin group are run by as few as six people.

The principle applies to the federated units as much as to the centre, forming a cascade of responsible units which can also be provided by franchising. Handy goes one further by suggesting that each unit consists of three elements, like the three parts of a shamrock leaf. The first consists of the hard core of professionals and others, without which a business could not function; they are essential to the direction, the creation of business, delivery of product and customer payment.

The second part comprises those skills or services the centre does not possess. For example, the company might buy in marketing skills from an outworker, a franchise specialist to advise on the viability of a licensing programme or a janitoring service to clean buildings and the surrounding grounds or buying in supplies. The final leaf consists of temporary skills to cover holidays or a seasonal surge in business.

One example of a federated structure is Boots, the British pharmaceutical and retailing group which divided its many divisions into ten business units – each with their own defined market, competitors, management team, logo and so on. Each is responsible for presenting its own annual 'prospectus' to the group centre, detailing its strategy and the required resources; when agreed, this becomes a performance contract between shareholders and management; this is similar to the relationship, described in Chapter 10, between New Zealand ministers and their civil service departments. The Boots reorganisation was not just a rearrangement; reported profits increased by 20% in the first year from cost savings and improved incentives at the operational level.

This 'business' relationship marks a considerable improvement on each division submitting a budget for central approval, then allocating resources through a series of deals; the company's management believes that the new system avoids the board being browbeaten by the most powerful subsidiary managements. Like other businesses mentioned earlier, the head office of Boots has been reduced to 100 people which now can adopt a much more strategic approach aimed at maximising shareholder value.

Concentrating on specific markets, getting close to customers and putting an emphasis on quality is another element to be worked on. Which is what one company did in the very difficult period during the 1930s, as recalled by Alfred P. Sloan in *My Years with General Motors*. He commented that 'new customers were hard to get and old customers were hard to replace' – chilling words for salesmen working on commission.

However, reality forced GM to specialise within the Chevrolet marque. The proportion of sales for this range which had been 66% in 1929 rose rapidly to 75% by 1932 at a time when overall volume declined by 70%. To differentiate Chevvies from competing makes at the lower end of the market, GM provided a range of alternatives to distinguish one model from another by colour, trim, engine size and accessories. This was so successful that GM made a profit during the Great Depression and never passed a dividend.

Sixty years later Tom Peters, the author of *Thriving on Chaos*, advises companies to forget 1980s' ideas of competing for market share and so-called economies of scale and concentrate instead on creating niches within various markets – just as GM did in the 1930s. Instead of cars he gives examples where these concepts have been applied to breweries, steel mills, photo processing laboratories, designer tomatoes and many other activities. Each one has created profitable niche positions within a larger market. Peters calls this market differentiation or creation. This is made possible by the Japanese ability to produce small volumes economically, so transforming a company's ability to 'duck and weave' using highly miniaturised and adaptable plants specialising in meeting customers' needs within a very tight market place. But all this investment will fall flat unless it is appreciated by the customer. For example, if a certain innovation is ahead of its time it could have a limited appeal and only serve to alert competitors. When money is tight customers have the dilemma that they did in the 1930s. Either the result is so good that the additional cost will be paid for by the rewards for superior performance, or the purchase can be delayed in the hope that the same product will be cheaper next year.

Keeping customers is also effective because it costs five times as much to create a new account than keep an existing customer. There may be many customer interfaces; they could be waiters in a restaurant, service engineers, delivery drivers, salesmen or telephonists. Technology enables each contact to provide information through a common database making each company/customer interface more precise. No matter who deals with a customer, each contact point has the same information and is responsible for answering questions, so avoiding run-arounds.

But customers do not buy from systems, however responsive

these may be to orders, requests for information, questions on pricing, order or quality. They buy from people. This multiplies the number at the 'sharp end' of an organisation having an interface – be they sales, service, accounting, technical, production or truck drivers. Each one has the responsibility to make a quality response. This is a policy matter that can be inspired only from the very top of the business.

Hammer and Champy describe in *Re-engineering the Corporation* how Hallmark Cards Inc totally changed their operating procedures by becoming closer to the customer. The company dominated the market, with mainly specialist outlets, before Wal-Mart and K Mart required their own tailored products. Designs were taking two or three years to reach the market; printing was also becoming a problem with a proliferation of short runs making the presses uneconomical. Hallmark's solution was to set up point-of-sale bar-coded terminals in 250 of their stores to receive direct feedback of sales, which enabled them to redesign store layouts, 'pull' the slow movers and target promotion activity where it could be most beneficial. Another innovation was to form design teams after it was found that 90% of the gestation period was time spent in someone's in-tray; this reduced the creative cycle to around three months – a remarkable achievement.

There are always some people who never learn. One medium-sized engineering company had a policy where board members never visited customers. By operating remotely through their general managers, they had almost no idea of market needs and had little idea why their heavy investment in one division or another always showed 'disappointing' results. By contrast, in another business an independent director insisted on regularly attending meetings between customers and sales people. He worked on the principle that unless he knew how a product or individual was received he was unable to make a constructive contribution at a board meeting. He believed that any director can cluck over board paper, but that his advice was valueless without direct contact.

Peters reminds managers that it is folly to reduce customer contact when times are difficult during a recession. That is the moment to move technical, service and where possible administrative and production staff into the field after appropriate training. This has two direct consequences: first and foremost it increases sales penetration at a critical time. Almost of greater significance, it gives normally office or factory bound staff a rare insight into how customers themselves can be harassed by lack of orders.

Customers will also look for quality. Gone are the days when manufacturers ran sub-quality models off the assembly line, leaving the distributors to make the final inspection and remedy any defects before delivery; it was a sick joke if a customer was unlucky enough to receive a 'Friday' car or appliance. No longer. The Japanese introduced the concept of strict codes of supplier quality and inventory levels through 'Just in Time' programmes that reduced quality defects to a minimum. Quality becomes an individual responsibility where there was no question of defective assemblies being removed from a production line for later remedy. In the Japanese system the whole line stops until the root cause of the problem has been identified and remedied.

High quality performance goes with good profit ratings. Peters gives the example of when TRW, the semi-conductor and car component firm, asked customers to rate 148 of their products alongside 560 competitive items. It was found that *on customers' criteria* those scoring over 90% out-earned those ranking in the bottom third by a three to one margin. One major contributor is the saving on service charges within the warranty period; one study into the room air-conditioning market showed that the worst American manufacturers spent 6% of sales costs on service calls compared to 1% for those of Japanese origin.

The number of credit notes demanded and processed is another definition of quality. One firm, a metal window maker, acquired a poor reputation for quality and was obliged to issue vast numbers of credit notes before customers were prepared to pay. The plant quality assurance systems were found to be sound but when delivered, components were often distorted and damaged; costly hand-made items such as sills were often lost, unmarked or unusable.

Eventually one senior manager accompanied the truck driver and was horrified to learn that the loading sequence did not match the delivery cycle – quite often the truck driver had to move half the load before the correct shipment was found. In many cases he was then in such a hurry to resume his schedule that the components were left haphazardly on site. It was a relatively simple matter to synchronise the drops with the loading and package the loose components.

When cash is tight during a recession customers are prepared to buy quality items and make them last knowing that spare parts will be available to keep their purchase working. In the 1930s customers had a choice: they could either buy a second-hand product and keep it running or wait a year and buy a new article in the knowledge that it would be cheaper.

Quality is something defined not by the company, but through the eyes of customers. As such, Peters urges that any executive wishing to be successful in difficult markets should put quality near the top of the agenda – it is not something delegated to a nominated individual specialising in soft answers. Quality is total. It covers any grievance concerning poor product service or durability, inferior customer service or an offhand manner by a member of staff. It should be defined as a series of measurable objectives that are well understood by those responsible for implementation and supervision, and any fall below the accepted level should be corrected. The same standards should also be a benchmark for rewarding superior performance.

Quality is generally best furthered through a continuous series of small improvements which are identified and implemented; this is more efficient compared to launching a grandiose programme which can quickly die out because of other priorities. In the best-rated companies the programmes are managed by inter-disciplinary teams which ensure that several departments and suppliers cooperate as a team. Supplier involvement has often resulted in fewer but selected subcontractors, the policy of successful buyers such as Marks and Spencer.

Make customers and suppliers an extension of the business. The days are nearly over when orders or purchases are sent by post, processed through the relevant departments and acknowledged by mail. Once the goods or service have been supplied they are then invoiced, the cheque paid on receipt of statement and sent to the bank in settlement. The practice is still efficient for some firms or contractors but now much more direct techniques have been introduced.

Individual buying, selling and settlement loops have been extended and linked together in the 1990s by supermarket stores. Now a process called Electronic Data Interchange (EDI) joins the head office, suppliers and distribution depots with an automatic system which starts at the checkout and ends with a cleared cheque. When merchandise is sold an automatic debit system reduces the store inventory until it reaches a re-order level when another signal is passed to the supplier for another shipment. When the goods are received, an invoice is automatically raised and the cheque electronically cleared.

One major user of EDI is Tesco, the British supermarket operator which trades electronically with over 1200 companies of all sizes representing more than 95% of the products sold. Each supplier is sent a 13-week sales forecast allowing them to schedule their own production and suppliers; they can then respond quickly to delivery schedules. The company reports that inventory levels, improved stock availability, increased sales and the operating costs all improved; in addition there are savings on telephone, fax and mail bills. EDI benefits are not just confined to retailers, the computer manufacturer ICL reports reducing the time from manufacture to invoicing from 20 to 3 days with considerably lower inventory levels, cash-flow benefits and a cut in administration costs by 70%.

A variant of EDI has been introduced by a large Swedish supermarket group called ICA Retailers. In the very tight marketing conditions during the early 1990s recession, the group sought savings not only in linking suppliers, depots and retailers electronically but also by thoroughly revising their ideas on distribution. Moving against the trend of requiring suppliers to feed depots directly, they set up their own strategic distribution points which cut shipping costs and hence lowered prices. The group also experienced more efficient loading factors by using their own transport from the strategic depots to a fewer number of distribution points.

A further variant of EDI is by making suppliers an integral part of the chain in what is called Efficient Customer Response (ECR). Its purpose is to integrate the planning of manufacturers and retailers to improve product introductions and promotions and tighten the feedback of customer preference, and information to the vendors. Instead of a three month sales forecast, suppliers can actually run the supply depot or deliver when their own estimates tell them another delivery is due.

Hammer and Champy describe how Proctor & Gamble, the supplier of Pampers (a disposable nappy), actually *managed* the Pampers' depot *on behalf* of the supermarket chain Wal-Mart; sensibly, the retailer reckoned that P & G could manage the merchandise better than they could themselves and were paid to supply the stores whenever inventory levels so demanded. Both sides benefited. Wal-Mart had a positive cash flow from the deal while P & G was a favoured supplier with preferential space given to their products and a direct feedback of customer preference.

The next stage of integrating customers into the retailers 'loop' is to link their PC into some sort of electronic superhighway, even employing virtual reality as a store guide. As a halfway house the Americans have introduced what they call Home Shopping Network (HSN), a telephone linked system. When replying to an advertisement or a personal order, HSN will arrange delivery and agree methods of payment from one call; in this way advertisers can make a rapid judgment of the 'message', shifting brands if necessary should the response not be up to expectation. Some systems are able to build up a database of thousands of customers, using as a main source credit cards to identify the sort and size of purchases made by individual card holders.

Electronic communications need not just apply to retailers. In America, a sophisticated weather reporting system found difficulty in providing information in a form that could be readily processed by their customers, which ranged from retail stores, oil distillation units, food processing plants, utilities and so on. The forecast of temperature and rainfall only became usable by the customer when a special program keyed the weather information directly into management, sales or production decision systems. Other direct linking systems have been devised for tailoring where the client's measurements are fed directly into the material setting-out and cutting machines, so considerably reducing the time between ordering and first fitting.

Although these techniques improve the response and accuracy between firms they have an even more serious dimension during a deep recession. There were reports that during the 1930s orders were only given to those suppliers which could respond rapidly to an opportunity; this meant that companies only stood a chance of receiving an order if they and their subcontractors were able to react immediately to a tender request. In general this can most often be achieved from the type of 'flat' responsive organisation described earlier.

Necessity is the mother of invention. It was suggested earlier that in war the aggressor always has the advantage because the opposition is still on a peacetime footing and can only respond effectively when a new generation of politicians, generals and admirals are appointed. So it is with business. One leading insolvency practitioner believes that it requires one type of chief executive to run a business in a boom and another in a recession. The first is primarily interested in the operating statement, the second in the balance sheet. It is an advantage for the 'company doctor' or insolvency specialist that he is detached from the policies that have driven a company into financial distress.

Stress and danger have a wonderful way of breaking down the rigid departmental barriers which may be adequate for more leisurely times but are hopeless in an emergency. It is said that one of Winston Churchill's first tasks in 1940 was to cut through the peacetime 'red tape' that so delayed vital decisions being implemented. It is the same thing when a new team comes in to 'turn around' an ailing business. In the drive to cut costs and improve efficiency all the old rigid distinctions between functions have to disappear as new inter-departmental teams are formed to make decisions about eliminating the unprofitable work and giving fresh life to products or services. These drastic changes have to be introduced and tested very quickly if the business is not to fail.

For still solvent companies *Thriving on Chaos* urges innovation by small changes, arguing that the most profitable activities are those probably needing the greatest attention. Peters compares the Japanese approach of introducing and testing small innovations to the American practice of assembling large teams to introduce the 'big idea'. There is little doubt that the American genius for mass-producing ships and aircraft was a major contribution to the winning of the Second World War for the Allies, but in peacetime a competitive edge is kept by making continuous improvements.

Of course, large teams can still be created to introduce a major project but these should include all the disciplines needed to break down departmental delays. Peters gives the example of the Ford Motor company's Taurus. Here a group consisting of designers, engineers, production people, marketeers, lawyers, dealers, suppliers, insurance representatives and customers produced a winning design on time with budget savings of $500 million. The team swept aside departmental barriers. For example, insurers gave their opinion on future claims by describing which components usually needed changing after a crash, potential customers suggested accessories that they would find useful and suppliers were consulted on the optimum method of producing items such as panels and castings. All these actions showed how the traditional sequence from design to engineering to production engineering to manufacturing and marketing can be succesfully integrated.

There is also scope for innovation in the market place, for it can be very lonely and unprofitable waiting for something to happen in times of rapidly moving markets, difficult economic conditions and scarce orders. One obvious source of intelligence is the business cycle, another is the customer database. It is a truism that a number of resourceful and innovative accounts can often see a better use for one's product than the company's own marketing people. Some customers may be suspicious of talking about their business but the information will be kept confidential and in any case, each business is distinctive and every interpretation will be different.

Another method of canvassing is by using the tele-sales team to glean information from a wide range of people. Very often delivery truck drivers, if properly primed, can be a wonderful source of data, particularly if a customer is about to fail; if a shipment yard is full of returned material then the business is in trouble and the goods inwards staff will know all about the problems. They have either a quality or payment problem – perhaps both!

The need for customer feedback in product development is vital as competitors force ever shorter life-cycles. One classic example is that companies in the business of gaming machines need to produce a new model, a new game, every three months otherwise the players weary of the old programme and go elsewhere. These are sophisticated computer-based 'fruit machines' offering punters the chance to pay for their evening drinks by winning a challenging game; these devices are also profitable for the café or pub managers, perhaps generating as much profit as bar takings. It is quite a challenge to produce a new product every quarter after measuring player reactions around the country. But that is the level of feedback that many more companies might be forced to adopt for their survival.

Networks have also become very fashionable, and rightly so, as a source of intelligence where people, often with different interests and contacts, are regularly in touch either on the telephone, fax or over casual meetings. Each group will vary but usually they include like-minded people with at least one person who challenges conventional wisdom. One of the rules of networking is that everyone has to make a contribution.

Make the most of even the humblest product. Companies such as Hanson Trust made a feature of taking over businesses producing relatively simple products or services and making them profitable; it's a well-trodden path and requires the attention of specialist managers. It also requires flair.

During the Second World War one contribution to fuel saving in Britain was to recycle the hot water from condensed steam back to the boiler; fuel was also saved by returning the steam condensing in supply lines. The solution was to fit a steam trap (a device that lets water through, but not steam) at low points in the pipe run where the hot water collected and then recirculated. The device was really quite simple but it needed the marketing genius of Lionel Northcroft of Spirax Sarco to prepare the definitive manual on the application of steam traps. What was before a relatively unknown (but essential) item now became accessible to every heating engineer with the Spirax manual – an essential reference book. Northcroft's company became the internationally acknowledged leader in steam distribution and the business was very profitable.

Although Spirax Sarco made steam traps, they were in fact in the fuel-saving business which considerably helped the company's development and marketing policies. This awareness is sometimes absent for quite often a customer is more perceptive about product applications than those running the business. The secret, as always, is to be close to one's customers and to ensure that the sales people report on new uses for the same product.

Another company that has turned a basic product into a profitable success is the American company Crown Cork & Seal, one of the smaller players in the can trade. The business was nearly insolvent when John Connelly joined the board in 1957 and was rapidly made president in a last attempt to avoid bankruptcy. He found the usual litany of errors, including something unique in business life – 'the customer was always wrong'. By investing heavily in Crown's strengths and insisting on a culture of service he was able to cut severely into his competitor's market share to such an extent that they sold him their operations at a rock-bottom price.

In the mid-1990s Crown acquired Carnaux Metal Box, a Franco-British company whose own merger had failed through internal bickering, to create a truly international business where more than half the operating profit is generated outside direct operations. The company's policy, unlike those of its competitors is to diversify within the packaging business into aluminium cans and plastic containers. Connelly died at the age of eighty-five and his successor William Avery, knowing the dependence of his customers on the weather, has a policy of meeting rapidly the fluctuations in customer demand.

Set up an intelligence unit. Just as an intelligence group is essential to a military staff, so it is to industry and commerce working within a tight and difficult market where orders are very difficult to win and a lost customer is hard to replace. A unit can be either located within a company and built along the detailed blueprint of *Competitive Strategy* or subcontracted to a specialist looking after several non-competitive clients. Whoever runs the service it is essential for senior managers to build up a competitive picture.

Putting together competitive information, by definition, is fragmentary. It may be gleaned from customers, published data such as press articles, product and staff advertisements, published accounts, trade directories, analysts' reports, a request for literature, inter firm comparisons and the like; data may also be gleaned from sales contacts or engineering staff at exhibitions or trade associations. Another excellent source can be from interviews with competitors' staff, who are usually only too pleased to show off their knowledge should they want another job.

Assembling knowledge will be fragmentary at first but in due course information about competitors can be assembled and collated in an appropriate software program such as a relational database like the ones used by the police for analysing and sifting evidence. The data is normally categorised under four headings:

Goals and objectives

These can be defined in several ways: one is financial in terms of profit margins or return on capital. Alternatively some other yardstick might be chosen, such as market share or price leadership defined by senior management. Another goal may be technological or quality leadership differentiating it from competitors. Yet another objective, adopted by Bic Pen, may be to manufacture at the lowest possible cost then organise wide distribution supported by heavy advertising. The priorities within an organisation may be defined either by the pecking order of different departments reporting to the chief executive or from the aims of an integrated parent company.

Assumptions

These may be more difficult to glean because they are often not stated and can only be inferred from the way a company conducts its business. For example, a specialised manufacturer of components for coin handling worked on the principle that it had only four customers that could be handled by the sales director; in fact an examination of the sales ledger showed a much more structured pattern which lent itself to a broader spread of accounts and the appointment of distributors. Similar assumptions might apply to its relative position within the industry, a historical or emotional approach to certain products or customers, cultural or regional differences or industrial trends. Once a competitor analysis has been completed, it is often salutary to look at one's own business through the eyes of customers, suppliers, sales staff – and competitors.

Current performance

This is a measure of such things as market share, profitability, return on capital, growth, export efficiency, quality and number of credit notes issued. Where it is not possible to categorise by figures one can sometimes apply qualitative yardsticks, such as judging relative performance on a rating of one to ten. The analysis might be helped by comparative performance databases such as PIMS (Profit Impact Market Strategies); subscribers receive details and rations of competitive businesses worldwide divided by specialisation and category. There is also benchmarking, which sets industrial standards.

Capability

This is an analysis of strengths and weaknesses, again rated on a scale of ten for excellent and zero for useless. The enquiry should cover matters such as products, distribution, marketing, development, profitability and financial strength, general administration and people management. These should be rated by customers, flexibility of response, adaptation to change and general regard among competitors.

Once this data has been collected it must then be kept up to date and expanded as new sources become available. The management access the information primarily for making strategic decisions but also for such matters as marketing, distribution, development, production, personnel policies and public relations.

Retain a manufacturing edge when up against the newly-industrialised countries around the Pacific rim. Despite the very low relative labour costs of developing nations, western factories can compete where a specialised response is needed. For example, an engineering company using computer-aided design (CAD) techniques can now reduce the time between design to a first prototype – a process that used to take months – is reduced to days or even hours. Even something quite complicated, such as machining the contours of a three-dimensional shape, can be produced directly through a computer input through a technique called stereolithography. A laser will cut the contours from a block of photosensitive resin which, when hardened, can be a pattern for a lost wax casting. Other shapes can be made from a CAD output applied directly to a machine tool.

A revolution in manufacturing may also be found in the potteries where companies like Royal Doulton have a long history of quality, design, artistry and craftsmanship. It has also been labour intensive with items like tableware being made by forming plastic clay on plaster of Paris moulds. No longer. In new technology called granulate pressing, the clay is converted into almost dry granules which are then pressed into plates and hardened in new fast-firing kilns. The whole process is less costly, there is a reduction of work-in-progress and more immediate quality control.

The ideas expressed earlier of integrating design, marketing, engineering and production have been incorporated into what is known as 'Agile Engineering' – or the ability to be able to meet several niche markets concurrently. Here the business is organised around a process which is a set of coordinated activities to meet a customer demand, with all functions including purchasing now under a single manager – instead of being under functional supervisors. Agile Engineering adopts an approach similar to Re-engineering.

As the group now handles design, engineering, scheduling and quality control, the processes that were sequential now become concurrent, and for optimum benefit should be linked together with an appropriate computer information system enabling standard modules to be used wherever possible. Agile Engineering not only reduces lead times by around 50% but it boosts sales per employee, reduces inventory turnover, cuts cost and 'flattens' the organisation by employing fewer managers. These are some examples of how Western companies can produce engineering and design performance unmatched anywhere:

> Chaparral Steel of Midlothian, Texas, is a pioneer mini steel mill with the lowest costs of any in the US steel industry and half the cost of the typical Japanese plant. Unlike many present industrial leaders, the founder Gordon Forward is a technologist, not an accountant or lawyer. The focus is not on the development centre or marketing department but the shop floor where the metallurgists and engineers work alongside operatives to produce specialised alloys and shapes. Forward makes the plant the centrepiece of his marketing effort and often includes a supervisor to accompany the sales representative if the customer has quality problems. Chaparral maintains its position at the leading edge of technology by drawing on the support of universities and outside researchers.

> Another example is Rotork, a British company based in Bath, making valve actuators serving almost recession-proof customers in the oil, water, sewerage and power generation industries. Of the company's 750 employees over half work in sales, many of them in seventeen overseas subsidiaries including a permanent office in Beijing. The company assembles components from subcontract suppliers in Britain and believes the key to its success is gathering and using intelligence. They believe they know more about their end users than their immediate customers, the valve-makers.

Continuous innovation is the theme of another British company called Cirrus Technologies based at Redditch in Worcestershire. The company was started by Harold Hayward in a two-storey slum house. Its first order was for £5,000 from Rolls Royce for a turbine blade encapsulation machine (making a metal casting of a low melting alloy to hold a turbine blade accurately for machining within an aerofoil section). One part of the business developed by applying new technologies to an existing process.

One such was buying the Automotive Division of Hymatic, but instead of purchasing the company (because Cirrus did not have the cash) the vendor agreed to take 10% in royalties on sales for five years in exchange for the assets. Cirrus then redesigned a tyre fitting and inflating product which reduced the cycle time to make the product a world beater. Like Gordon Forward, the company believes in close ties with universities and training colleges to receive the latest in applied technology and to provide employees with continuous training. The result is a remarkable return of sixty-two times the called-up share capital.

Learn to roll with the cycles. The message from earlier chapters is that the principles of planning and running a business can change drastically over the 60-year cycle. For example, in the middle of the 1990s the principles of free trade are taken for granted, just as they are before the *downwave* of any cycle. But history shows that if there is a slump of severity similar to other downwaves then there could be a public outcry against low-cost imported products as suggested by Sir James Goldsmith in his book *The Trap*.

Goldsmith shows that although Britain and France grew between 50% and 80% from the early 1970s to the present, unemployment actually *increased* largely through the ability of multinational companies to manufacture in the cheapest area. He advocates a system of managed trade to prevent whole swathes of western jobs being transported to the East. He may be right. Tariff barriers have been raised by governments at the low point of every cycle, so trade protection may be seen as a popular alternative to mass unemployment.

In any case conventional management styles will undergo considerable changes in the wake of Michael White's

'Cybernetic Revolution' or Alvin Toffler's 'Third Wave', where knowledge-based businesses will dominate. Peter Drucker, in his book, *Post Capitalist Society*, believes the business of the future will be run like a symphony orchestra where each instrumentalist is responsible for their own performance under the conductor. This is similar to the ideas of the 'bottom up' organisation described later where individual employees take full responsibility for their own performance supported by supervisors.

Make a virtue of necessity. Difficult times generate their own styles of innovation – just as they did in the 1930s when businesses were forced to respond rapidly to every opportunity thrown up by the market place. As we saw earlier, innovation is also forced on a business required to restructure as an alternative to failure; as Doctor Johnson observed, 'Depend upon it, Sir, when a man knows he is to be hanged in a fortnight, it concentrates his mind wonderfully.' All the old excuses of 'we tried that before and it didn't work then' are dumped, so are the constrictions of 'not invented here'. Quite suddenly poaching – or adapting – ideas from competitors suddenly becomes acceptable.

One classic restructuring which swept aside convention as an alternative to receivership was carried out at the British cycle firm of Raleigh by Frank Ruhermann, a specialist from the parent company Tube Investments (TI), plus a small head office team. Raleigh was losing £18 million a year when Ruhermann was instructed by the TI board either to sell the business, turn it round or close it down for the cost of £40 million. The company, located on a sixty-two-acre site in Nottingham, had been the graveyard for the reputation of several 'company doctors', but something had to be done. As an alternative to closure the team considered a trade sale to competitors who were then Merida in Taiwan, Huffey in Chicago and two Raleigh subsidiaries in Canada and Holland. However, the bicycle market was so thin at the time that returning the business to profitability was the least costly option.

It was agreed that the company could only be rescued by being calibrated against world-class players. To this end Ruhermann created a task force of specialists led by a McKinsey consultant to visit the major competitors and produce a brief which defined a practical competitive blueprint. The results were fascinating. For example, the best companies took 100 minutes to assemble a bike whereas Raleigh took 140; the Nottingham plant needed 54 people to complete an assembly while Huffey needed 9 – and so on.

Using these international comparisons, Raleigh set up manufacturing modules to make tubing, spokes and so on in batches of 500 using Japanese quality cycle techniques. Ultimately the same number of machines were assembled from half the work force in a third of the space with a lead time of ten days compared with the Taiwanese three to four days. Raleigh, now profitable, was sold to the management team in a buy-out; but by then business had picked up and they could sell all the machines they could make.

Learning from the competition is what Peters calls 'creative swiping' which is just what happened in the Raleigh example, even though in this case the competitors made it easy by co-operating with the investigating team. When the market is tight there are many ways in which firms can scramble for a diminishing pool of business: some will seek an advantage in price cutting, others on service, some on quality, yet more on innovation. Whatever course is chosen, each must have a feedback from the market. For example, the games machine business described earlier needs regular, timely, rapid and systematic intelligence from customers to ensure the innovative three-month cycle is maintained.

Support the front-line troops and convert fixed into variable costs. We can now expand on Drucker's suggestion that the business of the future will be run like an orchestra. This leads directly to what Peters describes as a 'bottom up' organisation where the management are there to support those at the coalface. A supervisor's job is no longer to hand down company policy but to support those whose job is to design, sell, fashion and deliver the end product or service.

Likewise, all information needed to produce a quality product or service should be directly available to support those principally responsible for making the necessary decisions. Peters gives several instances such as the Chapparel Steel example described earlier where the shop floor is the focus for innovation, change and delivery – the place which decides customer satisfaction. An organisation that might have been right for the upwave or directing a nation at war now becomes no match in the downwave for a small responsive group highly tuned to respond.

Another advantage of the 'bottom up' organisation is cost. If the focus is on those who are selling, making and delivering a product or service, then wherever possible other services should be bought in. In this way many costs normally considered fixed can become variable; they should only be incurred when there is something to be done, an order to be fulfilled.

Coping With the Collapse of an Industry

Up to now, the concentration has been on business ideas applied to a recession that are already in use either directly or in another context. They have not encompassed the collapse of a whole market, as happened in the 1930s and in each of the previous downwaves. This chapter ends with a review of the present housing market and, drawing upon a programme that was successful in the Great Recession, shows how similar ideas might be applied today.

The real-estate market has fallen during every downwave and the latest slowdown started in the early 1990s. This time the deflation was first felt in Japan where house prices, forced up in the speculative bubble of the 1980s, collapsed and there were also falls in Britain; in Australia the total value of all real estate in 1989 peaked over A$ 1 trillion but had declined 25% by 1993. The sums of value involved in Britain are considerable. By the middle of 1995, Britain had nearly 10.5 million outstanding mortgages funded by loans totalling over £380 billion of which the largest lenders were the building societies (£236 bn) and the commercial banks (£120 bn). House prices then staged some recovery in 1996 following the business cycle.

Traditionally UK house purchases have been financed through the capital repayment (or annuity) type of mortgage paid off over 25 years. As an alternative, a mortgagor might be offered an endowment insurance policy which not only protected the household in the event of death but provided a capital sum at the end of 25 years to repay the loan. This contract was popular in the upwave because it assumed that house prices would go on rising and by 1992 over 75% of all mortgages were still financed through insurance companies. Unfortunately, if a mortgagor was forced to suspend payments after the initial 5 years, there would be no refunds for the early money received would be needed to pay off hefty front-loaded agent's commission.

The great worry is that in the event of a downwave similar to previous long wave cycles the total worth of Britain's housing stock (which in the early 1990s could have been in the order of £1.5 trillion) would be at least halved. This would not only put at risk the loans secured on the properties but destroy a major part of the owner's capital. This means that towards the end of the 1990s over five million households could suffer negative equity – many of whom could no longer afford to make repayments. The main loans to the housing market outstanding in early 1996 had risen to nearly £390 billion and unless something is done to refinance mortgages, many householders will be forced to quit their homes with accompanying appalling social problems.

By the end of 1995 the US mortgage market had outstanding loans of around $4.4 trillion of which over $3.5 tr was lent to family residences. The main lenders were the major financial institutions such as the commercial banks, deposit savings institutions such as the Savings & Loans, and life insurance companies. The government-funded agencies such as the Federal Housing Association (FHA) occupied some 10% of the market.

Unlike Britain where most mortgages are held by the lender (be it a bank or building society), over 50% of loans in the US are securitised, implying at least three tiers of financing. The first is the interface with the borrower called the retail market which is either a deposit taking saving & loans (like a building society) or a mortgage banker. The latter borrows funds in the open market then finds home buyers with whom they will originate, process, then close a loan contract. The next tier is the wholesale market where groups of similar mortgages are pooled then sold to outside investors through agencies so refinancing the retail lenders who have borrowed in the open market.

The most prominent of these organisations is called 'Fannie Mae', a private corporation, which refinances around 20% of all outstanding mortgage loans. Originally it specialised in government backed agencies but since 1981 it has dealt with mortgage bankers. Next in size with over 15% or the market is 'Freddie Mac' which deals primarily with savings and loans associations. Although both are government agencies, their investors are not guaranteed by the federal government. Next in size is 'Ginnie Mae' with nearly 13% of the secondary market which provides funding for two Federal programmes specialising in cheap housing for poorer lenders and veterans of the armed forces; shareholders in this case are guaranteed by the federal government. Private mortgage backed security (MBS) houses make up the balance of the refinancing market.

Contrary to experience in Britain, Japan and Australia, US house prices rallied in the first half of the 1990s but these levels are additionally vulnerable in the event of a downwave from two directions: first there is a reduced demand from a rapid decline of 25-year-olds as first-time buyers. There is also a fall in the secondary post-war baby boom that reached its peak in 1990 and is now declining. A crash in the market could place at risk half the additional homes bought on mortgage from 1980 to 1994; this means that around 9 million contracts could suffer from negative equity and possible repossession.

A housing meltdown would not only impact on the mortgage banks and the refinancing houses but also the federal government. The US taxpayer has already had to spend $120 bn, through the Resolution Trust Company, bailing out the 745 savings and loans which failed in the late 1980s. There could be a further liability for a good part of $600 bn should the government guarantees of Ginnie Mae be called.

Anatomy of a housing rescue operation. As the US discovered in the early 1930s a downwave spiral of housing values could be arrested, not by lowering interest rates, but by providing a floor for house prices. In 1933 Roosevelt's Home Owners Loan Corporation (HOLC) created a public fund for refinancing defaulting loans at an affordable level. Repossessions were then running at 1,000 per day, and the HOLC raised the funds to salvage 20% of the mortgaged market so earning the undying gratitude of millions of Americans who contributed to the president winning the next election. The fund was wound up in 1942, its debts repaid.

In the indebted state of most western nations, few states would be able to mount a rescue operation similar to the HOLC although governments might encourage mortgage lenders themselves to set up a HOLC-style fund with the authorities providing tax and other allowances (and possibly some minor guarantees) to offset the losses. It is evident that the rescue programme would be considerable; for example, in Britain the total value of home lending is the equivalent to well over 80% of the total government expenditure in a year. The UK is not alone. In Europe, Ireland has the largest number of owner-occupiers with 81%, a number of nations (including Britain) has around 65% and Germany has the least at around 40%.

In the early 1930s the average value of houses in the United States fell over 80%. Should a similar fall take place in the 1990s then one could estimate the level of refinancing needed by Britain and America to bale-out insolvent mortgage holders.

Assuming 25% of mortgagors had to be rescued and British average house prices fell at least 50% from the 1990 house prices peak, then some 2.6 million homes would need to be baled out at £36,145 (50% of the 1990 average price of £72,290 – as reported by the Halifax Building Society) for a cost of over £90bn. As some of the houses in the early 1990s would have been bought below the peak, the total write-off might be nearer £80 bn – over 20% of the total balances outstanding by mortgage lenders in July 1995. It should be noted that this is still only one third of the Japanese 65% of irrecoverable debts and may be highly conservative.

The housing market in the US could take an even greater tumble than in Britain. Unlike the UK where house prices had declined by 1995, those in America have risen nearly 10% in the five years since 1990 and the total borrowings have increased by over 25% in the same period. Additionally, the practice in a number of households of taking a second mortgage has meant that by October 1995 household debt was 90% of disposable personal income. If, as expected, there is a decline in house prices the fall could be rapid. Taking the same scenario as in Britain, if there is a drop in prices of at least 50% (average new house price over five years of $155,000 falling to $77,500) and an estimate of 25% of the homes in danger of repossession then the refinancing needs will be around $700 bn – or some 20% of the outstanding loans.

Anatomy of a rescue plan. Roosevelt's HOLC, described earlier, was a model for millions of borrowers who would otherwise have lost their homes to cause potentially terrible personal upheavals and a real danger of civil unrest; it also avoided a free fall in house prices. By refinancing mortgages for those in danger of repossession, it gave thousands of families with genuine financial problems an opportunity to keep their homes at an affordable repayment programme.

Any latter-day programme to prevent a housing meltdown

would require the present lenders to set-up joint funds to act as a lender of last resort to buy houses in danger of reposession at an agreed level of housing prices; in Britain this might be 50% of the 1990 purchase price, in the US, 50% of the average house price mid-1996. The fund would not be available for those still solvent although there would be potential losses when houses changed hands. Most lenders would suffer a loss of assets with many of the small lenders being in danger of bankruptcy.

When a banking institution failed in the US, the Federal Deposit Insurance Corporation (a Federal organisation started in the 1930s and funded by participating banks) took possession, paid off the creditors, wrote off the bad debts, then sold the remainder of the business on to a willing buyer. The FDIC proved adequate for rescuing banks such as Continental Illinois in 1982 which was the largest support operation in history refunding $30 bn of depositors' cash. There was a similar organisation called the Federal Savings and Loans Insurance Corporation which itself failed in the 1980s, when it was unable to bail out the fiasco described earlier costing the US taxpayers $120 bn.

The threat of failure is real. The IBCA, the European credit-rating agency, has predicted that only 30 of the present 90 plus societies in Britain will survive the 1990s (a possibly optimistic estimate due to highly competitive pricing policies in 1996), hence any remedial programme must enable the strong societies to absorb the weak without being overburdened by bad debts – just as the Woolwich Building Society absorbed Town & Country without themselves being put at risk.

To construct a latter-day HOLC in Britain and America it would be necessary to focus on the most recent mortgage loans: in Britain this would be the 2.6 million contracts made from 1987 through to 1990 and for the US nearly 9 million negotiated since 1987. In the absence of a state funding package, a buyer of last resort is needed primarily to refinance existing mortgagors likely to default but also to take into ownership the bad debts of failed lenders. In a previous book, *Meltdown*, the author suggested this be called the National Home Owners Relief Fund (NHORF).

In Britain the size of the fund needed to bail out failed mortgagors, clear the bad debts of defunct institutions and put a floor under the market would be in excess of the £80bn. The equivalent fund in the US would need to be at least $700 bn to allow for the same role to be performed plus any additional funds needed to rescue depositors from additional defunct savings and loans. As the bail out would be partly political, the government might need to give tax and other incentives to mitigate at least some of the losses. The fund might work as follows:

If a borrower defaulted, the lender could offer the house charge to NHORF as an alternative to taking possession. Assuming a price could be agreed at or above the initial 50% threshold, the security would pass to NHORF and the borrower could be offered the chance to refinance annuity payments at the house transfer price. The loan arrangements would continue to be managed by the original lender for an administrative fee.

The fund would act as a buyer of last resort for a lender likely to fail through non-performing loans, low volume or inability to attract funds. As excessive liabilities might deter a take-over by a more soundly based mortgagee, the bad debts could be sold to NHORF before the acquisition – not unlike the FDIC action described earlier. When the new institution was taking over a failed bank, the bad debts would be removed from the balance sheet in order not to weaken the acquiror.

As an alternative to NHORF, bad debts could be securitised and subsequently traded at a discount in a similar way to the US mortgage security market described earlier. This solution would be similar to trading non-performing Third World debt at discounts of their face value. Setting up NHORF would not please everyone as lenders and the insurance companies would stand to suffer very considerable losses. It would also mean a substantial contraction of mortgage lenders.

The almost certain winners would be NHORF and the government's popularity, as Roosevelt discovered in the 1936 election. When the housing market recovers, as it assuredly will in due course, fund managers holding mortgage securities bought at a discount might profit from selling these back to the lenders; alternatively they might hold the mortgages to maturity. There are, however, two silver linings for investors in housing: the first is that in the event of a crash, there is a good chance they would hold their value better than stocks. The second benefit would be a revival of the house rental market once the legal and tax restrictions were swept away.

CHAPTER 9

MANAGING INVESTMENTS IN TURBULENT MARKETS

John Exter has had a remarkable career; an American, he was appointed Governor of the Bank of Ceylon in colonial times, following which he held senior banking positions which included serving on the Federal Board. Exter maintained that the liquidity of investments could be likened to an upside-down pyramid. If one can imagine an inverted pyramid with its apex buried in gold, then all other securities would be less liquid as they move upwards from the point. To give an illustration: with bullion at the bottom of the inverted pyramid, a nearly gold-backed currency like the Swiss franc would be next to the apex, then moving outwards and upwards one would find Swiss government securities, then possibly company debentures. Moving out still further there would the currencies and securities of the less conservative nations until at the top there would be the most risky unsecured paper. The value of securities moves with the long wave.

During the upwave investments would first be locked into the most stable securities next to gold – just as they were in the late 1940s. Then as the expansion gets under way the more adventurous investors move into equities; as the boom continues there is a proliferation of choice until at the peak of the boom speculators will be attracted by the least secure securities such as junk bonds and Third World debt at the top of the inverted pyramid.

The position changes as an economy slides into the downwave. The first securities to fail are the highly leveraged speculative ventures. Caution now forces investors further down the pyramid to the more blue-chip equities, sounder commercial paper and mortgage-backed bonds. Initially government securites are considered liquid but then when a nation like Mexico defaults there is a move to the less risky debt instruments such as American T-Bonds and DM denominated Bonds. In the classic downwave all the illiquid securities become progressively worthless as the pyramid shrinks down towards its apex leaving only gold-backed currencies, then finally the metal itself.

This is exactly what happened during the Weimar Republic, when so much paper money was printed that all other German securities, with the exception of some stocks, became totally worthless leaving only some commodities and gold with any residual value. It is also happening today; fund managers, having lost money in Mexico, are holding many fewer securities in the highly leveraged nations such as Canada, Sweden, Belgium and Italy. Instead they have greater holdings in the more soundly run companies on the principle that when the going becomes difficult, competent managers are likely to correct weaknesses more swiftly than politicians.

The Federal Reserve Chairman, Alan Greenspan, understands the value of gold. In answer to a question on the relevance of the yellow metal at his half-year Humphrey Hawking Testimony on American monetary policy in July 1995, he said:

> It is an issue which I think is relevant, and if you don't believe that, you always have to ask the question why it is that central banks hold so much gold which earns them no interest and which costs them money to store. The answer is obvious; they consider it of significant value and indeed they consider it the ultimate means of payment, one which does not require any form of endorsement.

Greenspan knows his economic history. Britain had a gold-backed currency from 1669 when Sir Isaac Newton, as Warden of the Mint, established a standard index of 100 which held until 1913; it was known as fractional reserve banking when gold reserves underwrote 40% of the issued currency. During that time the UK came off the gold standard once from 1800 to 1819 during the Napoleonic Wars.

The United States Congress adopted a bimetal gold and

silver currency in 1792 priced at $19.36 per troy ounce and America remained on the gold standard except during the War of 1812 and during the Civil War. The purchasing power of the dollar has varied over time, touching the original 1792 level briefly for the last time in the late 1930s, then slipping below the 50% level during the Second World War. Richard Nixon took America off the gold standard in August 1971 and by the mid-1980s the US dollar was barely 10% of its original value and the British pound less than 3%.

Gold has been an uncertain investment during the 1980s and early 1990s, largely because many of the producers sold their gold output forward to bullion brokers to 'lock in' a forward price for sometime in the future. The brokers in turn borrowed gold from central banks for a sum known as the lease rate (or gold libor) to supply the market. One complaint about owning gold is that it pays no interest, hence many central banks (which collectively own 30,000 tonnes – nearly one third of the total gold mined by 1994) – take the opportunity to lend the yellow metal forward. It was a tidy arrangement until heavy buying from the East and Far East in November 1995 drove up the spot price of the metal, the shortage pushing up the leasing rate to over 6% – an all-time high. Should the buying continue, for reasons of political or economic uncertainty, and the metal supply remain tight, then gold could make a rapid positive move, as it did in 1972 and 1979.

Currency is clearly an important factor in making stock-market decisions as German investors discovered during the early 1920s. Then, although the stock market rocketed, it fell in dollar or sterling terms, and German money would have been better deployed in strong currencies or in foreign stock markets. Japanese investors recently rediscovered similar truths after the value of their real estate or company acquisitions collapsed by well over 50% as the US dollar weakened against the yen. Historically gold-based securities have been a good hedge during rapid currency depreciation such as when the dollar was devalued in 1934 and during the inflation of 1974; on both occasions the rise ran against the level of other investments.

The Early Investors

The first traders or merchants dealt in commodities initially from home grown European products such as grain, timber, hemp, skins and cotton. Later exotic foods and fabrics were added like sugar, coffee, tea and silk. Even more important for town dwellers were peppers, for keeping meat tolerably edible, and scent, for those who could afford it, to mask the terrible odours in towns without drains. Merchants initially bartered their goods but later gold and silver became accepted all around the Roman Empire. Cities like Venice became established as the focus for the overland routes to India and China, with the area around the Rialto Bridge being famous for its merchandising community.

Investing *per se* was not possible with perishable commodities although fortunes were made hoarding grain during a famine until the price rocketed. The Florentine merchants who had discovered the secrets of dyeing wool in rich colours set up a considerable trading and banking network for buying wool from the sheep-grazing areas of the Low Countries and England. The Florentines and Venetians invested their wealth in magnificent homes, public buildings and sponsoring works of art.

In Europe the practice of usury was forbidden by the Roman church through edicts from the Councils of Lyon and Vienna; the ban was not total for certain banks, such as the House of Fuggers, were permitted to lend to the church or monarchs. The rules were relaxed in Elizabethan England when voyages of discovery (or plunder) were often financed by loans. There was also an active currency market in Antwerp in Tudor times where Sir Thomas Gresham was able to reduce King Edward VI's debts through shrewd currency dealing.

The focus of investment stayed in the Low Countries when the Dutch East India Company was launched in 1602 with a share capital of 6.5 million florins – equivalent to 64 tons of gold. As Far East trading grew, the size of the company was ten times that of the British East India Company created in 1600, which made it one of the first growth stocks with dividends equivalent to between 20% and 30% of the initial capital. As British power increased in the east, the Dutch company waned and by 1780 it filed for insolvency and was acquired by the government.

In Britain the first irredeemable bonds to be issued were 3% consols in 1729 but some shares were also traded in the London market in the early part of the 18th century. There was a market for stocks in several businesses, including the

Bank of England, Million Bank, Irish Lands, Royal Lustring and the Old East India, African and Hudson Bay Companies. But by the year 1800 some issues like the Million Bank and the African Company had disappeared after the South Sea Bubble, but these were replaced by stocks such as London Assurance and the Royal Exchange.

Investments Follow the Long Wave Cycles

Since 1792 there have been three of the long waves. The first, called K1, reached a peak around 1815 and a trough in 1848. The second, K2, attained a high point around the start of the American Civil War in 1861 and a bottom in 1889. The last full cycle, K3, reached a peak in 1916 and a trough in 1942. The upwave of the last cycle K4 ended around 1974 and the downwave started in 1990. The object of the remainder of this chapter is to trace commodities, bond and stock markets in both the United States and Britain through successive long waves.

Over the history of the long wave a lift in commodity prices has led to a rise in inflation to be later reflected in bond yields. As the yield on stocks partly follows bond yields one might expect the two to move in unison – to break apart only when stocks are regarded as a hedge against inflation. These three elements for K1 through to K4 are shown for US markets on Figures 10 to 13 (see pages 144–150). Where no continuous data exists, such as the early US bond yields, the Foundation has created a substitute series from British consols.

The size of these three markets varies considerably according to a Goldman Sachs report produced in 1994. Then the commodity market was valued at around $25 billion, the stock market $4.75 trillion and the bond market $15 trillion. By 1995, Martin Armstrong of Princeton Economics estimates the size of the bond market at around $20 trillion which proportionally would value the stock market at over $6.25 trillion. During this time commodities have remained within a tight trading range so their proportion of the market will have declined. To illustrate the relative value of some markets, Dr Marc Faber, editor of the *Gloom, Boom and Doom Report*, estimated in July 1995 that the market capitalisation of Intel, the hi-tech share was worth the combined value of all the North American and Australian quoted gold-mining stocks.

These have been the investment phases of the first three Kondratieff cycles:

The First Kondratieff Wave – K1

The first cycle started around 1792 at the time of George Washington's second term as president. In the continuing euphoria after independence a rise in output pushed commodity prices up and bonds followed. As Chapter 10 explains, the upwave continued after farms, bought on loans, were being settled in the west following the Louisiana Purchase in 1803 and later in the territories freed after the War of 1812. There was a hiccough in both commodity prices and bonds during the War, and the recession which followed marked the end of the upwave and the beginning of the plateau; bonds and stocks rose until around 1832.

The latter part of the plateau was marked by increased speculation from property and farm investment during what was known as the 'era of good feeling'. In the early days of the Republic there were a few private industries in lumber, fishing and ocean transport but the main investments were in American and foreign bonds, often British consols.

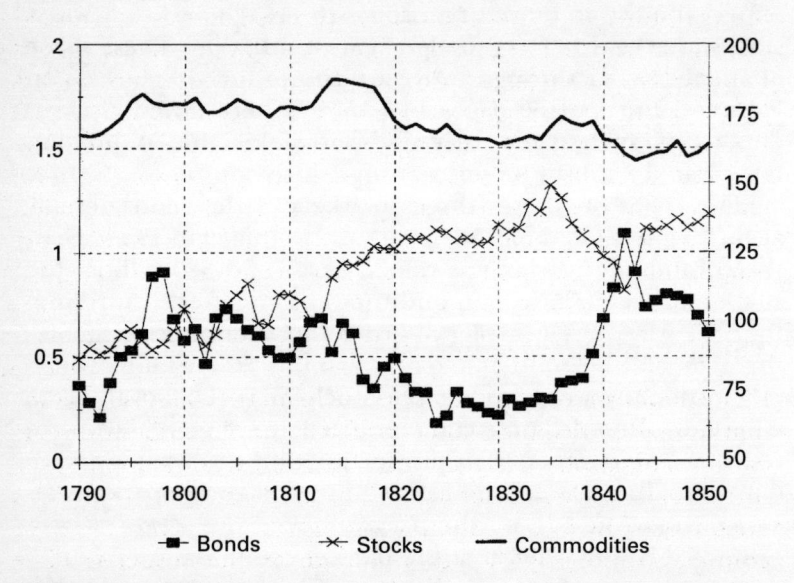

Figure 10. Market action during K1. (Courtesy the Foundation for the Study of Cycles.)

Bonds were increasingly used to finance ventures after the War of 1812 when textile industries were started in New England and the construction of canals and roads was opening up the infrastructure. In the decade before the 'railway mania' in England during the 1830s there was a 'road and canal fever' in America which encouraged numerous flotations and quoted stocks soared; for example, the Index of Bank and Insurance Company Shares rose from $2.50 to $12 per share by the end of the plateau phase which ended around 1826.

The end of the speculative fever was accompanied by increased failures and, in the beginning of downwave recession, the number of bad debts multiplied. This culminated in the 'Panic of 1837' when the banks were disallowed from redeeming debt other than in specie – or physical gold. In the latter part of the downwave many banks failed and bonds declined by 80% and almost all foreign debts were repudiated. By the early 1840s there was no market for bonds, when the federal government sought to pay off its debts. By 1841 the stock market had fallen to a thirty-year low point.

The 1840s were a difficult time in the western world. The debris from the volcano Cosiquina had caused weather patterns to shift so ruining crops in what were known as the 'hungry forties'. There had been severe famines in Ireland during the 18th century and before, but the potato blight *Phytophthora infestans* left fields of perfectly healthy tubers black and stinking within days. The fungus also attacked stored potatoes so creating starvation and disease. Although the Repeal of the Corn Laws allowed cheaper grain into the country, it was too late to save over half the Irish population who either migrated or died. Finally in 1848 there were anti-establishment rebellions in France, Germany and Austria.

The Second Kondratieff Wave – K2

K2 probably started around 1848 although the American stock market had anticipated an economic recovery some five years earlier. The advance of the index was helped by the popularity of railroad stocks – some of which had risen 70% by 1852 – encouraged by foreign money and government incentives to connect with the newly acquired lands on the west coast. The upwave was accelerated by the first gold rush in the early 1850s and the development of such new industries as steam-driven sewing machines and the licensing of the British Bessemer steel-making process.

The New York stock exchange came of age during this upwave, fuelled by the demand for railroad stock and the funding was accelerated by share offers to individuals, many of whom had benefited from the surge of exports to England after the Repeal of the Corn Laws. By the late 1850s, the economy was overheating, inflation was rising and interest rates increased when, in order to initiate building projects, the government competed for the same funds as the private sector. Stock prices declined when the Union went off the gold standard with the issue of 'greenbacks' to fund the War Between the States. Bond yields initially fell with the increase of money but then rose sharply, accompanying the inflation induced by the war, as shown in the rise of commodity prices.

The plateau phase started with the Civil War and was followed by the usual recession and recovery. As the opportunity to open up the interior of the United States grew so did the demand for railroads and the associated need for steel, engineering products and telegraphs; investment accounted for 20% of the national product and was largely foreign funded. As Chapter 13 explains, this was also a booming

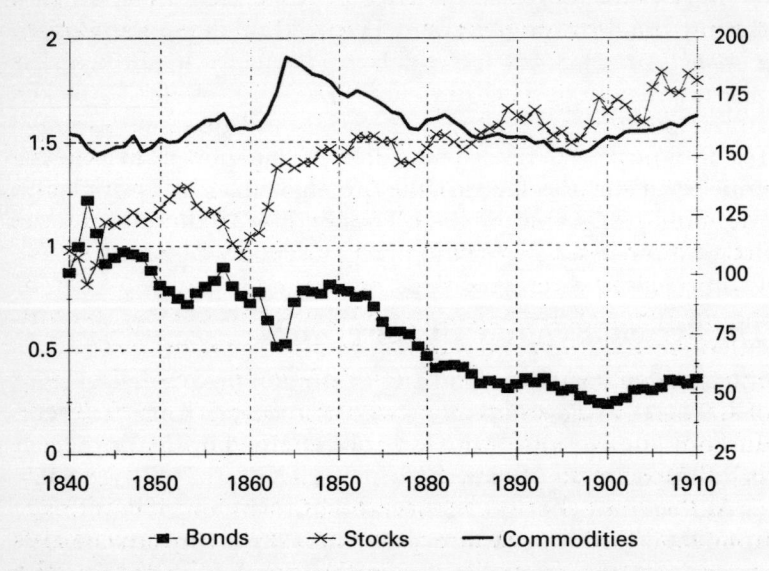

Figure 11. Market action during K2. (Courtesy of the Foundation for the Study of Cycles.)

time for innovations such as Graham Bell's telephone, McCormick's reaper and binder (which enormously expanded the output of grain) and Edison's light bulb.

The Civil War had increased the role of industrial unions who demanded protection against foreign imports by lobbying the government to raise tariff barriers. As the demand for foreign goods fell, fewer American products were bought overseas; there was a sharp recession in the late 1870s accompanied by a stock-market fall, which hit railroad stocks in particular. In the subsequent rebound in the 1880s these shares increased by over 100% although stocks in agriculture, mining, metal, real estate and construction declined. However, as can be seen from the chart, bond yields declined with falling commodity prices and large capital gains accrued to the banks and others holding these securities.

The recovery did not last. The second deflationary depression ending in 1896 was caused by a series of major loan defaults both in America and Europe accompanied by political unrest. The defaults spread to Latin America where a failing Argentinian railway brought Baring Brothers to the brink of insolvency before it was rescued by a lifeboat assembled by the Bank of England. By 1894, over 180 railroad companies and half of American basic industry failed, stock prices collapsed and many of the fortunes built up during the cycle were wiped out.

The Third Kondratieff Wave – K3

The political drive of 'Teddy' Roosevelt gave America the impetus to start K3, the cycle being dominated largely by the automobile and the genius of Henry Ford in setting up the first mass production plant using the techniques of F. W. Taylor. Almost single-handed, Ford boosted the number of cars in America from less than 100,000 in 1907 to over 10 million in 1922. The automobile gave the opportunity to other entrepreneurs such as Rockefeller of Standard Oil, Carnegie of US Steel and Goodyear Tyres. Fortunes were made by the du Pont family, Edison of General Electric, and bankers such as J. P. Morgan and Peabody.

As the chart shows, common stocks rose almost continually from 1896 to the peak in September 1929, with retracements around the time of the Boer War, the First World War and the sharp recession of 1920 which marked the beginning of the plateau phase. Bond yields rose throughout the upwave but then fell steadily from 1920 in what must have been the longest bond rally in history lasting nearly thirty years. The main performers in the early part of the century were transport stocks led by the railroads and later by Ford. There was a setback during the War but the trend was bucked by property, farming and technological stocks covered by strong patents.

After the sharp setback of the 1920 recession, the stock market broke through its previous highs rising from 50 to its peak of 386 in September 1929. When the Dow Jones Industrial averages broke through the level of 200 in 1927 most stocks had done well including synthetic fibres up 275%, drugs up 70%, insurance companies 90% and banks 70%; oil stocks such as Standard Oil, Exxon and Standard Ohio also performed well. Despite the popularity of the new issues, the capitalisation of rail stocks was larger than all the public utilities, over double the iron and steel industry and ten times larger than the motor issues.

The hi-tech stocks of the age were RCA, Zenith and Western Union which had sold radios into five million homes by 1929. Of these RCA rose spectacularly from $10 in 1926 to $114 in September 1929 – but then fell just as rapidly reaching

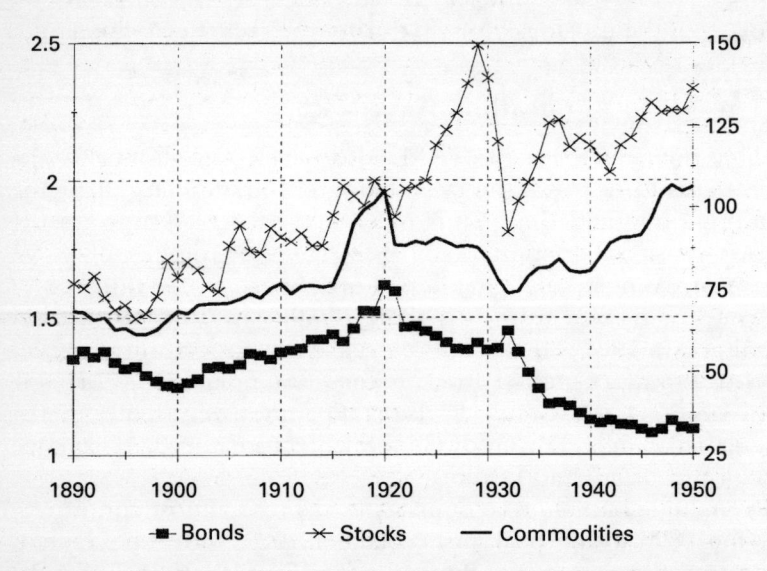

Figure 12. Market action during K3. (Courtesy of the Foundation for the Study of Cycles.)

a low point of $2.50 in 1932; it rallied to $14.5 in 1936 but never reached its previous high. The Zenith Radio Corporation recovered somewhat better: it peaked at $61.75 in 1929 and rallied around two thirds to $43.75 in 1937. As Dr Marc Faber comments in his *Gloom, Boom and Doom Report*, the present 'shooting stars' such as LSI Logic, Tellabs and KLA Instruments could fall just as sharply in a major reversal.

The United States suffered as badly as any country during the 1930s. Apart from those laid off in the Great Depression, the unemployed reached nearly 25% of the working population when falling commodity prices forced farmers to increase productivity through mechanisation – so forcing a massive flight of people from the land. Apart from the rally in the bond market the stock-market did not stage a rise until 1936 before there was another crash in 1937. There were a few counter-cyclical stocks. Gold shares staged a spectacular rally in 1934 after Roosevelt devalued the dollar from $20.67 to $35 per troy ounce in order to make the dollar-priced goods more competitive. Otherwise there was a steady demand for household appliances, which benefited shares such as General Electric, Frigidaire and Edison.

The Fourth Kondratieff Wave – K4

There are differing views as to when K3 ended and K4 began, depending on whether the low point in commodities or debt mark the turning point. If commodity prices are the yardstick then the next cycle started around 1932 according to the chart. However, as the debt depression lasted until America entered the War, then the recovery is more likely to have started around 1942.

Defence stocks such as Boeing, McDonnell Douglas, North America Aviation and General Dynamics were popular after the eruption of the Korean War, the start of the Cold War and the beginning of NATO. Technology shares such as Xerox, Memorex, Honeywell and Control Data were also in demand with IBM around that time having a capitalisation of $41 billion, accounting for over 5% of stocks quoted on American Exchanges. Bonds held their own in the early 1950s but then started to fall as the post-war expansion became inflationary.

The growth of the hi-tech stocks continued into the 1960s and early 1970s with the addition of other companies such as

Control Data, Digital Equipment, Motorola and Wang Laboratories, all of which, once again, suffered horrific falls in the 1974-1976 crash; even IBM, which had a capitalisation of $734 billion in 1971 fell nearly 60%. Faber reports that the technology stocks quoted on the OTC market at that time had very steep falls – some disappearing completely. Over this period the chart shows rapid rises in bond yields in the late 1960s when the Vietnam War was funded increasingly by borrowings – which continued during the commodity panic of the early 1970s.

The Gloom, Boom, Doom Report then lists the personal computer, word processing and CAD as the rising stocks of the 1980s including Apple, Commodore, Computervision and Micron – one or two rising thirty fold from their early 1980s low. Most of them peaked then lost more than 80% of their value by 1989. Bond yields peaked with the commodities in 1981 then recovered over the course of the 1980s to retrace values similar to those of the early 1970s.

The 1990s stock-market favourites have been concentrated in information technology, software networking, communication and electronic mail shares – some of which have risen well over ten times since the low in 1990. These include such stocks as Microsoft and Intel which together are greater than

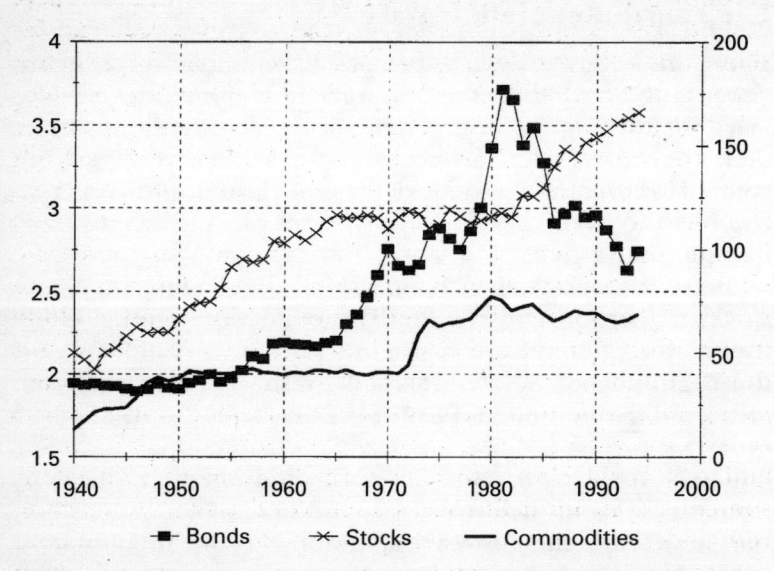

Figure 13. Market action during K4. (Courtesy of the Foundation for the Study of Cycles.)

the combined capitalisation of oil-related shares such as UNOCOL, Chevron, Amoco, Arco and Schlumberger. The manic behaviour of some stocks is exemplified by the Netscape issue on NASDAQ during August 1995. The 5 million shares on offer which were aimed at between $11 to 14 quickly rose to between $22 and 24, rocketed to $74 before closing over $50; in all, the total stock turned over nearly three times reminding some market historians of the behaviour of stock issues in 1929. Meanwhile bond yields fell to a 1970s low point in 1993 so ending a twelve-year bond rally.

Investment Performance During the Stages of the Long Wave

Although each wave is different, there seems to be a pattern of the upwave, plateau and downwave of the cycles K1 to K4 which might be replicated in the future.

The upwave recovery, coming out of a recession. The great cycles' guru Joseph Schumpeter believed that the 'bunching' of innovations took economies out of recession, although the evidence is somewhat patchy. If the investment in these ideas accompanies a stock-market recovery, then one would expect it to be present in each of the four cycles. A look at the figures shows this to be the case: the stock market led K2 by some five years in 1842, in 1896 in K3 and 1942 in K4. There are also other factors.

Low interest rates, low inflation and minimal debt levels usually stimulate a housing revival and employment; as incomes start rising the banks are increasingly willing to lend. As confidence rises, those with savings have an increasing choice of investments, including housing and real estate and stocks of banks, retailers, food processors and the clothing trades. Government *bonds* which were attractive investments during the latter part of a downwave now become less interesting compared to a rising number of selected stocks. As the recovery gets under way, there will be offers of redeemable and convertible loan stock or term bank loans as a cheap source of long-term finance, either to raise new funds or to refinance existing costly debt. *Commodities,* or the stocks of companies mining or handling raw materials, are unlikely to be good investments at the early point in the recovery but will come into their own at the early part of the plateau as they did in 1919 and 1972.

As the recovery continues there will be increasing evidence that more firms are becoming profitable and cautiously increasing their dividends. The rising prosperity will start to attract corporate raiders looking for undervalued assets such as property or poorly run businesses. Analysts will now be recommending interesting 'situations' as potential takeover candidates. Other entrepreneurs will be investing in new products or developing different markets using venture capital funds to fuel the new stocks being issued. The original recovery stocks will now be joined by those making consumer durables, insurance companies and utilities. There will also be the latterday railway, automobile or technology stocks that emerged in K2, K3 and K4. With increasing demand for houses and commercial real estate, construction business will start to recruit staff and there will be a rising demand for building materials and land for development. Property stocks will again become attractive after being in the doldrums for a number of years.

Ten years into the recovery the price of many stocks will have doubled and will continue to rise, business profits will be high and growing and the recession will be a distant memory. The managers who steered their companies through the recession are often displaced by go-getters prepared to take risks in the new business climate. What were previously regarded as sound policies are now displaced by risk-takers with an enthusiasm for highly-leveraged balance sheets that offer stockholders very high returns. The euphoria increases when clever takeover artists stalk and buy lowly rated businesses with sound balance sheets, dump the unprofitable activities, strip out the unwanted assets then use the released cash to make more acquisitions.

Meanwhile other stocks join the recovery; machine tools are often the last to respond to a recovery or a recession. By now the boom becomes international with a worldwide investment community moving its money around to the nations with the most rapid growth, the strongest currency, the lowest costs or the greatest political stability. As the boom reaches its peak there is the general assumption that any enterprise will make money, any stock will achieve a high rating, property values will continue to climb and the scourge of unemployment recedes.

But amidst the euphoria there are signs that the boom is becoming stale. Labour unions grow more aggressive, demanding an increased share of the prosperity for their members; politicians often respond with prices and income policies in an attempt to stop union demands from becoming inflationary. Likewise politicians feel it safe to increase social security costs on companies and employees in the *then* reasonable belief that the expense can be absorbed. There will be other ominous signals: the demand for credit will raise interest rates, commodity prices will become firmer and one or two of the more aggressive entrepreneurs will fail. The end of the upwave will be marked by overvalued real estate and stocks, speculative ventures and wild press enthusiasm.

The end of the upwave and start of the plateau. Historically, the end of the upwave has often been marked by a major conflict which is almost always inflationary and bad for bonds. The War of 1812 marked the end of the first upwave, the American Civil War the end of the second and the First World War closed K3; finally the debt increase caused by the Vietnam War contributed to the end of K4's upwave. Certain businesses do very well in war but there are dangers. Conflicts create a demand for raw materials; governments, not wanting to increase taxation, are inclined to finance the war with debt – or new money which only accelerates the inflation.

The Hale drought cycle also contributed to ending K4's upwave when it reached a low point in 1972. Veteran commodity watchers will recall how soya beans and corn led the commodity prices followed by wheat, the precious metals and some time later – oil. History blames the 1972–1974 commodity price rises and subsequent inflation on the Organisation of Petroleum Exporting Countries (OPEC) jacking-up the price of energy, but the real culprit was the extraordinary change in the weather which ruined crops – in the USA, the USSR and China. A similar commodity price rise could have the same impact in the 1990s.

As we have seen earlier, the investment profile changes at the start of the plateau when even high flyers may crash. As commodity prices rise, bonds fall and the best inflation hedges are resource stocks such as food processing, mining and precious metals. As governments try to quell inflation by raising interest rates, stocks nosedive. This is a difficult time for those who are fully invested for many companies fail and only those with a high solvency profile will be reliable. Initially ordinary shares may be seen as an inflation beneficiary but, as interest rates rise to quell prices, the rally will first be halted then make steep falls – just as it did in 1974.

As the boom falters, banks rein back credit in an attempt to protect their loans, house mortgages being one of the first to tighten. This rapidly creates an inventory overbalance which is immediately felt by building-material manufacturers and suppliers. Other consumer industries relying on credit also slow down, creating excessive stock positions, among them the car, domestic appliance and home furnishing businesses. As the demand for inventory collapses, manufacturing slows down, employees are laid off, spending tails off and a number of companies go to the wall. As companies scramble for business, transfer prices fall.

Although the previous boom will have encouraged people and companies to increase their borrowings, the overall level will be still relatively modest but several of the most highly leveraged balance sheets will fail. Although unemployment will rise, the setback will have dismayed but not stunned businesses, who believe that growth will return after a period. The optimism is encouraged by increased government spending on work creation capital investment projects such as roads, railways, bridges, buildings and so on.

Although investors in the stock and bond markets will have suffered considerable losses, most are still solvent as the level of speculation during the previous boom was still relatively modest compared to the frenzy to come before the final blow-off. Stock-market recovery is often stimulated by a few companies making rights issues, taking advantage of low ratings to reduce the balance-sheet debt. As some confidence returns, entrepreneurs take advantage of the attractive interest rates to start new enterprises and quite soon the requirement for housing reasserts itself, carrying with it the demand for building materials and home furnishings. Low interest rates also stimulate the need for domestic appliances and motor cars which create their own demand for materials and components. The rising unemployment is arrested then falls steadily as more people are taken on.

As the plateau boom gets under way, the constraints provided by the sharp recession are forgotten when confidence comes flooding back. The rate of recovery is much faster than during the upwave because managers will be eager to resume growth and hire more staff as the boom gathers pace. As business picks up, profits will start to recover, dividend pay-outs increase and the stock market will move ahead. Once again, the first to recover will be the retail trade, then domestic appliances and transport, housing, construction and then capital goods.

In the rising euphoria, the previous credit constraints are discarded as every sort of industrial and commercial business borrows to take advantage of the low interest rates. The corporate raiders return with a vengeance, using highly leveraged paper to make rapid acquisitions; companies which would normally expect to have steady ownership now often find themselves with a succession of major shareholders each of whom wants to improve the profit performance.

There are also considerable opportunities for buy-outs. The managers of a subsidiary company might see opportunities that the parent company may neither see nor sanction. They might then approach a venture capitalist who, after making a detailed examination, may be prepared to assemble a package of equity and loans to buy the business on behalf of the managers. Given the considerable opportunities to earn capital sums, the new owners will energetically develop the business in the hope of negotiating a stock-market flotation. Initially most will attempt a minor exchange rising to a full quotation in due course. All these new issues will provide investors with increasing variety of stocks from which to choose. Some shares may double within months.

As the final stages of the plateau boom gather pace intelligent dealers will put together ever more sophisticated investment ideas. In the 1920s it was common for a stock to be bought on 10% margin on the anticipation that it would rise in price; in this way a buyer could repay the debt if the share rose by 10%. A number of syndicates could be put together to ramp up a share price attracting private investors to join the party; at some point the original players would slowly remove their original stake leaving the others to take the losses. Conversely, a fall of 10% could wipe out the investment.

During the 1980s instruments called derivatives and junk bonds came to be widely used: derivatives are so named because they are derived from an existing stock, bond, commodity, interest rate, stock index or currency. Originally they were used for the perfectly respectable policy of hedging risks against a fall in a portfolio value by taking an opposite position. They then became a method of speculation to the extent that the derivative markets became many times bigger than those of the basic stock. Junk bonds are a method of financing a new issue such as a buy-out but have no collateral security. A financier might be prepared to issue a bond at a deep discount on its face value. If the company is able to redeem the security from cash generated within the business, well and good; if the venture fails, the financier loses everything.

In the euphoric last stages of the plateau boom, banks vie with each other to lend for ventures that would have been regarded as almost inconceivable a few years earlier. Loans would be used to fuel a speculative venture into housing or commercial property; all manner of instruments would be used to boost the stock and commodity exchanges; interest rates would soar. The end of the plateau is marked by clear signs of overheating but probably only the old hands are wise enough to read the signals to lighten their load; most soldier on hoping for even greater gains.

The downwave. In 1929 there was a combination of events very similar to the 1890s and to the position in 1996–1997. During the 1920s American companies were shedding labour and keeping tight inventories during a stock-market boom so by 1929 the Dow Jones Industrial Averages was responding to a rise in profitability while personal spending was waning. By mid-1929 the recession was starting despite continuing stock-market enthusiasm which lasted three more months. By 1996 companies were still reporting rising profits through restructuring and the Dow Jones was again posting new highs although retail sales were weakening in the third quarter.

Weakness in the bond market usually foretells a stock-market decline. In 1837 a massive crash in the bond market heralded a stock-market fall; a similar (but less violent) event occurred in 1893. In the 1920s, US bonds were in a spectacular long-term rally and suffered only a short retracement at the time of the stock-market collapse. But as Martin Armstrong of Princeton Economics reports, the losses to bond investors in the early 1930s were some $90 billion (nearly the GDP of the US) compared to the stock-market write-offs of $6.5 billion – a ratio of nearly 14 to 1. As Chapter 2 showed, the downwave is always marked by a collapse of credit as the bad loans have to be purged from the credit system.

The beginning of the downwave is always accompanied by a loss of confidence. In the 1830s it was a collapse of farm prices in the US and the decision of the government to repay federal loans. In the 1880s a rise in US protective tariffs first choked off first imports which then led to a progressive decline in American exports. In June 1929, an early collapse in Florida land speculation, a slump in farming and lay-offs reduced consumer spending and lowered demand for industrial output. At the same time the government raised interest rates to cool the speculation and the loss of confidence eventually triggered the crash. When it occurred, the government hardly improved matters by passing the tariff-raising Smoot-Hawley Act and devaluing the dollar 70% against gold.

Investment Strategies for the K4 Downwave

Kondratieff's genius was to spot that each cycle differed, which is why, perhaps, he did not attempt to define the reasons for his long wave. The first cycle saw speculation in farm land, the next in railroads and K3 in real estate and stocks before the 1929 crash. In K4 there are different conditions: one is that food prices constitute less than 20% of family budgets in 1990s compared to nearer 60% in the 19th century. Another item common to each cycle is debt.

High overall debt in America in relation to GDP was one of the reasons why the Great Depression was so intractable, although initially the proportion run up by the government was less than 5%. Now in the 1990s almost every western government is highly indebted and all are finding it increasingly difficult to reduce the burden when economies are growing either very slowly – or even negatively. It is likely to continue for most countries. Even taking no acccount of the downwave, the OECD estimate that by the year 2030 Japan will have government debts to GDP of 300% and the USA, Germany and France will be 100%; the same study suggested the UK will have no debt because its state pension burden is lower than other countries. In addition, although shares could be traded on margin in the 1920s, now a new speculative trade has grown up in derivatives which some observers believe is larger than twice the world's GDP at nearly $50 trillion.

If the position in the K4 downwave were to replicate the investment profile of 1929 then it would be the right policy for funds to move out of stocks into bonds before the inevitable crash. But this would be doubtful policy for the 1990s as almost every nation runs a budget deficit with the exception of New Zealand and, as shown earlier, government debt now dominates the credit markets. A further factor affecting decision making is that instead of there being a secular decline of commodity prices as in the 1930s, the weather cycles are promising higher, not lower, prices.

It is most unlikely that the conditions of the mid-1990s can continue for long. It is possible to consider five scenarios around which, singly or in combination, an investment strategy can be planned for the late 1990s and into the next century. First, one should consider the possibility that politicians and central bankers could delay the impact of the cycles for several years. Second, even at this stage in the downwave politicians and might have the courage to balance their budgets and start actually repaying debt. Third, a major debtor nation is likely to default which would trigger enforced selling of government debt. In this event all other states would be forced either to balance their budgets (so forcing a deep recession) or to print money to pay for their debts – so causing a collapse of their currency.

In addition, a climatically induced drought could lead to a similar position to 1972–1974 when rising food prices drove up the price of other commodities. This gives rise to two further possibilities: the authorities either raise interest rates to fight inflation or they accommodate rising prices by printing money so monetising debt. In the first instance this would lead to a deep recession and civil unrest; in the second inflation would rage before a crash which would induce a recession similar to 1975 but much deeper.

Alternative One: the impact of the cycles is delayed. Despite historical parallels it is possible that central bankers could create enough credit to keep the bond and stock markets intact for a while without generating initial inflation. This would be a perilous policy placing at risk the world's financial system. In these conditions bonds might rally for a while as would the stock market with inflation hedging stocks probably performing the best.

Alternative Two: investments when budgets are balanced. It is still possible for the authorities to avoid the worst of their excesses by balancing their budgets as did Neville Chamberlain, the British Chancellor of the Exchequer, in the 1931 Coalition Government. Britain at that time was relatively free from debt allowing Chamberlain to assemble a package of measures that reduced the cost of government, increased social taxes and stabilised the currency through an exchange equalisation account.

The measures were reinforced by a system of Commonwealth Tariff Preference and bilateral trade deals. The regime introduced an era of low interest rates and a stable economy which encouraged the creation of many new industries. Although there were black spots of unemployment in the staple industries, those out of work in the UK never exceeded 15% (compared to 25% in the USA and high levels in France and Germany) and the economy grew by 50% in the 1930s – much faster than almost any other country.

A government cutback is not without its downside. Over the last 200 years a decision to balance the budget has produced sharp recessions/depressions in America. Balancing the budget in the ten years to 1836 led to the 1840s recession; some 50 years later a similar exercise induced the bottom of K2's downwave. Reducing the American debt after the First World War in the 1920s was followed by the Great Depression. A decision to balance the budget in the 1990s would effectively destroy the Welfare State. As spending was curtailed the number of public servants administering publicly funded programmes would fall rapidly – so accelerating unemployment.

If that occurred then the following might be good investments:

Bonds. Bonds would be an excellent investment in a regime of balanced budgets; in the 1930s $2^{1}/_{2}\%$ consols stood at £1.20 and American bonds saw the greatest rise in history. The rise in bonds would be accelerated if there is all party agreement in America to introduce a flat rate of income tax which exempted bond coupons from income tax.

Stock-markets. If the government were seen to balance budgets interest rates would decline which could be the signal for a rapid rise in the stock market in the late-1990s; historically there is a good correlation between falling bond yields and rising stock prices – as there was in the 1920s. Selected stocks of companies benefiting from a run

down in state services would be education and health care despite generally falling profit margins. Other useful sectors might include security devices and services, environmental technology and products for an ageing population, such as pension funds and retirement homes.
Direct investment could also grow rapidly as more services are provided by private companies. Among the growth areas should be firms specialising in personal or property protection, adult retraining for companies and individuals, and franchising to help people set up on their own.

Alternative Three: the impact of a major default. There is a considerable danger of a major national default if one of the highly indebted western countries fails to honour its debt interest payments. The most dangerous periods are when a downturn in the regular business cycle coincides with a downwave. By early 1996 the leading indicator in the USA is signalling a low point probably in 1998–9 which, if this was confirmed by the coincident and lagging markers, would signal the timing for such a default. Should this happen then major insurance and pension fund holders would be progressively reluctant to hold bonds and instead would buy sound equities on the principle that companies are more likely to protect their solvency than governments.

As the authorities found it progressively more difficult to sell bonds then they would be forced either to raise taxes or cut back on their own spending to balance their budgets. If they continued to run deficits and people became more reluctant to pay higher taxes then governments would be forced to monetise their debts so generating rapid inflation and a currency collapse. In these conditions the bond market would collapse but the stock market could rise. The best investments would be food processing, mining, precious metals or energy stocks and probably also physical gold.

Alternative Four: governments clamp down on rising inflation. The rare combination of cycles could now play a part. Unlike other downwaves described earlier, there could be an inflationary rise in commodity prices from a combination of drought rhythms that started in 1995 and could continue into the next century. Normally this would call for a switch out of financial to tangible investments but some governments may take strenuous action not only to clamp down on inflation by raising interest rates but also to balance their budgets.

Corrective action would place over-committed economies into a tailspin. For example, by 1996 the Canadians are paying in excess of 40% of government income on servicing the national debt, leaving little expenditure for public services should the budget be balanced. To avoid the electoral pain politicians might try increasing taxes but many electorates would so order their tax affairs that revenue would be hard to collect.

Such action would hit interest sensitive sectors of the economy such as construction or manufacturing and many sectors would default; one recent example was Mexico when forced to retrench. In these circumstances the stock market would collapse and the living standards of most citizens fall sharply. One good result, however, would be to rescue the bond market – so protecting the life savings of millions. In investment terms there would be a fine choice between buying resource stocks or bonds in the governments that had taken corrective action.

Commodities. These should prove good while the seasons remain dry, the price leaders being wheat, soya beans and corn (maize) followed by the precious metals like gold, silver and platinum. Crude oil tends to lag behind the grains but then could rise quickly to $30 per barrel. The most followed commodity measure is the CRB (Commodity Research Bureau) index which is continually computed from twenty-one commodities and reported daily in the FT and WSJ. There is a close correlation between the CRB and US bond yields.

Bonds. The initial inflation would be bad for bonds but they would rally when certain nations balanced their budgets or when inflation was under control. The credit markets are well over ten times bigger than the stock markets and being highly related to commodities there would be serious early losses in the long dated stocks as crop prices and defaults rose before bonds rallied.

Stocks. Initially resource stocks would rise but these would collapse with the rest of the stock market as higher interest rates added to the deflation.

In the event of a major volcanic eruption or a prolonged

drought, private investors could be attracted towards home food-growing techniques, specialised seeds, fertilisers and equipment as commodity prices rocketed. Among those benefiting would be mechanised garden equipment manufacturers and distributors, high intensity food growers using hydroponics, or suppliers of know-how and equipment for the more unusual permaculture programmes.

Alternative Five: governments accommodate inflation. Instead of clamping down on inflation authorities could attempt to spend their way out of difficulties, in the belief that they could eventually regain control. Britain adopted such a policy in 1972–3 accompanied by a prices and incomes policy, hoping that the inflation could be contained by legislation. Any such action in the 1990s would force prices upwards and outstanding loans would be quickly devalued – a move that would please politicians who have seldom looked after their debtors. As prices rose rapidly so would demand for higher salaries – pouring petrol on the inflationary flames. With the bond market collapsing, governments would be forced to accelerate the printing of notes to maintain soaring spending levels and in the process currencies would fall markedly.

The end result would be the same as Alternative Three but much worse because ultimately governments would be forced to raise interest rates to avoid a financial disaster. By then the damage to the bond markets would be complete and one has only to read about the great Weimar inflation to learn that the only tangible investments would be commodities; although the stock market could be firm, shares would in no way compensate for a currency collapse. In the end the only commutable investments would be physical gold, platinum or silver.

Scenario Facing Investors in the Downwave of K4?

As reported by Simon Hunt, the metal consultant, by 1995 we are in the early stages of an extended period of deflation when debt is compounding faster than income in many countries. He cites the example of the USA where increases of government debt every five years from 1980 have produced a smaller percentage rise in national output: in the five years to 1985 there was a $1.46 rise in income for an additonal $1 of debt and from 1985 to 1990 each $ rise in debt yielded a $1.33 increase in GDP.

If, as suspected, K4's downwave started in 1990 then one would expect any rise in debt to yield only negative results. From the four years to 1994 for every $1 debt increase the GDP rose only 66 cents, conforming to the experience of the 1930s. If rising prices are superimposed on deflation the result is stagflation. In this condition highly borrowed industrial and commercial companies would be faced with falling sales and rapidly increasing real costs of interest rates – the worst possible outcome and a recipe for a vicious wave of corporate failures.

The implication of this policy has been described by John Pugsley of Phoenix, Arizona as the 'deadly anomaly'. Pugsley argues that government debt is bound to be inflationary if, having borrowed money from the pool of savings, the central banks then print the equivalent sum of cash to avoid a recession. As the diagram in Figure 14 shows, consumer price rises kept pace with American federal debt until 1982 when it then diverged; instead of price rises, surplus cash was invested in the equity, bond and real-estate markets while federal debt went on rising geometrically.

Pugsley postulated two alternative results: either at some point consumer prices (and with them bond yields) rise to meet the debt line, which by 1996 is now well over 1,300% from 1950 levels; or the debt line collapses to meet the prices curve. In the first scenario this would suggest that the government decides to take Alternative Five described earlier when, in order to avoid a depression, the authorities print money creating a major inflation. In the second scenario debt could become worthless from the defaults described in Alternative Three.

Investors will recognise whether Alternative Two, a balanced budget, is being actually adopted (rather than postulated) by countries other than New Zealand. The third alternative suggested by Martin Armstrong of Princeton Economics will also become evident if or when one of the most highly indebted nations defaults in a downturn in the latter part of the 1990s. If the bond market does crumble, as it did in Europe during the 1930s, then a loss of 50% (some $10 trillion) would be equal to over 40% of the world's GDP. Those worst hit in Britain would be the insurance companies holding nearly 40% of gilts followed by overseas investors which, in 1994, held 20% of a total issue of over £200 billion.

A similar stock-exchange loss would wipe out some $2.5

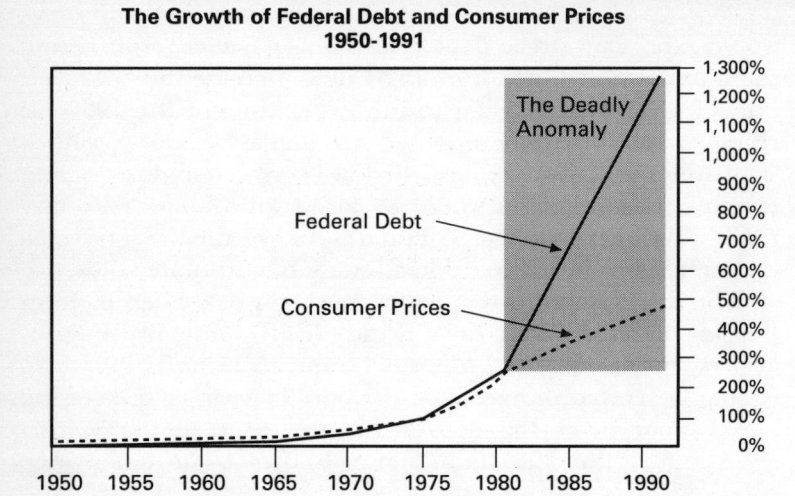

The Growth of Federal Debt and Consumer Prices 1950-1991

Figure 14. J Pugsley's Deadly Anomaly.

trillion, much of it the savings of individuals in mutual funds. In addition, there would be huge defaults to other credit markets in housing, personal and business loans – most of which would be at risk and much too large to be bailed out by impoverished governments.

Unfortunately, inflation has been used throughout history as an excuse by politicians and rulers to destroy their indebtedness and there is little reason to believe it will be any different in the downwave of K4. By the autumn of 1996 commodity prices still had not forced the CRB index above 270. If that were to happen governments will be forced to implement either Alternatives Four or Five; if the latter is chosen then Pugsley's deadly anomaly will be fulfilled sending consumer prices rocketing to the debt line before both curves finally collapse.

This chapter has considered events that fall naturally from a study of cycles but even the best prophecies may need to be modified. For example, another major Tokyo earthquake could suck cash from the world's stock and bond markets; alternatively a civil war in either Russia or China could revive ailing economies by stimulating arms industries.

CHAPTER 10

ENDING THE EUNUCHS' REIGN

The Ming Dynasty eventually fell when starving crowds led by the rebel Li Tzu-chan'g overran the Chinese capital Beijing in 1644 and drove out the corrupt civil servants and palace eunuchs who had plundered the country. Something similar happened to the Roman Empire in the 4th century after Diocletian divided the Roman Empire into east and west under a ubiquitous civil service. Attacks by the Francs, Huns and Visigoths did not daunt the emperors who made great proclamations to show how important they were and struck commemorative medals, but the invasions continued and in 410 AD Rome was sacked by Alaric.

Not much has changed in the last decade of the 20th century if the 500-year cycle is still working. Since the Second World War every western nation, with the possible exception of New Zealand and Switzerland, has developed a government that now manages enterprises as diverse as railways, health services, road programmes, the armed forces, education, pensions, unemployment insurance and so on. The public sector in most Western countries spends more than 40% of national income and where these huge sums cannot be raised from taxation, politicians and central bankers have resorted to borrowing – not in penny packets, but in high amounts. For example, there are several nations such as Canada, Italy, Sweden and Belgium that have borrowed over 90% of national income.

It is not now a question of government spending being

adjusted to what can be afforded. Before 1914 it was deemed that everything belonged to the individual with the state taking enough to pay for defence and maintaining law and order. Now politicians have become so arrogant that they talk about tax loopholes as if the government graciously allows individuals to retain a proportion of their income; in Canada, for example, the average person works for the state nearly six months of the year and the interest on the national debt is rising to nearly half government expenditure.

Traditionally all governments' programmes have been administered by huge bureaucracies employing between 20% and 30% of the working population, but now some functions are being farmed out to agencies which, by law, charge for their services. In Britain, some of these devolved groups are inspectorates enforcing European directives, charging business-scale fees which the luckless 'clients' have no option but to pay. Like the Roman Empire and the Ming Dynasty before them, politicians and their ministers meet in expensive conferences and make fine declarations but achieve little to interest the people they are supposed to serve; in fact they have become much like the bureaucrats they nominally control. This is an unhealthy state of affairs symptomatic of the corruption that always accompanies the end of eras like the longer-term cycles described in Chapter 2. How far matters have gone is shown in the following examples:

Britain joined the (then) European Economic Community (EEC) in 1972 with the best of intentions to become good Europeans and contribute to a free trade area. However, things have not gone well for many British enterprises who suddenly find themselves subject to a host of regulations which do little to help – and for the most part hinder, often at considerable expense – their regular business. A hair-raising account of how Whitehall bureaucracy, supposedly under the control of politicians, has implemented Brussels directives will be found in Christopher Booker's *The Mad Officials*.

The then British Prime Minister, Edward Heath, accepted the Common Fisheries Policy (CFP) when he signed the European Act in 1972 without it ever being ratified by Parliament. By doing this he accepted that the British fishing grounds, yielding some 80% of the European fishing stocks, would be a common resource. In 1983 this was allocated to member nations by quota; the British share was 1,750 tonnes around the south-west coast compared to the French share of 18,000 tonnes. Overall British fishermen received 30% of the total allowed catch – 12% in value terms of their original take.

The laudable aim of the quota system was to conserve fishing stocks but fish move with their food source so often it was not possible to catch any one particular species. With quotas rigidly enforced by the Ministry of Agriculture, Fisheries and Food (MAFF), fishermen exceeding their quota either have to dump thousands, if not millions of tons, of dead fish back in the sea or else land them as a 'black' catch. Fishermen are also subject to the Department of Transport's Fishing Vessel Survey Department where inspectors, who know little about fishing, go through a checklist with often bizarre results. In *The Mad Officials,* Booker describes how a 32-foot boat was required to fit an escape hatch to an engine casing that could not possibly be entered; another boat was disallowed going to sea because there were only forty-nine bandages in the first-aid kit, not the regulation fifty.

The Brussels and Whitehall bureaucracy could, of course, be dissolved and unnecessary laws rescinded – they contribute little or nothing to increase safety or hygiene; it would be more difficult to reverse the manipulative laws being imposed on American citizens that most regard as being not only silly but downright insidious. As Ronald Reagan opined in the early 1980s the problem for America was not the people but the government.

The Democrats held a majority in the House of Representatives for at least the last 30 years, passing legislation which did not apply to them; unsurprisingly this seems to have alienated much of white middle America – something called Whitelash. They regard an interfering government as their remote enemy which in affirmative action programmes discriminates against the majority, supports deviant sexual lifestyles through welfare spending, and has created an underclass dependent upon state support.

This alienation is particularly strong in some parts of the west where people are invoking the Tenth Amendment to the Constitution, which defines that all powers not specifically allocated to Washington are reserved by the states. Ambrose Evans-Pritchard reports in the *Sunday Telegraph* that a

Hawaiian-born federal judge issued an injunction prohibiting all mining, logging and ranching in five national forests in Idaho to protect the chinook salmon – effectively destroying the livelihood for people living in towns 900 miles from the Pacific. Many of the streams are too small for the fish to live – even if they avoided being chopped to pieces from hydro-electric turbines downstream.

Another example of state alienation for many people in the US is the elimination of school prayers in an effort not to impose Christianity on everyone. This has led to questions whether a town can decorate public areas during the Christian season with lights; when Jewish decorations were placed side by side with Christian nativity scenes there were still complaints that this offended minority religions. Does this really mean that the state is sponsoring a form of tribal atheism where no overt signs of the indigenous faith can be displayed for fear of upsetting minorities?

Are Politics Also Influenced by Cycles?

There seems to be no good reason why politics, like investment, business, technology and so on (all subjects of other chapters) should not conform to the cycles described in Chapter 2. The primary influence is likely to be the Kondratieff long wave but others such as the 179-year climatic cycle, identified by Rhodes Fairbridge and described in *Riding the Business Cycle* could also be significant. The book explains how people become aggressive towards their rulers in cool climates, demanding a greater degree of freedom and independence; conversely, warm conditions make people more cooperative, willing to be led and inducing greater creativity.

There is another cycle, now becoming important, identified by Alvin and Heidi Toffler as the 'Third Wave', or the transition from the industrial age to what the international consultant Michael White describes as the 'Cybernetic Revolution'. The Tofflers describe the Third Wave as three successive phases of mankind: the first established settled agriculture, saw the growth of market towns and the rise of the guilds. The second wave created the Industrial Revolution where people, dispossessed of their rural homes, were obliged to converge on the then centres of energy, operating machinery driven by mill streams and later by steam. The Third Wave reverses the previous trends, introducing the era of new information and technology which frees individuals from the constrictions and centralisation associated with the second wave.

We can now start to analyse what these cycles have meant to the political policies of Britain and America, the two oldest English speaking democracies. Although both countries have quite different histories there have been remarkable points of convergence.

Political changes during the 179-year sun retrograde cycles. It became very cold late in the 16th century and into the 17th century, when the sun retrograded in 1632, creating what was later known as the 'little ice age'. The event contributed to the violence of the Thirty Years War in Germany, the overthrow of the Ming Dynasty in 1644 and the conflict in England between the king and parliament which gave rise to the English Civil War. Charles I, who wanted to help the Spanish against the Protestant Dutch, inflamed the attitude of the largely Puritan London parliament who refused the supply of funds. Matters reached an impasse when the king tried to arrest four elected leaders, so setting the scene for the future conflict.

The English Civil War, like the American Civil War two centuries later, started slowly, both sides needing time to gain support. The king was backed largely by most of the nobility, the gentlemen and their tenants – drawn primarily from the North and West of England. Puritan squires and farmers were the backbone of the Parliamentary cause, supported by the town and city merchants. On their behalf, Oliver Cromwell and Sir Thomas Fairfax created a proficient 'model army' drawn from the South and East of the country; this force prevailed at two decisive battles after suffering early reverses.

After the king had been captured and imprisoned in Carisbrooke Castle on the Isle of Wight, Parliament hoped that he would accept the position of a constitutional monarch but it was not to be. Discovering that he was secretly encouraging the Irish to invade England and restore him to the throne, Parliament brought the king to trial and duly committed him to death as 'a tyrant, traitor, murderer and public enemy to the people'. He was executed on a very cold morning on 30 January 1649. Oliver Cromwell then ruled as Lord Protector (through 12 military districts in England and Wales, each governed by a major general) and abolished the monarchy, the House of Lords and by-passed Parliament. Cromwell died nine years after the king, to be succeeded by his son before the monarchy and the House of Lords were re-established in 1660.

The 179-year cycle showed itself again in 1811 about the time Napoleon's empire was at its peak, but was being undermined by Wellington's successful Iberian campaign; if he had known about the cycle the Emperor would never have embarked on his disastrous invasion of Russia. After the mighty eruption of Tambora in April 1815 the cool climate triggered several liberation movements. In the rising tide of nationalism, Greece was freed from the Ottoman Turks and by 1825 Simon Bolivar had liberated Venezuela, Colombia, Ecuador and Peru from Spanish rule. San Martin helped to free Peru and liberate Chile, while Brazil declared independence from Portugal in 1821. Encouraged by the protective doctrine of President James Monroe, Mexico declared itself free from Spain and in the same year Florida was ceded to the United States.

Political Changes Around the Kondratieff Long Wave Cycle

The long wave Kondratieff cycle had probably the greatest detailed influence on the politics of America and Britain over the three completed long wave cycles (K1, K2, K3) that divided into the upwave, plateau and downwave phases. (Each cycle is illustrated in Figures 15 to 18.)

The exuberant first cycle

K1 started in America after Congress had replaced the old Articles of Confederation with the present-day Constitution in 1787 and the First Bank of the United States was formed with a gold-backed currency. George Washington had been elected president in 1789 and again in 1792 after angrily rejecting a call by some army officers that he should become king. The new government created the offices of State, Justice, War and Treasury and passed laws to regulate seamen, the militia, Indian affairs and the creation of a post office.

About this time two political parties emerged. The first, led by Thomas Jefferson and calling themselves Republicans, believed that the rights of the individual could best be preserved by minimum interference of the states by federal government. The other group, centred around Alexander Hamilton, called themselves the 'federalists', believing that securing the strength of the nation was no threat to individual rights. Two hundred years later, one can only appreciate how right Jefferson was.

After a nasty recession at the bottom of K1 following the euphoria of the British defeat at Yorktown, the American economy boomed in the early 19th century, stimulated by the Anglo-French War which broke out in 1803. That same year the Louisiana Purchase was negotiated from Napoleon during Thomas Jefferson's presidency for $15 million in gold so doubling the American land mass; this not only gave the president enormous prestige but added to the production of war material for Europe. However, free trade to the Continent did not suit Britain which was blockading French-controlled ports and led to frustrated American sailors being turned away. Increasing acrimony after the 1811 elections brought aggressive men into power. In 1812 president James Madison declared war on Britain – an action effectively starting the first *plateau* phase.

The War of 1812 consolidated the north-east states within the republic, gaining valuable extra territory, increasing the prestige of the fledgling navy and also of General Andrew Jackson who soundly beat off a British attack near New Orleans. After the Treaty of Ghent, the 1812 war ended with America consolidating its gains but still unable to trade with Napoleon's empire which was then in decline. There was an 'era of good feeling' when America found stability, the second Bank of America provided a stable gold-backed currency, and land settlement continued in the then new territories in the west.

The 1812 war had also created new political alignments, with a more self-confident projection of national power through the foreign policy doctrine of the next president, James Monroe. It also revived protectionism to support America's nascent industries and provide the revenue to build canals; the tariffs were quite severe, imposing 25% on imported cotton and woollen goods and 20% on pig iron. The moves destroyed the old 'federalist' party but created instead a new Republican alignment which contained the elements of the future Civil War. The cotton industry, which was barely alive in 1784, was transformed by the invention of Eli Whitney's cotton gin in 1793 and by 1805 was shipping over 40 million pounds a year in bulk to Liverpool where it was processed by newly developed steam-driven spinning and weaving machinery.

The *plateau* phase ended in 1826 when the preceding boom had over-extended the banking system, defaults became increasingly common and a steeply declining economy forced debtors out of business. There was also a political sea change with the selection of Andrew Jackson as president in 1828, the first to be elected by a genuine popular vote without the direct support of Congress. Jackson had a remarkable career. He first fought in the revolutionary war then practised as an attorney in Tennessee before being appointed a judge. He came to public notice after defeating the British at New Orleans and subsequently fought the 1824 election unsuccessfully. Old Hickory Sticks, as he was known, was the first president to hail from west of the Appalachians and was perhaps of humble origins.

Sales of land by the federal government in the west had brought in revenue of $36 million by 1836, over twice what had earlier been paid for the Louisiana Purchase. Individual states received some federal income but also took part in land speculation as did foreign investors. Quite suddenly individual authorities, used to agonising over investing $100,000, found they could now invest millions in roads, canals and railroads. The speculative orgy, spawning dozens of 'wild-cat' banks, could not last for ever. In 1836 the hard-money Democrats under President Van Buren required payment in 'specie' (gold or silver) for the land sales; this the borrowers could not provide and those banks still with specie refused to honour paper money. This started the 'panic of 1837' when states defaulted and foreigners refused to hold American securities.

First the panic, then the depression as all the poor credit risks and debts were wrung out of the system. The decline continued until 1848, the low point of K1. But other strains were appearing in the body politic. There were mounting claims from South Carolina to withdraw from the Union in defiance of the tariff act of 1832, but Jackson replied by sending a naval force to take possession of Charleston harbour. The issue was defused the following year when duties were reduced over time to 20% and the state dropped the nullification order. The state of Texas had beaten the Mexicans to become a republic in 1842, and in 1845 joined the Union. Continuing aggravation triggered a declaration of war leading to General Zachary Taylor defeating the Mexicans, and to an agreement to cede the territories that are now New Mexico, Arizona and California to the Union.

Expansion and tragedy during K2

The euphoria of the additional states joining the union and the discovery of gold in the west considerably increased agricultural capacity, which found a ready market after Britain repealed the Corn Laws in 1846; output was helped still further by McCormick's invention of the reaper and binder, the machines being drawn by teams of horses. Confidence in all parts of society improved and capital was available to expand construction in western real estate and in railroads whose shares had risen 70% in the four years to 1852. However, the expansion was troubled by growing political dissent in the south-east.

Texas was the last slave state admitted to the union, an issue that dogged policy in the recovery upwave of K2. In 1790, there was near equal representation in government from slave or 'free' states but with the huge influx of migrants to the north the balance had swung away from the south so that by 1860, there were 147 'free' House members to 90 from slave states. The old Whig party under stalwarts like John Calhoun gave way to Jefferson Davis and Alexander Stephens who now formed the new Democratic party.

Lined up against them were the progressively anti-slavery Republicans, competent people such as Charles Sumner,

KONDRATIEFF CYCLE K1

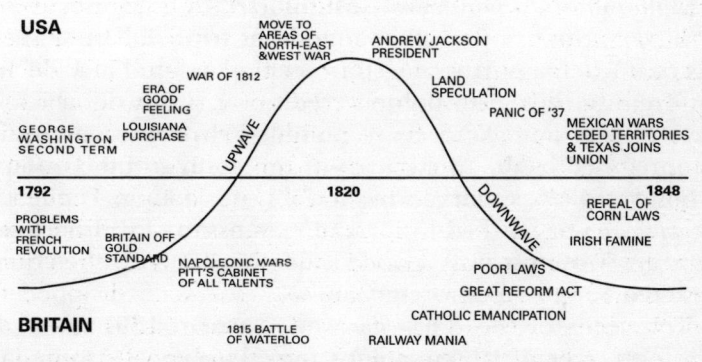

USA

MOVE TO AREAS OF NORTH-EAST & WEST WAR
ANDREW JACKSON PRESIDENT
WAR OF 1812
ERA OF GOOD FEELING
LAND SPECULATION
PANIC OF '37
GEORGE WASHINGTON SECOND TERM
LOUISIANA PURCHASE
MEXICAN WARS CEDED TERRITORIES & TEXAS JOINS UNION

UPWAVE

1792   1820   1848
                                          REPEAL OF CORN LAWS
PROBLEMS WITH FRENCH REVOLUTION
BRITAIN OFF GOLD STANDARD
                                          IRISH FAMINE
NAPOLEONIC WARS PITT'S CABINET OF ALL TALENTS
DOWNWAVE
POOR LAWS
GREAT REFORM ACT
CATHOLIC EMANCIPATION

BRITAIN   1815 BATTLE OF WATERLOO   RAILWAY MANIA

Figure 15. Historical events associated with K1 in the USA and Britain.

William Seward and Salmon Chase. The rivalry between the parties became more acute when Congress passed the Kansas–Nebraska Act which allowed each new state to choose whether to be slave or free – a blunder that was to create unwanted political pressures within any new territory applying to join the Union. The two parties became even more polarised in the election of 1855 when James Buchanan for the Democrats advocated the greatest possible state freedom for John Fremont known as the 'Pathfinder', a soldier and explorer who achieved fame prospecting railway routes through to the west.

The final split came at the *plateau* phase of K2, when in 1859 the Republican Abraham Lincoln was elected president. In October 1860 Governor Gist of South Carolina received a favourable reply from the other cotton states to secede from the Union – a decision ratified at a Confederate convention. The War Between the States started on April 14 1861 when southern troops fired on and captured Fort Sumpter near Charleston, South Carolina. The Civil War that followed was the most bloody ever undertaken by Americans, accounting for some 800,000 dead, a terrible loss for a growing country. It was also at times a remarkably sophisticated conflict, more ably fought than the Crimean War only a few years earlier. It was also for its time particularly well documented and its study will handsomely repay students of American history.

The beginning of the war coincided with growing strains from a banking system which had expanded by an astonishing 55% in the seven years to 1857. The supply of credit was accelerated when in 1862, the Union Congress authorised the issue of $450 million 'greenbacks' unsupported by gold and, as with most wars, the price of all commodities tripled. The position reversed when a northern victory seemed assured in 1864 and the Treasury began to tighten credit, war industries slid into receivership and land sales tumbled by 84%. This was accompanied by the usual post-war recession and the collapse of bond and stock markets but it did not last long. The rest of the *plateau* was marked by a rapid expansion of railroads and farming, business was good, stocks rose and the boom attracted $2 billion of foreign capital.

The seeds of the *downwave* were sown in 1861 when the growing power of labour unions forced politicians to apply a 24% increase of tariffs on most foreign goods; by 1864 the duties had risen to a prohibitive 47%. In ten years retaliatory action from Europe virtually stopped all trade and a worldwide recession started as the post-war recovery lost momentum. It is said that the Civil War cost the Union $12 billion and a huge debt servicing cost that was a drain on private savings; as money became tighter, prices declined by 40% and railroad stocks lost 50% of their value. As the recession bit harder, political and social unrest demanded government relief to which Congress responded with price support measures and lower tariffs.

After the war the south was placed under a military government and the Thirteenth Amendment was passed abolishing slavery. But the agony of war did not end for the ex-Confederate states; their currency was worthless, their transportation destroyed and freed slaves roamed the country obliging plantation owners to repair the damage on their own. No love was lost with the north when 'carpet-baggers' set about organising the newly enfranchised negro vote to becoming Republican supporters. This so antagonised whites that secret societies like the Ku Klux Klan were formed to intimidate black voters. By 1868 some of the southern states had sworn allegiance to the Constitution and rejoined the Union; the rest would follow.

Not surprisingly the Republican presidents who dominated the post-war years continued the policy of tariff protection – encouraged by the growing labour unions. However, the tariffs did have their positive side by raising the funds to pay off the national debt. The southern recovery later surprised many when cotton cultivation was made more efficient by using white labour. The former Confederates also benefited from

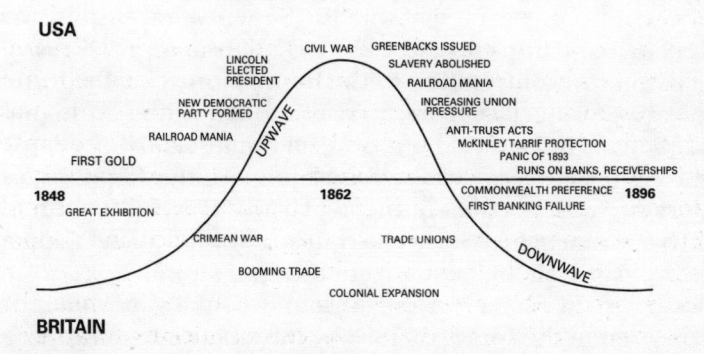

Figure 16. Historical events associated with K2 in the USA and Britain.

the discovery of coal and iron ore deposits at the southern end of the Appalachians which, when developed, rivalled the output of New England.

By 1883, the Republican administration was becoming corrupt with complaints that government officials were found fraudulently conniving in the collection of whisky duties; also the Secretary for War was forced to resign to avoid impeachment for his conducting of Indian affairs. The system was partly reformed by introducing competitive examinations into the civil service but the changes did not go far enough and in the election of 1884, Grover Cleveland was elected. Cleveland was the first Democratic president since the Civil War and had the support of the 'solid south' and large states such as New York and Connecticut. Cleveland's main contribution was to lower some of the import duties, so reducing federal income but also encouraging business in a depressed economy. But lifting tariffs only lasted a short time before the next president took office with a mandate to increase protection and introduce fresh legislation such as the Sherman [Anti-Trust] Act of 1890. The aim was to break up industrial monopolies like the Standard Oil Trust and large banks to increase competition. There was also the Interstate Commerce Commission to control the railroads and there were laws regulating securities.

Again the tariff issue, which had surfaced at the trough of the K1 cycle, became important politically with the McKinley Tariff Act of 1890 aimed at protecting farmers. The huge volcano Krakatoa had gone off in 1883 causing an exceptional blizzard four years later which devastated livestock; it also caused the rain belts to move south – resulting in very hot summers for ten years that made it nearly impossible for farmers to grow crops in states like west Kansas and Nebraska. The failed farms only added to the depression. The Tariff Act did not just protect farmers, it also applied duties to manufactured items that could be produced domestically.

The distressed conditions were blamed on the Republicans who lost the next election, returning Grover Cleveland again in 1892. No sooner had he started his administration than a disastrous panic hit the nation from the agricultural depression, reckless railroad financing and unsound banking practices. It was triggered in the spring of 1893 by the failure of the Reading Railroad and the collapse of the National Cordage Company. There was a run on the banks, loans collapsed and 22,000 miles of track went into receivership. Labour troubles at the Pullman Car Company, and other sympathetic strikes, accelerated the decline which marked the low point of K2 in 1896.

K3 tracks euphoria to despair

K3 began in 1896 with new gold-mining finds in Alaska which, through improved chemical processing, produced higher yields than before. The population had grown rapidly to total 76 million by 1900 through European and Far East immigration and America was able to project power overseas through the building of a formidable navy. Disputes with Spain in the 1890s had led to the Spanish-American War after which, for the consideration of $20 million, Cuba and Puerto Rico in the west and Guam and the Philippines in the east were ceded to America at the Treaty of Paris in 1898. A purchase of land in present-day Panama allowed the building of the canal across the isthmus.

This new-found confidence was given vigorous leadership when the vice-president Theodore Roosevelt became president after the assassination of the elected William McKinley in 1901. Teddy Roosevelt, as he became known, had a career of public service before being appointed assistant secretary of the navy in 1897 when he led a volunteer group of 'rough-riders' to clear the Spanish out of Cuba. As president he completed the Panama canal after the first failed enterprise and was instrumental in ending the Russo-Japanese War in 1905. During his administrations, competition was promoted

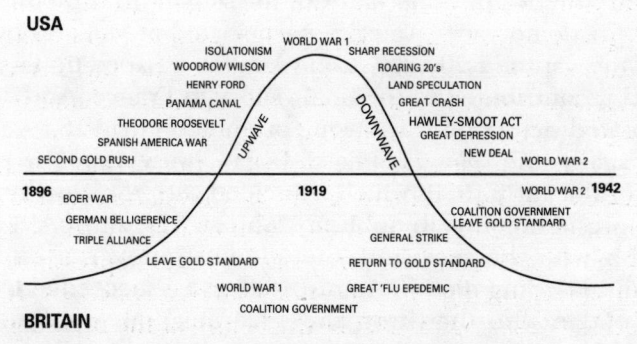

Figure 17. Historical events associated with K3 in Britain and the USA.

by trust-busting and breaking up monopolies. In 1912, unable to gain the Republican nomination, he stood as the candidate of the independent Bull Moose party against the Republican candidate. The Republican vote was split, which let in the Democrat Woodrow Wilson.

The *upwave* of K3 was one of the most remarkable in history with the rise of industrialisation and the spread of trade to the growing markets in the Far East and to Europe. The upwave also saw a naval rivalry between Britain and Germany which developed into an armament race. As confidence soared, businesses invested in plant and machinery, attracting additional immigrants and people from the land. The recovery was stimulated by the Payne-Aldrich Tariff Reduction Act of 1909 and the growing output of mass production enterprises pioneered by Henry Ford.

President Wilson was a genial man of Scottish Presbyterian background who strongly believed in the power of ideals to arouse and inspire people. This gave him a certain aloofness and with it a reluctance to confer with Congress or to meet people. He was also against war and although determined to keep America out of the forthcoming conflict, the nation was encouraged to sell war material to the allies during the early years of the First World War, bringing in large profits and a positive trade balance of $3 billion by 1916. However, neutrality became more difficult after a German submarine sunk the *Lusitania* in 1915 with the loss of American lives and Wilson still won the 1916 election on a ticket of continued neutrality.

The continued sinking of American ships, and an attempt by Germany to bring in Mexico on the side of the Central Powers, precipitated America into the war with the slogan 'to make the world safe for democracy'. America participated at sea, and by the end of the war the 1,200,000 strong American Expeditionary Force (AEF), contributed to the final victory in France. Americans celebrated victory by introducing prohibition in 1918.

Once again the *plateau* phase began with the sharp recession of the early 1920s which coincided with the election of a new president, the Republican Warren Harding. After dealing ably with the recession, the administration ran into scandals and Harding died in August 1923 to be succeeded by Calvin Coolidge who then won the 1924 election – polling nearly double the votes of his nearest rival with the slogan 'keep cool with Coolidge'.

The 'Roaring 1920s' were a typical *plateau* story of booming business after the sharp 1920 crash. Initially interest rates were low and there was a benign economic environment; however, towards the end of the decade there was rising speculation in land like in the 1820s and 1860s but this time accompanied by a booming stock market. Just as farms were traded in K1 so now were land plots in Florida, and quoted stocks on the New York exchange rocketed when leveraging allowed large investments to be owned for just 10% of their value.

The real-estate crash started in 1927, two years before that of the stock market – but both were very real. The Dow Jones industrial average fell 50% from October to November 1929 before rallying into the first quarter of 1930. There was then a slow collapse to the second quarter of 1932 after the averages lost nearly 90% ($6.5 billion) of their value; those who were holding General Motors stock in September 1929 did not see it reach the same value until 1952. Severe as the stock-market losses were, the crash of the world bond markets cost $90 billion.

The Great Depression was one of the worst periods in American history, shattering the myth that free enterprise could overcome any difficulty. As Dorothy Parker observed, the bankers, investors and industrialists who had been the heroes of the 'roaring twenties' now suddenly became the villains. Likewise the pro-business president Herbert Hoover totally failed to understand the change and served only one term in office. To compound America's problems Hoover was obliged to sign the Smoot-Hawley Act, one of the most comprehensive tariff packages ever enacted; the tariff wall was rendered almost unscalable for foreign importers after the next president, Franklin Roosevelt, devalued the dollar nearly 70% relative to gold fixing it at $35 per troy ounce from $20.67.

The New Deal enacted by Roosevelt and supported by a Democratic congress was one of the first attempts to stimulate an economy by government action on the principles of Maynard Keynes. In the 1920s the federal government spent only 3% of GDP (compared to the 22% in the 1990s) giving the state ample borrowing powers to rescue failed mortgage holders, initiate major public building and to run job-creation programmes. Many mistakes were made, including the start of welfare dependency which is dogging America and other countries six decades later.

One particular fiasco of Roosevelt's New Deal was the National Recovery Administration (NRA), an organisation headed by ex-general Hugh Johnson, which attempted to stimulate the economy during the Depression. It became a form of state administered fascism that mercifully was declared unconstitutional by the Supreme Court when four poultry dealers, the brothers Schechter, were given short prison sentences for disobeying poultry regulations. The code stated that if a buyer took less than a full coop of chickens he was not allowed to select the fowls but must pick a random selection.

The K4 *upwave* probably started soon after America entered the Second World War and provided the motive power for the allies' victory. The country then had to reduce the huge post-war debt and at the same time initiated what Winston Churchill called one of the most selfless acts ever undertaken by a nation. The Marshall Plan, enacted under the presidency of Harry Truman, provided the funds and material to rebuild the war-torn nations of Japan and Europe and in so doing created the basis for their future prosperity as democracies. As America grew in confidence it also undertook to act as the main bulwark against the rising might of Soviet communism. Pax Britannica administered by the Royal Navy gave way to America's Strategic Air Command and the US Navy.

The euphoria at the end of the *upwave* encouraged the belief that the nation must have, and could obviously afford, a new wave of liberal legislation. Lyndon Johnson's 'great society' built on the New Deal and there followed other bills

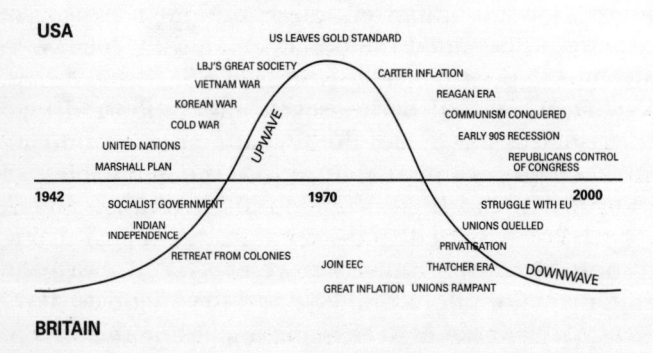

Figure 18. Historical events associated with K4 in Britain and the USA.

such as the Environmental Protection Act, the Occupational Safety and Health Act and the Comprehensive Employment and Training Act. Legislation continued when the Republican, Richard Nixon, passed the Family Assistance Programme and minimum wage legislation. All these measures forced America to leave the gold standard in 1971.

The Vietnam War, followed by the mid-1970s recession, probably started the *plateau* phase with America undergoing a period of great uncertainty when one president was assassinated and another impeached within 10 years. However, after the dip in the mid-1970s, booming business conditions once again took over in the 1980s, accompanied by wild market speculation and the build up of excessive public and private debt. The consequential downwave is likely to have begun in 1990 with increasing signs that the classical Kondratieff downturn would reach its low point early in the next century. By 1996 the nation's debt to GDP ratio was equal to that of 1931 with the prognosis that, with other indebted nations, the downturn will be as severe as the 1930s.

Does British Political History Also Run in Cycles?

By the 1790s Britain was a settled democracy already reaping the benefit from early industrialisation. The principles of the economist Adam Smith were well understood by politicians and were being applied in a regime of free trade. Private enterprise promoted the digging of canals while the steam engine took over from the mill stream as the prime motive power for the thriving textile, coal mining, iron smelting and other industries.

Politically the country had not moved on much further from the heated struggle in 1679 to exclude the Catholic James, Duke of York, from succeeding to the throne. His accession was resisted by the Whig party while there was support for the hereditary principle from the Tories. After the 'Glorious Revolution' of 1688 which put the Protestant William of Orange on the throne, the Tories were obliged to change their position, although they still tended to be known as the king's party. Conversely, the Whigs were the party of the nobility – a division which possibly could be traced from the days of Magna Carta.

Democracy in the 18th century was lopsided, with the nobility controlling most of the parliamentary seats through what were known as 'rotten boroughs'. Under this set-up a sparsely populated county like Cornwall had 400 seats while the emerging industrial towns of Manchester and Birmingham were unrepresented and the City of London had only two members. However, although there was a Whig majority, distinct party positions did not crystallise until 1784 with a new Toryism led by the remarkably able William Pitt the younger. The Whig party was still that of the nobility but starting to attract radical ideas and some industrial interests.

K1, the age of reform

At the start of K1, Pitt's government had reformed much of the British and Indian administration, reconstructed the nation's finances, passed the Canada Act, founded the colony of New South Wales and simplified the tariff code. At first the news of the French Revolution and the fall of the Bastille had been almost universally welcomed but approval turned into alarm when France fell prey increasingly to disorder and bankruptcy – then to horror when Louis XVI was guillotined in January 1793. This led to a division within the Whig party, the 'new' Whigs under Charles James Fox becoming more radical. They supported the French Revolution and stood for the abolition of slavery, Catholic emancipation and parliamentary reform; they won few friends at court by offering the toast 'our sovereign, the people'. For this Fox's name was removed from the Privy Council list.

The war with France started with a dispute over Britain's ally, Holland, but then engaged other countries such as Austria, Prussia, Spain and Portugal. However, by 1796 all the allies with the exception of Portugal had fallen away leaving Britain to continue the struggle. First of all, the war went badly for Britain with the loss of Toulon and Malta but things were reversed by Nelson's stunning victory of the Nile in 1798, the recapture of Malta in 1800 and the crushing of an Irish rebellion at about the same time. The end of Irish hostilities encouraged Pitt to recommend the emancipation of Catholics which the king refused to countenance. The prime minister tendered his resignation when the French war was temporarily suspended by the Treaty of Amiens. But the new British administration proved incompetent and Pitt resumed office when Napoleon appointed himself Emperor and the war resumed.

While Napoleon was still winning conquests in the east which destroyed the Alliance (and indirectly led to Pitt's death), Britain was gaining control of the seas following the Battle of Trafalgar in 1805. After Pitt's death a 'ministry of all the talents' was formed including remarkable names such as George Canning, Lord Castlereagh, Charles James Fox (for a brief period), Henry Temple (later Lord Palmerston), Sir Robert Peel and others. (One might marvel how another equally talented group of men some thirty years earlier had won freedom from Britain to create the new American republic.) The new ministry gradually prevailed against Napoleon, firstly with the Emperor's exile to Elba then later with Wellington's victory at Waterloo. The subsequent Treaty of Vienna restored most of the old frontiers, created the new country of Belgium and kept France a sovereign state. After the treaty (at the beginning of the *plateau*) Britain was unchallenged on the seas with numerous possessions abroad and a growing industrial might.

The end of the *plateau* and the start of the *downwave* were marked by a financial crisis in England in 1825 with widespread industrial and commercial failures. As unemployment rose the Poor Law Amendment Act of 1834 was passed, a draconian measure that gave relief only to those who were admitted to a workhouse on the grounds of unfitness for work. Two years earlier the Reform Bill had been passed by a reluctant Tory government, led by the Duke of Wellington, after the king threatened to swamp the House of Lords with supporters. Amidst a cascade of other reforms that had been simmering for years, the Catholic Emancipation Act was passed in 1829 allowing Catholics to stand and hold almost all public offices.

The end of K1 was marked in 1851 by a low point of the Rousseaux Price Index (a register of English agricultural and industrial prices which showed a high point in 1814), and also a low for births per thousand. In the clamour for cheap food at the beginning of the Irish potato famine in 1846, the Corn Laws were abolished allowing grain to be imported primarily from the USA.

Global expansion during K2

The seeds of the K2 *upwave* had already been set in 1851 when the Great Exhibition in Hyde Park was opened by the queen. The display of exhibits from all over the world dazzled visitors with products and machinery which were the last word in technology and excellence. Joseph Paxton's exhibition hall was itself a masterpiece of design and construction, employing prefabricated cast-iron sections bolted together. One of the few remaining exhibits is the handsome cast-iron entrance gates made at Coalbrookdale in Shropshire which now divide Hyde Park from Kensington Gardens.

The *upwave* was also accompanied by a vigorous foreign policy to extend Britain's global influence. During Lord Aberdeen's administration in 1854 war was declared jointly with France against Russia to defend Turkey's hold over the Bosphorous. A successful action in the Crimea forced the Russians off the peninsula but showed dismal gaps in military organisation when four times as many men died from disease than in combat. During the recovery phase to 1861 the price index rose one third as output of the staples such as coal and iron increased nearly 100%. Although exports like cotton cloth more than doubled to over 2,000 million yards by the 1860s, Britain's balance of visible trade remained in the red throughout the century but was positive overall after invisible trade from banking, insurance, investment income and other services were taken into account.

The *plateau* and *downwave* phases of K2 saw the contrasting administrative styles of the flamboyant conservative Benjamin Disraeli and the reforming Liberal William Gladstone in the latter part of the 19th century. Disraeli, creator of the modern Conservative party, embraced electoral reform and projected British power by making Queen Victoria Empress of India, buying the Egyptian Khedive's share of the Suez Canal and encouraging British interest in Africa. Conversely, Gladstone was responsible for home reforms by introducing (but not passing) Home Rule in Ireland, the first Education Act and recognising trade unions.

The beginning of the *downwave* was not as marked as that in America because Britain had not been involved in a major war. However, from a peak in 1872, prices once again fell to reach a low point in 1899 but this did not destroy growth in agriculture, industry, commerce and investment. National income rose 23% in the ten years to 1891. Although the movement from country to town continued, cattle rearing, arable farms and market gardens became increasingly organised and thrived with improved distribution to the towns. Industrial production boomed with steel output double that of Germany. Craftsmen were much in demand even beyond their normal retirement date, being valued for their skill and experience.

There was also considerable investment in the infrastructure. The Albert and Tilbury docks were built, the Forth Bridge was opened by the Prince of Wales during the 1880s and the Manchester Ship Canal was started in 1887; tunnels were also dug under the Mersey and Severn. Despite the recession in other countries, the gross tonnage of ships built increased by 23% during the 1880s, probably accelerated by the switch from sail to steam as the proportion of mechanically propelled vessels increased to 84%.

As in America, tariffs were raised in Germany, France, Russia, Italy and Austria-Hungary during the downwave, but although protection was mooted in Britain and exports fell, protectionism was rejected and did not become a major political issue until 1931. Unions had represented skilled craftsmen in agriculture, textiles, gas, mining, railways and other industries but new associations were formed to represent the unskilled workers to improve their terms of contract. Although there were restrictions on picketing, union strike funds were protected by law. In 1893 an Independent Labour Party was set up as a political offshoot of the Trade Union Conference.

The torch is handed to America during K3

Britain started K3 still a major power but the industrial base was too biased towards the staple industries of coal, iron and textiles to take a lead in the newer industries pioneered by Germany; these included electric power, the internal combustion engine and chemicals. Politically, the Conservatives still held power in 1900 although the party was split over Commonwealth preference tariffs and for the first time there were two Labour members in the House of Commons. As with previous *upwaves* the Liberals were returned to power in 1906 on a reforming ticket to pass an Old Age Pensions and National Insurance Act – years after Bismarck's similar legislation in Germany.

Overseas, the world's peace was still held by the Royal Navy's battle fleet which was transformed by the revolutionary dreadnought which could outgun any capital ship afloat. The benefits were two-edged, however, as the design also allowed Germany to create a new and modern navy in competition. The long wave started with the Boer War which was fought on behalf of the British settlers in Cape Province against the

Dutch farmers. Peace was signed after two years fighting and several humiliating defeats against a wily and determined foe. As the *upwave* continued Britain formed alliances with France against an increasingly belligerent Germany and Austria.

A Liberal government with all-party support led the country at the start of the First World War – another cabinet of all talents. It became a brutal and costly slugging match along the western front and Gallipoli, where tens of thousand of tons of metal and high explosives were pitted against men in trenches. It decimated the young men of many nations and the only people who benefited were those supplying the armaments, food and other stores.

The *plateau* was not a happy time for Britain. It started with the terrible influenza epidemic of 1919 which wiped out as many people as all those lost in the war. The Prime Minister, Lloyd George, had promised 'a land fit for heroes' but the nation was war weary and hardly profited from the 'roaring twenties' as did America or France. The country's woes were increased when the pound was once again linked to the gold standard in 1925 but at too competitive a rate; the result was deflation, a squeeze on wages and the General Strike of 1926.

Surprisingly, Britain fared much better in the *downwave* during the 1930s than almost any other nation. There had not been the same degree of market speculation in the 1920s as across the Atlantic, nor the build up of debt, and although the country was still burdened with the old staple industries, these were largely protected by a regime of Commonwealth Protection negotiated under the Ottawa Agreement in 1931. In fact many new industries such as housing, transport, radio and domestic appliances thrived under the regime of a balanced budget, plus the low interest rate during the chancellorship of Neville Chamberlain.

Britain suffers from the arthritis of socialism during parts of K4

The upwave started during the Second World War saw the nation triumphant but in no position to take real advantage of the recovery because of measures passed by the Labour government of 1945. The administration increased the power of the unions; they delayed modernising some staple industries through nationalisation and retained war-time controls. Even though the Tory government of 1951 tore up many of the regulations, it too was committed to full employment and failed to redress the regime of wasteful nationalised industries and high taxation.

Britain reached the plateau phase in the mid 1970s with the stock and commodity markets working in harmony with America. It also coincided with a defeat of the Conservative Party which had unwisely taken on the powerful miners union; it was followed by the return of an aggressive socialist government with the full backing of the trade union movement. The plateau ended with a burst of free-market enthusiasm during the 1980s led by Prime Minister Margaret Thatcher, who was determined to unwind the corporatist state and to promote individual freedom. Fortunately the administration ran a budget surplus, which is why Britain had probably one of the lowest debt to GDP ratios in the free world – another surprising comparison with the 1920s.

The Patterns Associated With Political Cycles

A sequence occurred during the first three political cycles which is now being repeated during K4. Initially the patterns were most evident in America but with increased globalisation at the end of the 20th century each western nation is showing symptoms similar to those of America in the 19th century.

	Upwave	**Downwave**
Economic Outlook	Inflation	Deflation
Dominant Creed	Liberal	Conservative
Perception	International	National
Reform	Innovative	Static
Prevailing Trends	Collectivist Deregulation	Individualist Regulation
Successful States	Corporatist (Germany, Japan)	Individualistic (Anglo-Saxon)
Trade	Free Trade	Protection
Federations	Formed	Broken up

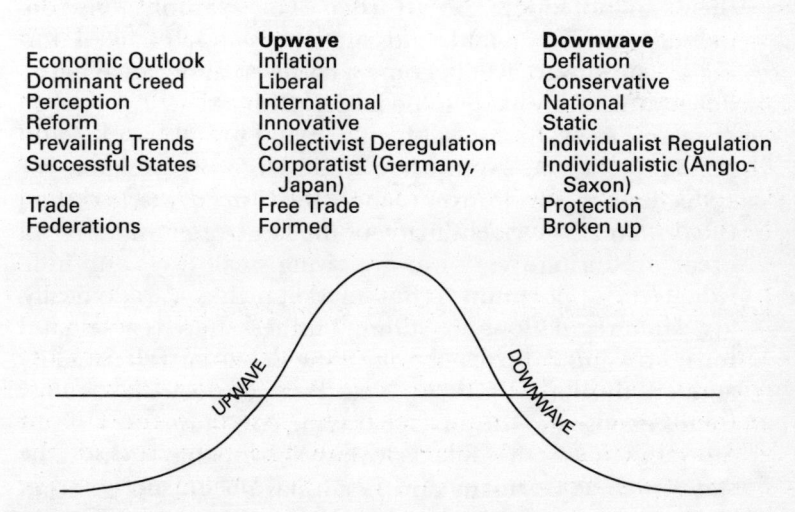

Figure 19. Summary of cycles influencing politicians during the long wave.

These observations have been summarised in Figure 19 under events that occur during the upwave and downwave:

Economic outlook: upwaves are inflationary while downwaves (on their own) are deflationary. This has been true for each cycle although K4 is likely to be an exception as it coincides with two powerful climatic cycles.

Dominant creed: liberal ideas including a greater degree of government involvement are acceptable in an upwave but it becomes increasingly obvious that state spending can no longer be afforded in the downwave. This then becomes a major problem. The electorate, expecting protection that can no longer be afforded, now becomes disillusioned and resentful of politicians and civil servants. Social policy only became an issue for America and Britain initially during K3 and then a dominant theme in K4.

Perception: international cooperation is encouraged enthusiastically during the upwave but is likely to suffer during the downwave. The League of Nations came apart during the 1930s but the more grandiose United Nations considerably expanded in the upwave of K4; there are growing signs that the UN as it is will not survive the 1990s downwave.

Reform: liberal reforms are more acceptable during the upwaves but these tend to be reversed in the downwave for they can no longer be afforded. For example, environmental, minority, health and safety legislation enacted during the downwave will become a costly encumbrance in the downwave and is likely to be largely disbanded.

Prevailing trends: there will be a demand for all barriers and regulations to be swept aside while large organisations or collections of people grow to meet the rising demand during the upwave. Conversely, many of the large organisations will break up during the downwave giving small firms and individuals the opportunity to find market niches. Paradoxically, just when regulations are stifling business there is a demand for increasing controls like the New Economic Plan (NEP) applied during the 1930s New Deal to regulate against frauds exposed in the adverse trading conditions.

Successful states: the K4 cycle has shown that corporatist states such as Germany and Japan have been successful in the upwave but both are already showing signs of being unable to weather the downwave. Expect the more individualistic nations such as America, Britain and Italy to be successful in the downwave.

Trade: tariffs have been lowered in the upwave but raised in the downwave. The farming lobby called for the Smoot-Hawley Act in 1930 to protect commodity prices which triggered Commonwealth Preference at the Ottawa Conference in 1932. By 1996 politicians seem to have learned from the 1930s although there is minority support for Pat Buchanan and Ross Perot. Any recession would strain trade blocs like NAFTA and the EU.

Federations: these tend to be formed in the upwave then disbanded in the downwave. The Russian Federation is already showing signs of strain and could break asunder early in the next century. Others could follow.

Other Cycles at Work

Analysts and historians over many decades have been fascinated by American political cycles and have reached differing conclusions. Those, such as Martin Armstrong, who relate the cycles of big versus small government have found they track well with the Kondratieff wave. Others such as Emerson looked at presidential innovative rhythms while Henry Adams identified a 12-year cycle of movements towards or away from Washington DC; Arthur Schlesinger Jnr has identified a 16.5-year wave between the forces of innovation and reaction – or presumably between liberals and conservatives. This is a summary of some of their views:

Martin Armstrong, the principal of the Princeton Economic Institute, has found that swings between big and small US governments jibe with investment cycles. An examination of presidential campaigns shows that thirty-one presidents were elected on a platform of less government and lower taxation while only twenty-one believed that big government could solve people's problems. As suggested earlier, people demand support from governments during the rough times of the downwave – which then cannot be afforded. The state borrowing that made possible the New Deal is unlikely to be repeated in the 1990s.

Ralph Emerson saw the political parties alternating between conservation and innovation. The conservatives stand for preserving what exists, while the innovators pass social legislation. He said 'we are reformers spring and summer, in autumn and winter we stand by the old'. His divisions are not between the Republican and Democratic stereotypes because several Republicans such as Theodore Roosevelt and Ronald Reagan were reformers.

Henry Adams defined the swings like the beat of a twelve-year pendulum between the centralisation and diffusion of national energy – the basis of the original dispute between Hamilton and Jefferson.

Arthur Schlesinger Jnr quotes from various sources listed earlier, plus John Stuart Mill the philosopher and the lesser known Frank Klinsberg. In his book *The Cycles of American History*, Schlesinger identified eleven periods of 16.5 years between the forces of change and reaction but identified an overall liberal trend, as conservative forces tend to consolidate at least some of the collective measures. If the economic and climatic forces described in Chapter 2 work as they have done in the past, the unwinding of the centralised state initiated by Newt Gingrich, the House Speaker, will be directly in the mainstream of history.

John Stuart Mill was one of the first to argue that each generation (of about 30 years) repudiates the one before which follows the Kondratieff tenet that wisdom skips a generation. Mill held that each generation brings with them attitudes prevailing in their youth; Woodrow Wilson made the same point when he commented that each generation can only raise their sights once above material things before reverting to an easy life which is why the radicals are in power for only a third of the time. Wilson's remark was borne out by his successors Warren Harding and Calvin Coolidge – both archetypal conservatives.

Frank Klingsberg has identified a periodic swing between 'extroversion' in foreign affairs and 'introversion' – which is another way of describing the internationalism of the 1980s and rising isolationism of the 1990s. Klingsberg comes to a similar conclusion as Martin Armstrong; his extroversions coincide with recoveries, and introversions with recessions, with timings almost exactly synchronising with the Kondratieff *upswings* and *downswings*.

Thomas Willett in his book *Political Business Cycles* has used a statistical approach to identify the economic factors most likely to appeal to electors when an incumbent is up for re-election; unsurprisingly Willett's time horizon is four to seven years depending upon the country. The writer identifies two political strategies dependent upon the likely result of the election.

When the result could be close, Willett comes to the rather obvious – though no less valid – conclusion that most electors, being non-savers, would vote for a moderate inflation to keep them in employment. Conversely, when the results are more likely to favour the right, it will be easier to sell ideas and a policy of low inflation to protect the value of savings. Conservatives might also emphasise ideological principles such as soundness in foreign policy, the value of international trading associations or large scale domestic investment programmes.

The researchers found that low inflation correlated with electoral success in the United States, Germany, Denmark and Norway. Low unemployment was the winning message in Sweden, while in France, and in America, the issues were low inflation, rising incomes and low unemployment.

Schlesinger correctly foresaw the election of Bill Clinton in 1992 but failed to spot the rise of an intellectual right-wing backlash in the mid-term election that challenged his liberalism. Some implications of this political revolution are considered later but for the mid-1990s it is becoming no longer intellectually chic to be a liberal. Scholars are returning to the nation's roots to discover why the country has deviated from the tenets of the founding fathers. This too has happened before. In the 14th century Giovanni Boccaccio set out to discover Italian origins in classical Greece before the Ottomans captured Constantinople. In America there is renewed interest in Alexis de Tocqueville, a young French aristocrat, who in the 1830s and 1840s tried to gain inspiration to help France evade the stifling centralism of the Jacobins, the dominant party in Paris.

What are the Political Cycles Telling us Now?

Earlier analysis has suggested people could expect more big government in the late 1990s which would normally be in demand during a downwave. But at the end of K4 'nanny' states could probably only be afforded by printing money – just as happened in Germany in the early 1920s. The printing of money to pay for public works programmes created hyper-inflation destroying the savings of the middle class and paving the way for Hitler's Third Reich.

An inability to afford public works programmes is not the

least of the problems besetting politicians and most are blithely unaware of the difficulties.

In his book *The Third Wave* Alvin Toffler portrays the transformation of an industrial society into a knowledge-based culture. With rare insight, Toffler describes the transition from a first wave, agriculturally based, economy to the second wave of the Industrial Revolution which concentrated people and machinery around a power source. Initially, water wheels driven by mill streams provided the power for the new spinning and weaving machinery but these gave way to the steam engine which was not only more reliable but could be operated away from running water. As machines supplanted craftsmen, there was a mass movement away from the country into the new industrial towns that grew up first in Britain then also in America and Europe.

The Third Wave could totally change the political relationships between the majority and minorities. The Tofflers explain that majority rule is a second wave concept needing the support of bureaucracies; they conceive instead a configurative society in which permanent and temporary minorities can co-exist, not unlike the communities which were the bedrock of New England societies in the 1840s and so admired by de Tocqueville – whose work is described later.

The Tofflers show that to accommodate minorities, the delegation of power to elected representation in Congress or Parliament should be replaced by much more direct consultation between the government and people, using sophisticated networks such as the Internet. They concede the danger of instant and sometimes emotional decision making, but suggest that this can be overcome by a cooling off period – similar to the Swiss system of referenda. As the Tofflers and de Tocqueville point out, local corruption and tyrannies can be just as damaging to local interest as the power of central government.

In a remarkable paper Michael White, an international consultant, describes how the Cybernetic Revolution is totally changing the nature of industrial organisation – and hence politics. *Webster's Dictionary* describes cybernetics as: 'the science of communication and control theory that is concerned especially with automatic control systems' – the sort of computer-based information and management systems which allow companies to downsize so successfully. White further argues that newly industrializing nations can provide valuable outsourcing of components, assemblies or material produced at a fraction of the price needed to produce a similar object in the west.

White's ideas are very similar to the Third Wave shift described by Toffler, which suggests that by the early years of the next century only 50% of the working population will be in full-time employment. The remaining 50% will be dominated by unskilled males (women, who tend to work flexibly and more cheaply, are preferred) and those prematurely retired who can look forward to no regular employment.

There is no way that politicians can avoid the drift of these changes which will divide nations between the haves and havenots. By early 1996 there are already recruiting problems for the 'cybernetically literate' top percentage but the danger comes from those without regular work who will expect to be supported by the state. However, as we have seen, government's ability to raise more revenue will be severely limited; not only will raising taxes above a certain level be unacceptable but politicians' ability to raise debt at low coupon rates will be severely curtailed by investors' fear of default. Governments have only to witness the movement of companies out of New York or the relocation of Japanese head offices to Hong Kong to realise their limitations.

Cybernetics will no longer enable politicians or civil servants to use totalitarian methods to deliver full employment through confiscation. Communications are now so sophisticated that wealth may be transmitted instantaneously around the world and individuals can choose their own tax-efficient domicile. As politicians will be unable to arrest the declining standard of living for the middle class (created by the Industrial Revolution), new political parties will emerge. Martin Armstrong forecasts that as the Democrat agenda becomes obsolete they will be replaced by a third party; trade unions, which were a phenomena of the Industrial Revolution, will also nearly disappear.

The present gulf dividing those able to use the new technology and those who cannot will widen, creating vast differences between those with knowledge and those without. As central and local governments will no longer be able to afford the Welfare State, this will perhaps encourage communities to become self-contained, with local firms providing a focus for community support for such things as health care, basic and adult education and unemployment. As more become independent, their spare cash will be invested, not in pension funds but in their own businesses. This would be similar to the days of guilds where individual enterprises were the focus of local life.

How Will the Status Quo Change?

There have been few recorded events in history when the ruling system gave up its power voluntarily; it may be forced to relinquish the reins through enfeeblement or violence but seldom by choice. The same is true for other institutions such as the church which has only ever been reformed by outside pressure. When theorists encourage those in power to change by giving up their authority voluntarily, they are actually expecting a form of political hara-kiri. Most unusually this may be happening in the United States where Congress is passing laws limiting the terms of legislators and trying to devolve power to the states.

Ironically the modern state (what Peter Drucker calls the Megastate) may have inadvertently sown the seeds for its own downfall through its spending excesses – not unlike an alchoholic who needs even more liquor to achieve oblivion. When politicians feel they can no longer raise taxes they have to increase borrowing to make up the spending shortfall. As Professor Bremner of Canada's McGill University recalls:

> The difference between Baring's inability to control Nick Leeson and the Canadian government is that in Baring's case, the bank's mismanagement forced the firm to default. In government there is no such responsibility: politicians can impose taxes to cover losses, print money when they can raise no further debt and wipe out their obligations by allowing their currencies to collapse.

He went on to report on a survey which stated that unless Canadians are able to take control of their own affairs, many would migrate to a more benign tax regime. [Note: since this was written spending exercises have been pared back but the debt remains.]

Perhaps the megastate will, like the church, be forced to change from outside. If a modern state has borrowed so much that it must default on its debts then no institutions will buy its bonds; if treasuries can no longer sell their debt they can either print money or reduce their own spending. Despite protestations about 'keeping a lid on inflation', most politicians would rather inflate than fail at the ballot box through unpopularity, hence the preferred alternative would be to 'keep the game going'. Eventually, like the aftermath of the Weimar currency collapse in 1924, a government would be forced into painful retrenchment – having wrecked the nation's savings.

A collapse in public spending would devastate the Welfare State in most western countries, leaving millions who relied on the government with no support. If most countries were forced into a spending cutback this would torpedo the European Community drive for federalism, with its agricultural support and petty harmonising regulations – leaving nothing remaining except possibly a free trade area. It would be difficult to continue other international treaties such as the World Trade Organisation and the North American Free Trade Area as each country would erect barriers in an attempt to arrest the rapid rise of unemployment.

A cutback of government spending will almost certainly torpedo the United Nations and associated agencies such as the World Bank, and the Food and Agriculture Organisation – but perhaps not the World Health Organisation for the reasons explained in Chapter 12. By August 1995 the contribution to the United Nations by member states was $3.7 billion in arrears, the main culprit being the USA where elements in Congress are increasingly hostile to international agencies. If the downwave continues, as it has in previous cycles, then an organisation which gives the 15,000 strong population of the Palau Islands the same voting rights in the General Assembly as China or the USA will not be viable.

Profiles for Change

It has been a post-war theme for all developed countries that politicians, released from the discipline of the gold standard, have increasingly borrowed to fund their spending programmes. For example, in the 1920s the US federal government spent only 3% of the country's GDP compared to a forecast 26% in 1996. This increase in spending might have some lasting impact if it were spent on capital projects or launching a massive programme to help the 60% of the population without regular employment.

However, out of the $1,612 billion of the 1996 proposed budget spending, 16% will go on servicing the government's debt, 21.8% on social security, 11.4% mandatory programmes and 16.8% on medicare. Compare this with the Swiss Federation where federal spending is around 18% of GDP, there is no figure for interest and 23% is spent on welfare, with nothing for medical support. However, even the prudent Swiss are not living within their budget; their deficit, which was almost zero in 1972, rose to nearly 13% of GDP in 1993. This did not prevent the Swiss in 1992 from having a GDP per head of population of $36,231 which was over 1.5 times that of America and double that of Britain.

There is a real danger that highly indebted western governments with large budget deficits could be destabilised either by a major national default or a commodity induced inflation. If there is to be a debt deflation similar to the 1930s then excessively leveraged countries such as Canada, Sweden, Belgium or Italy could default. This would make it virtually impossible for treasuries to sell bonds at anything other than a damagingly high interest cost; already America and other countries are vulnerable to rising interest rates as over one third of their debt has a maturity of less than one year. Rising commodity prices could be equally damaging – forcing many countries effectively to print money in a attempt to keep interest rates low. In either case, the present level of government spending would be under severe threat.

Although Peter Drucker, in his *Post-Capitalist Society* does not run a cyclical analysis, he fully recognises the need to reduce the power of central government and suggests an audit of the state, dividing the review into three categories:

Abandonment of the things that do not work. In this category Drucker places military and economic aid in which he can find few success stories and many disasters. He also asserts that governments have signally failed to end the business cycle. More important, they have failed to reform society through the redistribution of income – their sole achievement being a pork-barrel non-saving society. He might also have added that the state's foray into education, welfare and medicare has only politicised services that would be much better handled at a more local level. In 1776, Adam Smith in the *Wealth of the Nations* expressed matters more forcefully:

> It is the highest impertinence of kings and ministers to pretend to watch over the economy of private people and to restrain their expense, either by sumptuary laws, or by prohibiting the importation of foreign luxuries. They are themselves always, and without any exception, the greatest spendthrifts in the society. Let them look well after their own expense, and they may safely trust private people with theirs. If their own extravagance does not ruin the state, that of their subjects never will.

Concentrate on the things the state does well. Drucker points to countries such as Germany, Japan and the Asian tigers who have created the environment for 'investment in knowledge and in the human resource, in productive facilities in the infrastructure'. He did not point out that keeping a nation on the gold standard during the 19th century probably did the most for restraining politicians. (A pound's value today represents about 1% of when Britain went off the gold standard in 1913.) In many nations only the armed forces are a credit to state management.

Analysis of successes. There are not many examples today but during the 1930s, one of the New Deal's greatest successes was the Civilian Conservation Corps (CCC). In March 1933, the president combined the resources of several government departments to create work and training for young men from deprived homes who volunteered for service. The CCC succeeded in creating national parks, clearing forests, building flood levees and providing emergency services. Today the same principles might be employed in helping the many millions of people being made redundant by the Cybernetic Revolution or Toffler's Third Wave doing useful community work as an alternative to becoming self-employed.

The most important political contribution is to encourage those millions of people with no possibility of a regular job to make an independent living without preying on the 40% who remain at work. It will not just affect the unskilled because many white-collar managers and professionals such as lawyers, accountants and teachers could find landing a settled job difficult in the next few years. The possibility of social unrest into the next century should exercise the best minds but little can be done without a political infrastructure to launch any constructive programme.

Role Models for the Present

Nations have prospered without high government social spending as the Roman Empire did in its early days; however, it later became corrupt when the nobles divorced themselves from politics and the proletariat were bribed with food and wine hand-outs. Very little has changed in the modern world. Great nations like the United States were once led by high-minded men but their successors were less principled; privileges were used for personal gain, earning the contempt of a growing number outside the Washington beltway.

The final part of this chapter is devoted to investigating several ways in which the modern state may reform. These models include the early American experience as seen through the work of Alexis de Tocqueville, the modern Swiss state, the New Zealand of Jim Bolger, the thoughts of speaker Newt Gingrich and the Confucian ethic.

New England in the 1830s and 1840s

Alexis de Tocqueville has been mentioned earlier as a French aristocrat who, in despair over the excessive centralism of the Jacobins, sought to rediscover individual rights by researching mid-19th-century America. Like present-day conservatives in the west, he was appalled by the growing power of the state and wanted to create a more compact and less costly methods of government – a return to days when people took responsibility for their own affairs. He noted that France had a degree of local autonomy before the guillotine eliminated many of the nobility, to be replaced by bureaucrats. The Jacobins, the revolutionary leaders and later Napoleon, followed Rousseau who held that the happiness of the individual was inferior to the wants of the majority.

This meant that it was the duty of the French state to create a set of rules for its citizens. They challenged private ownership of property and reserved the right to shape opinions – as de Tocqueville quotes, 'making people a flock of timid and industrious animals with the state as the shepherd'. The Christian tenet of equality in God's eyes was despised by politicians who themselves became the sole source of wisdom in a centralised state – and the only means of social progress. The Jacobins had a lot to answer for – Lenin based his communist state on the same principles.

Initially de Tocqueville looked to England as his paradigm but in those days decentralisation of power often flowed down through the nobility and not upwards from the people. Continuing his quest he travelled to New England where he discovered what he believed to be was the ideal society for his native France. The French aristocrat provides us with the most acute observations on America in the 1830s and 1840s, which could be a model if we wish to change today's centralised state.

De Tocqueville discovered that American habits of local responsibility (where the public interest was a sum of individual interests) was adapted by the founding fathers from Benthamite ideals. Holding that religious freedom was the most basic of all institutions and that all were equal in the sight of God, people could work out their own ideas within the context of shared civil and religious beliefs. The first responsibility was within the family then outwards to the town; later these were grouped into counties and then states in a series of widening concentric interests. In the Jeffersonian concept, the central government was to deal only with matters of general concern.

This shared belief was the ultimate source of social stability without which there could be no sense of justice. This gave the New England middle-class settlers a sense of equality, the confidence to run their own affairs and to deal with public needs as they arose. It also provided an agreed standard of morality and self-interest which was quite contrary to de Tocqueville's experience in French Canada. There the people, still wedded to the idea of a centralised state, lacked the passion for self government and the independent commercial drive of the Anglo-Americans. This independence gave the Americans a spirit of local sovereignty enshrined in the Tenth Amendment which states that 'The powers not delegated to the United States by the Constitution, nor prohibited by it to the States, are reserved to the States respectively, or to the people.'

Sovereignty in New England stemmed not from the states but upwards from private citizens. Each individual authorised the introduction of new taxes, and the supreme court of each state not only applied laws but judged whether basic rights were preserved from the tyranny of the majority. The importance of local autonomy meant that laws were created, and if necessary were changed, to suit the people, who became willing observers – or even magistrates. Quite different from the bureaucratic megastate where in many cases people regard the law as their enemy.

The civic spirit fostered by local autonomy was the final guarantee against the encroachment of the remote and bureaucratic state that de Tocqueville had observed in France. The American blueprint might not have bred uniform behaviour and administrative tidiness but it created something much more powerful. It generated not only well-founded schools and a sound local administration but people had a self-interest in their local community – and were concerned with such matters as crime prevention, condition of local roads, halls and churches.

Whereas an autocratic society imposed obligations without choice, a democratic society created a series of unwritten or defined contracts which bound people of different talents together. De Tocqueville admitted that individual ambition could run roughshod over the rights of others but observed that free societies spawn a myriad of associations starting with the family. Within these, people could receive confirmation of their own judgments and reinforce their moral or intellectual convictions; people like this do not look for the state to 'brush away every danger from their path'. In this way the citizens can enjoy the power of a great republic and the security of their community.

Can Switzerland be a model?

The Swiss republic has an enviable record of stability and efficiency; unlike the USA of today, they have implemented the spirit of the Tenth Amendment by retaining a high degree of local authority devolving only necessary powers to the federal government. The present republic goes back to 1291 when the 'forest cantons' of Schwyz, Uri and Lower Unterwalden formed a league in defence of their liberties against their Habsburg overlords and successfully broke away in 1389. The entry of Lucerne, Zurich and Berne with others brought the number of cantons to eight by 1353, just when the Black Death was ending. Switzerland's neutrality was guaranteed after the Treaty of Vienna in 1815 when Geneva and other territories joined. There are now twenty-six sovereign cantons (only subject to federal laws) which compete to make themselves attractive to business by keeping taxes low; they do not charge capital gains tax, and estate duty is 10% in most cantons. The Swiss are some of the highest savers, encouraged by a stable, almost gold-backed, currency.

The powers delegated to the central government are controlled by the Federal Assembly of two houses, the federal council which runs the government and the federal judges. Members are elected every four years to the national council which meets for several weeks, four times a year. Unlike most other countries they are not professional politicians and receive only expenses and no salary. The upper house is the Council of States which, like American Senate, has two members from each canton. The federal council is elected from seven members of the Assembly for a four-year period of office with one of the seven elected president every year. It is hardly surprising that few Swiss know the names of their federal representatives – let alone their president.

In an enviable method of consulting the people, the Swiss have the right to a referendum dating from 1874. Under this rule, 100,000 citizens can submit a written proposal to add to, or change, the constitution. The initiative is then discussed by the Assembly who may accept, reject or modify the request before it is put to a referendum. Likewise 50,000 citizens together can challenge laws and treaties that have lasted more than fifteen years. This means that 1.5% of the total Swiss population (6.8 million in 1992) can demand that the Assembly debate their requests. The same proportion of voters in Britain would be about 900,000 and in America under 4 million. Unsurprisingly the Swiss saw Brussels bureaucracy and the European Assembly as flawed and voted against membership of the EU.

The basic economic and political units are the 3,000 Swiss communities not unlike the New England townships of the 1830s. Their rights and responsibilities differ, but the local units tax their residents through the community town or district councils; in addition, they look after such matters as schools, local traffic, refuse collection and sport. Above them each canton has an elected assembly and a five to nine person executive. Their size varies: for example, Zurich was the only canton with over 1 million people in 1992 and some like Jura were below 70,000.

The cantons provide free primary schooling for which attendance is compulsory, plus fee-paying higher education. There are only two federal universities at Zurich and Lucerne, the others being shared by cantons with a common language or faith. The cantons are obliged to conform to national standards but are otherwise autonomous; they decide the types of school, the length of term, teachers' salaries and the like. After leaving secondary school, pupils go on to qualify either at vocational or academic establishments.

Social security is based on a principle of a minimum wage which continues through to old age. These services are funded through the Old Age and Survivors Pension Scheme, the Disability and Unemployment Insurance Schemes and Pension and Health Insurance Funds. These services are paid for by the individual, the employers and to a lesser extent, the cantons and federal government. There is strong opposition from the elected centre right majority to a full-blown welfare state which could dangerously inflate the federal deficit that has been growing since 1972.

The Swiss run a remarkable citizens' army where all fit males are required to attend a seventeen-week recruit's course at the age of twenty. This is augmented by eight three-week refresher courses up to the age of thirty-two which reduces to three two-week courses from the age of thirty-three up to forty-two. After completing military service most men transfer to the Civil Defence Corps. Perhaps even more remarkably, the men eligible for active service keep their equipment, weapons and ammunition at home; they are required to attain a certain proficiency at regular compulsory target practice sessions (not unlike Henry V's archers who were required to practise archery after church) and their kit is inspected.

New Zealand reforms the Welfare State

New Zealand used to be one of the most socialised countries on earth until in 1990, the Prime Minister, Jim Bolger, introduced a radical cost-saving budget to be implemented by Ruth Richardson, the Finance Minister. The reforms were based on the simple principle that those individuals and families with reasonable means (the top one third earners) should attend to their own needs. The overall aim was to reduce government spending of the GDP to 37.5% by 1994–5 – at a time when most other states were increasing their spending and borrowing.

New Zealand has a national health service although, unlike Britain, patients are required to pay a consultation fee which is paid in full by the top earners as are prescriptions, and dental and optical charges. Those who can afford to pay are also charged a contribution towards hospital care and the richest pay for all, including emergency treatment. The health service is organised, as in Britain, into regional health authorities and up to 25% of health funding is through insurance plans. Income support for those out of work has been turned into a proactive method of helping claimants by encouraging a training programme aimed at helping individuals achieve their own goals in life.

Education has also been reformed by giving schools control over their own budgets, the more enterprising offering fee-paying services such as adult training and places for overseas students. Higher education is paid for privately, 10% being charged to students, the balance through a repayable loan. The reforms also affected social security which was cut by 10% and is not payable to those less than eighteen years old and on a reduced scale up to the age of twenty-five. Even pensioners are required to pay added taxes on unfunded state programmes, although this may be modified.

The state has also been reformed by distancing ministers from their departments and introducing the concept of asset accounting just like a firm. Before the budget, each minister will negotiate with their head of department for the precise budget spending and services for the coming twelve months. Failure to meet the goals will come in for censure; this also applies to an independent central bank if it fails to meet the inflation target. To make the banking system more market orientated, the principle of *caveat emptor* (buyer beware) is being applied to bank depositors; bank regulators are being replaced by the scrutiny of independent directors and the regular display of financial statements.

Almost alone among developed nations New Zealand has run a budget surplus since 1994 and is starting to pay back the national debt with all-party acceptance; if needed, it has no difficulty in selling government bonds – unlike most other countries. Accounting for assets has sharpened the wits of the civil service departmental heads who now have to pay a return on assets to the treasury, this has often mobilised capital items such as property and led to a much more commercial approach.

Contract with America

One of the most remarkable changes ever to be launched on a nation has been the contract with America introduced into the House of Representatives by its speaker Newt Gingrich and the Republican majority. In its first session, the new House cut the number of committees, reduced support staffs by one third, limited the terms of those on the committees and implemented a rule that any tax increases needed a three-fifths majority. The House also required its members to obey the same laws as other citizens – previously there had been a number of exemptions.

Other bills included a move to balance the budget, stop violent criminals, strengthen family and parental authority and discourage single parents from having children. There is a thrust to roll back government regulations that strangle small businesses and discourage senior citizens from continuing to earn; there are also moves to cut family taxation and promote strong national defence. By mid-1995 nine out of ten proposals had been passed by the House and in addition the Representatives want to axe the departments of commerce and education, handing back responsibilities to the states. Even if only a majority of these bills become law, the political agenda of every western country will be changed. A similar agenda is promoted in Canada where Preston Manning leads the Reform party. Unfortunately, the public had lost much of their enthusiasm for these measures by the 1996 presidential elections.

The Confucian ethic

If there is to be a west to east shift in ethics suggested in Chapter 2 we should be aware of the legacy of the Chinese sage Confucius who was born in Shantung province in around 550 BC. The philospher bequeathed to eastern peoples a love of learning and wisdom, an emphasis on filial piety and respect for the family which, in part, has generated much of the work ethic of the eastern 'tiger' economies. Although the associated rule of authority may resonate with only a few in the west, the Chinese dedication to looking after the family will appeal to politicians committed to reducing the Welfare State and those with a taste for the puritanical values de Tocqueville found in New England.

Towards a New Politcal Agenda

In their own ways reformers like Bolger and Gingrich have set the agenda for the decades on either side of the millennia: Bolger wants to keep a reformed Welfare State while Gingrich wishes to disband the institution. Both also discern the implications of the Cybernetic Revolution and Third Wave by encouraging more people to take responsiblity for their own affairs.

Excessive debts have made it impossible for most countries to expand the role of government in the downwave as in earlier political cycles. Instead many have attempted to trim the Welfare State at the margin which has caused an electoral outcry and will be unlikely to produce the required savings. Even if centralised western nations do not suffer the potentially very damaging cyclical defaults or commodity-led inflation described earlier, a modern agenda must decide either drastically to reform state institutions on the Bolger model or to devolve most central powers to the states or regions. Politicians seldom make radical changes unless they are forced either by war or, for instance, the chaos of the Weimar Republic in the early 1920s.

The Cybernetic Revolution will place much more responsibility on the individual to run their own affairs wherever possible; if there are to be public services, those eligible will pay for these through some form of voucher. The large managing bureaucracies will no longer be either afforded or needed. Any remaining ministries will be there only to create policies, not to administer.

The basic administrative unit could be smaller than the present states, provinces, *Länder*, regions or counties because local bureaucracies will also have to be severely trimmed. A community on Swiss lines could be responsible for many first-line services such as health, education, crime prevention, dealing with the unemployed, encouraging the self-employed, business taxation and contracting for local services. Each community would compete to attract firms which could provide a focus similar to the guilds in Toffler's First Wave. Additional institutions such as secondary schools, universities and hospitals could be the responsibility of a community grouping on the Swiss model.

In a *Times* article of 15 May 1995, William Rees-Mogg argues that successful economies should reduce public expenditure (from 40-50% in Europe) to only 25% of national income in line with those of south-east Asia. Public and private consumption should not exceed 65% of GNP and there should be a top flat rate of income tax at 20%; there should be no tax on savings or capital accumulation. The Far East 'tigers' realise that you cannot help the poor by taxing the rich, you cannot thrive if the state consumes too much of the nation's income.

If, as suggested earlier, we are due to return to a more puritanical set of religious and moral values, then a case could be made for adapting the Confucian ethics that drive the eastern nations to a western context. This will have to happen in any case if the west is to survive. The spreading of Confucian ideas could spread into investment. In the likely convulsive stock markets, there will be more incentive for individuals to invest retirement income, not in pension funds, but in family enterprises where their future will be looked after. This will reduce still further the power of the state to control people's lives.

Fortunately, the usual downwave tariff barriers have been avoided so far, although the Americans have tried to restrict trade with countries like Cuba and Iran for political reasons. However, if the full impact was felt it is unlikely that the European Union could exist in anything other than a free trade area, which might also include North America and eastern Europe.

We shall have to see whether any but a handful of the present politicians have the leadership or stomach to introduce such a radical agenda. Their confidence ratings in America declined from over 40% in 1966 to only 8% in 1994 with the office of president at 12%. Unfortunately, the truth that the Welfare State will decline has been hidden from most people. When it happens many individuals deprived of their support and also out of work will turn their present resentment of politicians and bureaucrats from disgust to hatred.

CHAPTER 11

THE CYCLES OF WARFARE AND INTERNAL CONFLICT

It was the great Prussian military theorist Karl von Clausewitz who argued that war is an extenson of diplomacy, which is why there have always been, and always will be, wars or rebellions. Since the Second World War much international effort has been expended in avoiding war but this has not provided disagreements turning into conflicts – in Korea, Vietnam, Africa, the Middle East and in Bosnia. Anyone who believes that wars or rebellions are obsolete does not understand history.

Because wars are essentially either a rational or emotional reaction to events one would expect these to work in cycles following the climatic and economic patterns described earlier. They are also subject to the result of events, such as the great German inflation of the early 1920s, which destituted most of the middle class and paved the way for Hitler and the Third Reich.

That forces exist beyond man's control is the stuff of other chapters, our task is to try and understand these influences and make them work to our advantage. One of the first researchers to become aware of the war cycle was Raymond Wheeler, who analysed the relationship between climate and human behaviour. The team sifted through hundreds of thousands of data items relating climate to history, which were then recorded on to cards and into the Big Book at the Foundation for the Study of Cycles at Wayne, Pennsylvania.

Some of his work on the 500-year cycle has already been mentioned but he also extracted and recorded data on international and civil war battles related to climate. He concluded that an above average warm climate stimulates wars of aggression, and cooler than normal weather patterns encourage civil conflicts. He then prepared a chart rating battles according to their size and duration. This work was taken up by Edward Dewey, the originator of the Foundation for the Study of Cycles. Dewey was a statistician who believed there were clear rhythms of 57, 22.142 and 11.4 and 142 years which could be combined to provide a forecast. This chapter first explores Dewey's assertions then investigates the relationship between warfare and the Kondratieff long wave and the 179-year climatic cycle which have been so dominant in politics and economics. Taken together these should provide an insight into the nature of conflicts into the 21st century.

A 57-Year Cycle of International Conflict

Dewey first considered a 57-year cycle, which he examined over the relatively short period of 200 years from 1750 to 1950 taking his database from Wheeler's record of warfare from around 500 BC to 1950. Dewey worked on the premise that international wars occurred at the peak of the cycle and civil wars at their troughs. This is a brief record of the conlicts that coincide with the low and high points in the rhythm over the 200-year period:

The first peak in the 1750s. There was the Seven Years War from 1756 to 1763 when Austria, France, Russia, Sweden and Saxony joined a coalition to cripple the expansion of Prussia under Frederick the Great; he was allied to Britain which was already at war with France over colonial disputes. In a series of brilliant manoeuvres, Frederick picked off one foe after another using the advantage of internal lines. Although considerably outnumbered at the battle of Leuthen in 1757, Frederick encircled the Austrian left wing and put the rest of the army to flight. Britain made the most of the war by becoming dominant at sea. Some cynics might argue that the victories were due more to fear than patriotism, after the celebrated courtmartial and execution of Admiral Byng following his poorly-rated performance at the Battle of Minorca. The Treaty of Paris which ended the war settled very little although it left a militarily powerful Prussia and a France which renounced all claims to Canada, Nova Scotia, the Ohio valley and all territory east of the Mississippi. Further south, Spain traded Florida to the British in exchange for Cuba.

The first trough in 1775. There were numerous conflicts in Europe, India, Russia, central Asia and South America but by far the most important rebellion occurred in British North America where, after declaring independence, the former colonialists went on to create the United States of America. The main complaint against the British crown was England's imposition of taxes without appropriate representation in parliament. The cause had some validity because by the latter part of the 18th century, the number of colonialists was significant compared with the British population.

The war broke out at Lexington when Governor Thomas Gage sent 700 men from the Boston garrison to capture arms assembled by the local citizens at Concord, Mass. After an exchange of fire which left casualties on both sides, the colonialists under the command of Colonel George Washington then laid siege to Boston. On a high ground north of Boston at Bunker Hill, the Americans successfully held out against a British attack until the defenders' ammunition ran out. The war was fought in three areas: to the north by the Canadian border, in the centre around New York and the Jerseys, and south in the Carolinas. It was also fought at sea where the young navy, manning rather larger frigates than was normal for the Royal Navy at that time, gave a good account against the most powerful navy in the world. The Americans were also helped by France, a decisive influence at the concluding campaign at Yorktown. Here the French navy not only landed French soldiers but denied the British defenders relief from the sea so enabling Washington's troops to storm the garrison. The United States of America was recognised at the Treaty of Paris in 1782 and the war ended when the British troops left New York.

The second peak in the early 1790s. This was dominated by the wars of the French Revolution, followed by the Napoleonic Wars. France had been weakened financially by supporting the American colonialists during the revolution and in an effort to restore solvency raised taxation on the bourgeoisie; this was resisted by the merchants who, with support of some nobles, took control of the government. This led to the overthrow of Louis XVI. Although outnumbered by the armies of Prussia and Austria, there was enough professionalism in the old French army, supported by revolutionary fervour, to defeat the invaders and Louis was guillotined for acting as the focus against the revolution.

The king's execution did not end the wars which continued on land and sea. On land the French successfully combined a revolutionary rabble with professionals under General Lazare Carnot to repel their opponents. In the Italian campaign the little-known general Bonaparte took command of 45,000 ill-fed, poorly-clothed men by the Riviera and advanced into Lombardy against the Austrians. In a series of brilliant actions at Lodi, Castiglione and Rivoli, the general pushed the Austrians out of north Italy and in the process occupied Venice and ended its status as an independent republic. His reward for the Italian success was command of an amphibious force to capture Egypt when Alexandria was stormed in 1798.

The revolution had decimated the naval officer corps, which not only destroyed morale but robbed the navy of some devoted professionals (it is curious how dictators never learn from history for Stalin made the same mistake in 1940 with the Red Army). It is certain this loss contributed to the French fleet's defeat at the Battle of the Glorious First of June when Admiral Louis de Joyeuse, in an effort to escort a food convoy from the United States, was forced to break off action after the capture of several ships. Actually the delaying tactics worked, for the convoy reached harbour safely. Later a Spanish force was beaten by Admiral Jervis at Cape St Vincent and Nelson destroyed the French fleet escorting the Egyptian invasion at Aboukir Bay.

The year after the Battle of the Nile, Bonaparte became dictator of France through a *coup d'état* and once again tried to make peace with the allies. This failed and he then proceeded to defeat the Austrians and Prussians at the battles of Marengo, Austerlitz and Jena showing a dazzling display of speed, surprise and manoeuvrability. France then went to capture the Iberian Peninsula and his brother Joseph Bonaparte was installed as King of Spain. By 1809 France dominated most of west and central Europe only opposed by Russia in the east, the Royal Navy and a small British expeditionary force in Portugal under General Sir Arthur Wellesley – later the Duke of Wellington.

It is said that the only person to conquer Russia during

winter was Genghis Khan whose cavalry advanced up the frozen rivers. The French went overland and they were also riddled with typhus; Napoleon's army, after defeating Kutuzov at Boradino, reached and retreated from a burning Moscow harried by Cossacks and Russian irregulars. At one of the last rearguard actions at the frozen Berezina river, thousands of Frenchmen were slaughtered by marauding Cossacks and of the reputed 500,000 men only 10,000 survived as fighting soldiers. Squeezed by his Continental foes and Wellington's success in Spain, Napoleon was forced into exile at Elba but even that did not last; he escaped to France only to be defeated by Wellington's international army at Waterloo.

The second trough in 1825. By the early 1800s, the old colonial empires of Spain and Portugal dominated the Americas south of 42 degrees north, and the Balkans were striving to be free from the Turkish occupation.

The Balkans and Greece had been occupied by the Ottoman Turks during the second Islamic jihad that had swept across the Bosphorus, captured Constantinople in 1453 and surged around the Black Sea. The Turks later had seriously threatened Vienna in 1648 but were repulsed; from then on Turkish power was on the wane but nearly three centuries elapsed before it was seriously threatened. The Balkans were then, as now, a convergence of different interests: the Russians were co-religionists with the Serbs and Greeks and they also wished to control the Bosphorus. The Catholic Austrians had been influential as far south as Croatia ever since the split between the Roman and Orthodox faiths in 1054. By the 1820s both France and Britain were anxious to prevent the Russians from gaining control of the eastern Mediterranean.

The first of the Balkan regions to gain independence was the mountainous region of Montenegro in 1799. Although Serbia attempted revolts against the Turks these failed and the next to seek independence was Greece through the massacre of a Turkish garrison. The Ottoman Empire replied with an invasion from the north by Corinth and the occupation of the peninsula by Egyptian troops. Stirred by public opinion in England and encouraged by the romantic Lord Byron, a British and French squadron led by Admiral Sir Edward Codrington entered Navarino bay to defeat a Turkish and Egyptian fleet. The action effectively decided Greek independence confirmed by the Treaty of London in 1832.

Spain and Portugal had occupied Mexico and Latin America from the 16th century. But now that Spain itself had been invaded by Napoleon, it was in Britain's interest to assist the freedom movement encouraged by the independence of the United States some fifty years earlier. To start with the colonial militia beat off British landings at Buenos Aires and Montevideo but later Paraguay was the first to declare independence, followed by the remainder of Spanish-held territories under the leadership of two remarkable men, Simon Bolivar and José de San Martin.

Bolivar, who had spent most of his early life in Europe, was initially repulsed after capturing Caracas in Venezuela. However, he returned in 1816 and although suffering setbacks marched his ragged force of 2,500, including a British contingent, to Colombia where he entered Bogotá in triumph after routing the defence of regular troops. Then Bolivar liberated Venezuela, Ecuador and Peru.

The other deliverer was San Martin. Originally a Spanish soldier he organised and trained a revolutionary army at Mendoza, Chile. He then marched over the Andes and fought several actions but was unable to beat the Spanish troops while they still controlled the sea. The Spanish navy was defeated by a revolutionary force under the command of a maverick British Admiral, Thomas Cochrane, the 10th Earl of Dundonald, who had previously resigned from the Royal Navy under a cloud. Taking command of four ships he sailed into Valdivia, bombarded the defenses and so allowed San Martin to invade Peru. Taking Lima, he continued north where he combined forces with Bolivar.

The deciding battle was at Ayacucho, south-east of Lima, where Bolivar prevailed and the remaining Spanish forces capitulated. It was not the end of Cochrane's war for he was also instrumental in liberating Brazil where the Portuguese royal family had fled from Napoleon's invasion. By outwitting a Portuguese relief convoy to support beleaguered royalist troops, Cochrane captured Mananhao, their intended port of arrival, and the royalists had nowhere to go but home.

The third peak around 1860. This included several international wars, the most important being the Crimean and Franco-German wars. Amazingly, the Crimean War had its origins from the year 1054 when the Roman and Byzantine churches divided, but by 1853 the conflict was between France and Russia arguing who should have jurisdiction over the Holy Land – then controlled and within the Turkish Empire. As Russia also wanted control over the Bosphorus this brought in Britain on the side of France and an expeditionary force was landed on the Crimea to stem the Russian invasion. The subsequent war showed the administrative shortcomings in both armies – but particularly that of the British, when more died from cholera and semi-starvation in scant winter quarters and with hopeless medical attention. In all, the allies lost around 250,000 men, of whom only 70,000 died in action.

The Franco-Prussian War of 1870 was part of Bismarck's plan to unite Germany under the Kaiser of Prussia. This was to be achieved by several moves: the first was to neutralise Austria; next Bismarck planned to unite the previously independent northern and southern states by provoking war with France. These moves were coordinated by the superb officer corps created by Frederick the Great, who had learned their lessons from Napoleon's brilliant campaigns at Jena and Austerlitz. One general in particular, Karl von Clausewitz, wrote a treatise, *On War*, which became the handbook for all military staff colleges.

Clausewitz's ideas were implemented by the chief of the Prussian staff, von Moltke, who planned the campaigns in the most meticulous detail using the latest in weapon technology. Using breech-loading needle rifles, trench mortars, field fortifications and communications perfected during the American Civil War, the Prussians planned the unification campaign. Having neutralised the Italians, the Prussians started a limited action against Austria at the Battle of Königgrätz.

Thinking the French army invincible, Napoleon III was provoked into declaring war against the Prussians. It was no contest as 380,000 well-equipped men from the German confederation in three armies faced 224,000 poorly organised and supplied Frenchmen. The Germans prevailed in a series of actions before the French were soundly defeated at the Battle of Sedan on 1 September 1870 and the way was open to Paris. The capital fell after a siege and under the terms of the armistice Germany demanded reparations of 5 billion francs in gold and the territories of Alsace and Lorraine. It was said that Moltke only smiled twice in his life: once when he heard the besieged Parisians were eating rats, the other when he was told his mother-in-law had died.

The third trough around 1885. Surprisingly, the sequence of civil wars leaves out the American Civil War, or the War between the States, from 1861 to 1865, which created some of the weapons and tactics that were used with such deadly effect in the 1870 Franco-Prussian war. Instead, the rebellions around this time were largely outside Europe.

In Egypt the Khedive, Ismail, although nominally a vassal of Turkey, had borrowed heavily to modernise his country; becoming insolvent, his debts were paid off by Britain and France who now operated a system of dual control. This caused a rebellion led by Ahmet Arabi which subsequently turned into an anti-Christian conflict. Although Arabi was routed by a British force at Tel-el-Kebir, the rebellion spread to the Sudan where the Dervish tribesmen of the Mahdi Mohammed Ahmed of Dongola wiped out a British-led army of 10,000.

In an effort to stop the fighting the Liberal government of Gladstone sent out General 'Chinese' Gordon to evacuate Egyptian troops from the Sudan but the general's garrison at Khartoum fell and Gordon was killed. Horrified at his death, a relief force was sent against the Mahdi's successor Kalifa Abdullah, led by General Kitchener who defeated the Sudanese at the Battle of Omdurman, where for the first time the Gatling gun was used against mass troops. It was also the last time that a cavalry charge (launched by the 21st Lancers) was successful before being rendered obsolete by modern weapons. It is said that Kitchener delighted Queen Victoria by presenting her with the Mahdi's skull, with the eye sockets made into ink wells.

Further south in Africa, the Zulu chief Cetewayo, rejected British demands for a protectorate over his country, and deployed his 40,000 trained and fanatical warriors against an invasion. The British troops were divided into three columns. One of these, camping for the night at Isandhlwana, were attacked by a Zulu force of 10,000 and nearly annihilated. The British troops then fell back on Rorkes Drift where 85 fit troops from the South Wales Borderers were left as a rearguard. In one of warfare's great epics, the defenders fought off six full-scale attacks which lasted until the night when the

Zulus withdrew. The war ended at the Battle of Ulundi when a force of 10,000 Zulus attacked a force of mixed European and African troops and were soundly defeated.

The fourth peak, the Great War of 1914 to 1918. Germany, united by Bismarck and led by Kaiser Wilhelm II, feared a war on two fronts: from Russia on the east and the old enemy France on the west. Britain, threatened at sea by the Kaiser's growing fleet, joined the alliance. To cope with this dual menace, von Schlieffen, von Moltke's successor as chief of staff, devised a strategy for keeping the Russians at bay while the main thrust would be through the low countries then around Paris to the west so encircling the French army. Schlieffen's plan provided a simple and flexible blueprint for a two-front war.

History records that the First World War started when the Austrian, Archduke Ferdinand, and his wife, were shot by Gavrilo Princep, a Serb nationalist, in the Bosnian capital, Sarajevo, on the 28 June 1914. The extreme friction between Austria and Serbia's great backer Russia on its own would not have led to a German attack on France. However, the historian, AJP Taylor, argues that the German war plans were so integrated into the German rail network that mobilisation against Russia was impossible without also implementing the Schlieffen plan in the west.

In the event, the French invasion plan was amended so that instead of 90% of German forces being pitted against France, only 60% were committed, with the result that the German right wing failed to encircle Paris. This change of plan allowed the French army, supported by the British Expeditionary Force, to regroup and counter-attack at the Battle of the Marne – which some military historians describe as the most decisive battle since Waterloo. It resulted not in victory but a stalemate on the western front that consumed men, metal and high explosive like some horrible monster. But German staff excellence still lived up to its reputation on the eastern front where Hindenburg and his brilliant chief of staff Erich Ludendorff totally outmanoeuvred and defeated two vast and cumbersome Russian armies. In the west, in three weeks of war both sides had lost around half a million men either dead, wounded or captured.

Although there were some indecisive naval actions, the land war ground on for another four years with little territory being either lost or gained. There was one successful attack by the Germans in March 1918 which was eventually contained, but the real breakout by the allies in August of the same year forced the Germans to retreat and led to the eventual armistice. A war supposed to end all wars, it wearied Europe; in Germany the Weimar Republic was created, and arguably, the seeds were sown for the Second World War.

The fourth trough around 1950 saw the conflict in Korea whose antecedents went back almost fifty years to after the Russo-Japanese War, when the country was annexed by Japan. It was an unhappy occupation for the Koreans who had been promised their freedom at the Cairo conference in December 1943. On the fall of Japan, the country was divided at the 38th parallel, the North owing allegiance to communism, the South to the West. This was regarded by America as a purely arbitrary boundary and the United Nations was invited to organise elections which the USSR opposed. The South became the Republic of Korea with its capital at Seoul; in the North a puppet communist government was set up.

While the North had a Russian equipped army of 130,000 men with tanks and artillery, the South had little more than a national police force with few supporting arms. Sensing an opportunity, the North crossed the 38th parallel in June 1950 with seven divisions supported by tanks and aircraft. Outraged, America demanded that the UN Security Council condemn the North; the motion was carried as the Soviet representitive had boycotted the meeting and failed to exercise the veto. Other countries were brought in to assist. By early September, forces of the South plus those of its allies were holding the small Pusan enclave to the south-east of the country.

The allied commander Douglas MacArthur, launched a sea-born attack on the port of Inchon just near the capital Seoul after a preliminary bombardment. Surprise was complete and the invading force successfully overcame a very difficult landing site, which had a 30 feet rise and fall of tide and treacherous beaches that could only be used for six hours a day. At the same time the troops around Pusan broke out and by the end of September the capital was recaptured. By early November the North Korean capital Pyongyang had been overrun and the allied troops were at the Yalu river, the border between Korea and China.

The Chinese government had threatened participation once

the allies crossed the 38th parallel. MacArthur thought they were bluffing but being denied aerial reconnaissance across the border had no means of confirming the potential threat. The assumption was shattered when in late November, 180,000 Chinese troops were hurled against the advancing allies who, despite a spirited rearguard action, were forced to retreat against a foe who operated through infiltration and surprise attacks – the tactics learned from guerrilla fighting during the civil war. By early December over 100,000 American and South Korean troops were safely evacuated with much of their equipment. An eye-witness reports that this recovery was greatly helped by 16-inch guns on the US battleships, whose accuracy enabled them to pinpoint and destroy individual bridges.

The war of offensive and counter-offensive continued through 1951 and 1952, during which time MacArthur was dismissed by his commander in chief, President Truman. After several attempts at a cease-fire, the armistice was eventually signed in July 1953 leaving the country divided. The Korean War cost the lives of nearly 120,000 UN troops compared to some 1.5 million of their communist opponents. As is often the case with modern war civilians suffered the most with over 3 million casualties.

The Korean War was the first conflict to engage the latest jet fighters in combat and to employ helicopters for the rapid movement of troops, for the rescue of downed pilots and casualty evacuation. Unfortunately it also resembled the American Civil War for the treatment of prisoners. Of the 90,000 UN troops captured, some 60% died from torture or neglect and a number were brainwashed. This had not occurred during the Second World War and the American and British troops were totally unprepared for their ordeal.

The fourth peak in 1975. There were no major wars in 1975. Although there were many conflicts around the world, none was on a par with the other previous peaks. However, by the mid-1970s after America had ignominiously withdrawn from Vietnam, the Soviet Union might have been tempted to make a pre-emptive strike to reunite Germany and bring Yugoslavia into the embrace of the Warsaw Pact. By this time there was clearly no way they could have won the arms race but the threat of a nuclear exchange almost certainly held their hand. This was their last chance, for the Cold War was finally won in

1989 with the collapse of the Berlin Wall and the disintegration of the Soviet Union.

Dewey's series did track the Crimean War, the Franco-Prussian War, the Boer War, the First World War, and the Korean War but missed out important conflicts such as the Napoleonic Wars, the American Civil War and the Second World War. More consistently he held that international wars take place at the cyclical peaks and civil wars at the troughs of the cycle – although admittedly a certain amount of manoeuvring is needed to fit the dates on such a short time-scale.

The 22.142 and 11.2 Year Cycles in Warfare

Edward Dewey also identified shorter cycles of 22.142 years which, using Raymond Wheeler's battle analysis, traces the rhythms back to 1400 AD with a break from 1758 to 1827. This study tracks such international conflicts as Agincourt (part of the Hundred Years War), the Balkan Turko-Serbian War, the conquests of Cortéz and Pizarro in Mexico and Peru, the Spanish Armada, the Thirty Years War and the Wars of Spanish Succession.

In addition to the 22.142 year cycle Dewey also identified a 11.2-year cycle of conflict from at least 1750 to 1960 (excepting 1758 to 1827) which took into account the lesser international and civil actions.

Moving Averages and a 142-Year War Cycle

The statistician in Edward Dewey also identified a 142-year war cycle by constructing a 67-year moving average that filtered out the 11- and 22-year rhythms and also largely eliminated the 57-year cycle described earlier. He then found a remarkably good fit with Raymond Wheeler's record of battles. This is a brief account of the peaks and troughs of this rhythm since the birth of Christ; the peaks and troughs will be briefly described in separate sentences, peak first:

Cycle 1: the first peak coincided with the Roman invasion of Britain. There were civil wars in Rome and China at the first trough.

Cycle 2: there were a number of small international conflicts in the Roman Empire around 250 AD. There were also revolts against the Romans in Britain, Egypt and Spain and rebellions in China.

Cycle 3: this peaked when the Huns, Goths and Visigoths attacked the Roman Empire. The troughs coincided with numerous civil wars as the Empire collapsed.

Cycle 4: signals the First Jihad or Holy War when the Arabs overran Syria, Egypt, North Africa and Spain. At the low point the armies of Charles Martel stopped the Moors at Poitiers.

Cycle 5: the rise of Charlemagne and the creation of the Holy Roman Empire were both tracked. Some 70 years later Alfred King of Wessex halted the Danes.

Cycle 6: there were a series of small conflicts in China and in eastern Europe which allowed the Russian capital to be moved to Kiev. At the trough, England achieves unification under Edgar and the Sung Dynasty reunited China.

Cycle 7: the Normans invaded England and the schism of the Roman and Orthodox churches provoked wars of reunification; there was a secondary peak during the First Crusade. At the low point, the C'hins rebelled against the Sung Dynasty and overran northern China.

Cycle 8: the cycle peaked with Genghis Khan's invasion, first of Asia then Europe and the trough coincided with Robert the Bruce defeating the English at Bannockburn.

Cycle 9: there was a series of battles such as Agincourt, Tannenberg and Ankara at the peak and the trough; Joan of Arc begins her rebellion against the English.

Cycle 10: Babur conquereds northern India and founded Mughal dynasty; at about the same time the Mongol Altan-Khan invades northern China. Portuguese power is destroyed in North-West Africa at Kasr al Kabir and Dutch revolted against Spain.

Cycle 11: the peak coincided with the war of Spanish Succession ending with the Treaty of Utrecht. The low point tallied with the War of Austrian Succession and the Seven Years War.

Cycle 12: Napoleonic Wars and the Taiping rebellion in China are at the peak. The trough coincides with the Franco-Prussian and Crimea Wars.

Cycle 13: the next high point was around 1914 coinciding with the First World War; the Second World War and the Korean War were in the trough.

What Triggers War Cycles and Do They Work?

Dewey's 22.142 and 11.2-year rhythms have a remarkable resemblance to the sunspot cycles, implying that climate is an important factor in warfare, for starving people have an incentive to fight. Curiously, Dewey does not mention the economic 45 to 60-year Kondratieff wave and its contribution to conflicts for it picks up all the major wars over the four major cycles.

For example, the first cycle K1 started with the French Revolution as its low point and the 1812 War at the end of the upwave. This was a conflict between the United States and Britain provoked primarily by the Royal Navy disallowing American cargoes reaching the blockaded continent; there were also disputes when some British ships pressed American sailors into the fleet. America succeeded in gaining territory around the Great Lakes in what is now Michigan and Ohio; in turn America agreed not to break the European blockade. The downwave of K1 ended in the European rebellions of 1848.

K2's upwave started around 1850 and reached its peak in the American Civil War, the bloodiest ever fought by Americans. The background to the war has been covered in Chapter 10 and, like other major conflicts, arrested the recovery and triggered the plateau phase. K2 reached a low point with the Boer War and Boxer Rebellions, which could be described as civil wars; however, the American-Spanish War and the Russo-Japanese War were both limited wars in that they did not include a conflict directly between major powers. This latter strife was remarkable in that it showed the defensive power of the machine gun and field gun; it also destroyed the myth of 'white man's' supremacy.

The greatest conflicts the world has known occurred during K3. The upwave ended with the First World War, there was a delay of some twenty years before the next great war completed the business of the earlier strife at the bottom of the downwave.

Now in the fourth wave K4, the upwave ended with the Vietnam War and, if history is to repeat itself, will probably end at the bottom of the downwave with civil wars. The Kondratieff analysis (displaced some 20 years earlier) fits the pattern more convincingly than Dewey's 57-year cycle.

The known low points of the 22.4-year Hale drought cycles are picked up well by Dewey's 22.142 years including such known troughs as the Dust Bowl in the early 1930s, and the droughts in 1952 and 1974; it would also expect to pick up the dry conditions in the late 1990s. Logically one might expect wars of expansion when sufficient crops were available to feed armies (wars typically starting after the harvest); conversely, a food shortage is often a cause of civil war and rebellion such as the Paris bread riots during the French Revolution.

Wheeler also believed climate change triggered wars. A warm moist climate tends to trigger not only affluence – but also international wars. A cool dry period creates the aggression inducing civil wars. Although not mentioned by Edward Dewey, the 179-year sun retrograde cycle has created the cool dry climate which accorded with the civil wars in the mid-17th and early 19th centuries. There was the terrible Thirty Years War from 1618 to 1648 which ravaged Germany leaving hundreds of thousands either dead or displaced from a wretched conflict. The English Civil War and subsequent beheading of Charles I coincided with the latter decade of the continental conflict. This was not confined to Europe. In 1642 starving mobs overthrew the decaying Ming Dynasty which ultimately led to Manchu power. In the 1811 retrogration, there were the liberation movements described earlier, in continental Europe, the Balkans and South America.

Apart from climate, Edward Dewey suggested that, based on the work of Garcia Mata and Shaffer (described in *Riding the Business Cycle*), solar eruptions could also be a cause for conflict. It is generally recognised that solar eruptions and eclipses correlate with a marked increase in insanity, mental illness and suicide. They also create mental excitability that ends in warfare – but the impact is displaced by a year. A two-year shift gives a better correlation with maximum mental stimulus occurring *before* the sunspot cycle peak.

In general, Dewey was correct to track international wars at the peak of the cycle which perhaps creates national distortions so that civil wars occur at the troughs. Another contention is that the 'peak' wars leave the major powers so exhausted they are unlikely to intervene in the actions of the second tier of nations. Another distorting factor may be the introduction of nuclear weapons, which forces major contenders either into accommodation or into subsidiary actions such as the Gulf War; they fight by proxy when the first tier are not directly involved with each other.

The distinguished airman Sir John Barraclough has suggested that Dewey's definitions of warfare may be outdated. Instead of international and civil wars, the distinction might be between a general war such as the First World War or the Second World War and limited war which only involves a few belligerents. In this way the 'troubles' in Northern Ireland or the PLO/Israeli running sore might be designated as low intensity, whereas the actions in Chechnya or Bosnia have a much higher profile. Clearly the Korean War which caused millions of casualties would still be regarded as a limited war – by tacit agreement between the major powers.

What the War Cycles are Telling us

We can now begin to draw together the various strands of the earlier analyses to see what is likely to occur in the next century taking into account the cycles described in other chapters. First it seems that there is a discontinuity in the affairs of mankind every half millennia which should make the analyst cautious about drawing a straight line from the present post-Cold War era into the future. Whenever it seems that the threat of war has passed it is generally time to re-arm.

There have always been either limited or international wars and both displace huge numbers of people. Up to the Second World War, civil wars created the greatest tides of refugees as one faction, then another, claimed territory and displaced opponents. Before the Dayton Agreement this was happening in Bosnia and if this type of conflict spreads into Russia, India or China, the world would be placed in a horrific position of having to resettle and feed millions of people. As people move, they are either likely to carry disease, for which they might well be immune, into areas where there is no such protection; alternatively they can catch new disorders.

Wars damage food supplies which could anyway become a problem through the growing water shortage reported by the UN and Worldwatch Institute. Already many countries have reached the limit of grain production through the 'green revolution' which has considerably increased crop yields through the use of hybrids, fertilisers, pesticides and irrigation. There will be an urgent need to develop techniques such as hydroponics and perhaps even permaculture to make up for shortages. There is the additional problem that wars also destroy and disrupt the distribution of potable water and often leave untreated sewage as another source of cholera.

Based on the cycles described earlier, Edward Dewey combined the 142, 57, 22.142 and 11.2-year wars to forecast correctly the Vietnam War and possibly the Yom Kippur War of 1973. These predictions were made including rhythms of 12.3 and 9.6 years which he believed were also of significance. The result is the chart below from 1820 to 2000 showing the comparison of the forecast interrupted by the actual continuous lines.

On the principle that the peaks of the war cycles represent international wars and the troughs civil or limited conflicts, then the steep decline in the forecast towards the year 2000 could be significant for it tallies with the history of the 179-year

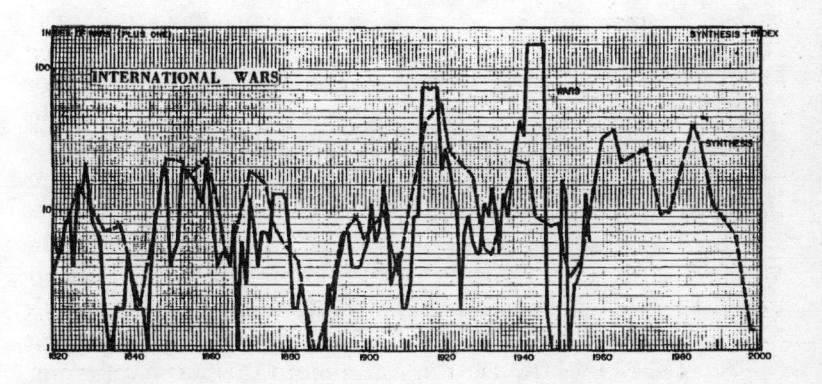

Figure 20. Comparison of cycle synthesis with actual battles taken from Raymond Wheeler's analysis. (Courtesy of the Foundation for the Study of Cycles.)

cycle and low point in K4 mentioned earlier. Even more important it also confirms the condition of the world in the mid-1990s where there are many simmering conflicts. If climatic history repeats itself, this disruption could also extend to China, India and elsewhere.

If the conflicts continue through the latter part of the 1990s and into the next century, they could create very difficult times for many nations which believe that such misfortune could never happen to them. Instead of disarming, countries will be obliged to increase the number of men capable of bearing arms, possibly through some form of territorial service on the Swiss model. Apart from military training, there could also be training in disaster relief – increasingly needed for humanitarian help overseas in the way the UN forces have provided help in Bosnia.

In addition, a parallel unit could be set up similar to the Civilian Conservation Corps (CCC) which President Roosevelt created in the 1933 to train and put to creative work young men from poor homes. This would harness those unable to find long-term jobs, to work on the infrastructure and for the community. Each country would then have available trained groups to work around the world to rebuild shattered infrastructures, repair damage and provide emergency services – as in its own way the CCC achieved during the 1930s.

CHAPTER 12

THE BATTLE BETWEEN MUTATING BUG CYCLES AND MODERN MEDICINE

Every animal reproduces at a greater rate than is needed to maintain its numbers. Disease regularly wiped out a high proportion of youngsters until the 20th century when mortality from measles, whooping cough, enteric fevers and tuberculosis dropped to at least one hundredth of the former rate. Throughout history many more people have died from disease than ever perished from war or famine.

The most notorious destroyer of population was the bubonic plague which was brought to Greece by the steppe nomads from central Asia in 433 BC. The nomadic Huns 800 years later swept all before them, triggering indirectly the sack of Rome by Alaric the Visigoth in 410 AD. Although the almost impregnable land defences of Constantinople held out against the invaders at the time of Justinian, the defenders caught the bubonic plague with the rest of Europe. This culled the population by nearly one half.

The 800-year cycle worked again in the early 13th century when Genghis Khan's warriors brought the plague once more to Europe. This time they were besieging Kaffa in the Crimea which was defended by, amongst others, Genoese sailors. The investment failed but as a parting shot the besiegers catapaulted into the fort the diseased corpse of a slaughtered prisoner, which infected the garrison. Once the siege was lifted, the sailors, accompanied by the flea-carrying rats, returned to European ports infecting people at every stop. The plague took three years from 1348 to surge through Europe destroying once again over one third of the population. Eight hundred years later we await the next invasion!

Few other diseases run in cycles but the trigger points for epidemics certainly do. One of these is the rhythm of warfare. They are great destroyers – not just from combat but from what they bring in train. Conflicts lead to massive numbers of displaced people, cause disruption of the water supply, sewerage system and public health arrangements that keep modern cities free from disease.

The main scourges of previous generations were typhoid, cholera and typhus – the diseases that felled many more people than combat. One of the least researched and probably the most important influence on the outcome of warfare has been – and probably still is – the impact of disease. Hans Zinsser in *Rats, Lice and History* shows that plague, cholera, typhoid, dysentery have decided more campaigns than Caesar, Hannibal, Napoleon or the German general staff. Other chapters describe how history was changed by the plague of Athens in 433 BC and how typhus reduced Napoleon's army from 500,000 to 10,000 men in the space of months in 1812.

Wars also bring malnutrition which reduces the body's capacity to resist disease; this is almost certainly why the outbreak of Spanish influenza in 1918 destroyed more people than soldiers that had died in the trenches. Researchers claim that flu pandemics work in 60-year cycles, each time the virus arriving in a form that overcomes the immunities built up in the population.

Other cycles relating to climate cause malnutrition such as the 179 and 22-year rhythms. Famine provides people with a choice: either they stay and starve or they leave; however, moving also has its hazards for they may be travelling to an area that has a disease for which they may not have immunity. Conversely, they may be carrying problems to their host country for which they are not immune – like the Mongols bringing the plague to Europe.

How these cycles could affect us in the future has been the subject indirectly of at least five books. Two are *Plague's Progress* by Arno Karlen and *The Coming Plague* by Laurie Garrett; both have provided the non-medical researcher with much information. Also helpful has been Burnet and White's *The Natural History of Infectious Diseases*, as has Henry Hobhouse's *Seeds of Change* and *State of the World 1996* by the Worldwatch Institute.

This chapter aims to describe in non-medical terms how diseases occur, the protection we have against them and the possible conclusions within the context of cyclical events.

About Disease

Infectious diseases are spread when foreign organisms enter the body and cannot be dealt with by the body's immune system. Like other animals, the human body is composed of cells which require the intake of proteins in the form of amino acids to keep in good repair; immunity declines through famine or malnutrition which is why epidemics often follow poor harvests. Apart from a healthy diet, the immune system is assisted in repelling disease either through surviving an illness or the exposure to a small quantity of the killed or altered virus through vaccination. Smallpox immunisation is not new. Infected matter had been injected into people in the east and in the Arab world for centuries before Edward Jenner introduced much safer vaccination based on his observation that the harmless cowpox gave dairymaids immunity from smallpox. Wellington had his army inoculated as did Napoleon several years later.

The body's immune system works on the principle that it can detect and produce material to counter a foreign body or antigen. At its heart are complicated proteins called immunoglobulins which, when stimulated by antigens, replicate to generate antibodies. These then usually envelop and destroy the interloper. If the balance of the immune system is compromised by disturbances such as malnutrition, chemotherapy, HIV or severe stress, then this mobilises microbes that were once harmless into becoming active and virulent. For example, in the days before antibiotics, pneumonia could only be cured through the immune system. An infected patient often became extremely ill for six or seven days before staging either a rapid recovery or dying. The survivors had a rapid fall in temperature and disappearance of delirium when the immune system generated an antibody quickly enough to overwhelm and kill the infecting bacteria. This was called recovery by crisis.

Bacteria are living organisms shaped as small rods or spheres a few thousandths of a millimetre across, which multiply rapidly in a propitious environment such as a cell; they can also copy their own genes. Like any living organism, bacteria need food for production of energy which, unlike plants, cannot come from sunlight and carbon dioxide in the air. They are great survivors, with a powerful ability to change their composition, or mutate, making them resistant to mainline antibiotics; it is said that Alexander Fleming's discovery of penicillin immediately set in train its own antidote, for even if a few organisms survived they would multiply to form a resistant strain.

This is now becoming evident in cases of gonorrhoea, tuberculosis and malaria where mutations continue to defy antidotes. One particularly resistant staphylococcus called MRSA causes sores over the human body and infects wounds. Penicillin used to be effective but a mutation produced an enzyme that dissolved the antibiotic. By the end of 1995, only the drug vancomycin remains effective against some of these resistant organisms.

Bacteria live naturally in the gut of animals where considerable competition occurs without having the slightest effect on the creature; other less propitious places are in the mouth and genitals. The more well-known bacteria are responsible for cholera, tetanus, the bubonic plague, typhus, chlamydia and syphilis. In principle all these can be treated by antibiotics but bacteriologists have found that not only do the bugs mutate but drug resistance can be transmitted within species. In his book *Power Unseen, How Microbes See the World,* Bernard Dixon reports how some incredibly resistant bacteria are able to exist in volcanic lava or in a glacier. They are also essential; life would not be possible unless they reduced organic waste back to basic matter.

Protozoa, the smallest animal organisms, are responsible for diseases such as amoebic dysentery and malaria, but the main causes of infections other than bacteria are viruses. These are tiny organisms that can only live, and duplicate, within cells; they are able to mutate a million times faster than human cells. Viruses were first identified by the work of the German bacteriologist Robert Koch who stipulated that they were responsible for a particular disease when its effect could be replicated either as a culture or when inoculated against in an animal. Viruses can only be seen under an electron microscope and are spherical in shape.

Apart from mammals and birds, viruses are also versatile enough to grow in insect cells which helps propagation via mosquito-borne sickness such as yellow fever. They are also responsible for smallpox, herpes, some forms of pneumonia, measles, influenza, mumps and AIDS. In addition, some of the haemorrhagic plagues such as Lassa and Junin fever are caused by viruses carried by mouse droppings. However, the most deadly of all, Ebola, has no known vector – or carrier.

The body's main natural defence against virus infections is a substance called interferon which is synthesised and liberated by cells in the course of infection; it then diffuses through the body fluids into unaffected cells to render them immune from viral damage. Immunity against viruses can be increased by inoculation and by stimulating the body's own immune system through the introduction of a substance called viral nucleic acid. Past infection with an epidemic such as measles can also create an immunity against it re-occurring.

The body is exposed to many childhood viral diseases like measles which are often caught directly through droplets carried by breath. There is a pause of up to ten days before there are catarrhal symptoms, then a skin rash. During the initial period the virus is carried around the body to the lymph glands, gastro-intestinal tract, the tonsils and appendix. The cell sites where the virus lodges also indirectly generate an antibody which then destroys both the infected cell and the virus. Immunity for the future is achieved through the antibodies that remain in the blood increasing the system's reaction to future attack.

Transmission of Diseases

We saw earlier how the mass movements of the steppe herdsmen, who were themselves immune to the plague, could infect and partly destroy a population. It happened also during the Spanish invasion of Mexico and Peru where infinitely more Aztecs and Incas died of smallpox and influenza than Spanish weaponry. It could be said they got their own back through the export of tobacco which goes on killing people while smallpox has been eliminated. Apart from mass movements of people, diseases can be caught in several other ways.

The ploughing up of new lands often disturbs an environment which has its own reservoir of potential pestilence. One such is the bacteria anthrax that can lay latent in soil for many decades. Later there will be a description of the Junin virus, released in Argentina when food shortages required the pampas to be cultivated. The haemorrhagic virus was carried by the Calomys mouse which, with the new source of food, spread rapidly; it then infected people through its droppings and urine. Like other viruses Junin caused bleeding, shock, then death.

Insects and other bugs are responsible for transmitting a number of terrible scourges. Rat-borne fleas infected with the plague carried the bubonic bacteria; however, its deadly pneumonic form is carried through breath aerosols. Lice carry typhus, while mosquitos carry malaria and yellow fever.

Animals and birds also carry disease and act as reservoirs for transmission to people: dogs can carry rabies, monkeys carried the haemorrhagic Marburg virus (green monkey disease) to Germany, Yugoslavia and America. Green monkeys are thought to have harboured the original AIDS virus, mice carry Lassa fever and it is known that some wild game carry tetanus, brucellosis and salmonella.

Sexually transmitted diseases (STD) such as syphilis, gonorrhoea, herpes or chlamydia are not new. Syphilis destroyed many people in the 16th century before its transmission was understood; only then did people change their habits. Since 1947 many STDs could be cured simply by antibiotics but this too is becoming more difficult as new mutations appear. Apart from the rise of the AIDS virus in the west, there has also been an increase of other sexually transmitted diseases including Hepatitis-B which, in acute forms and over a period, can form cancer of the liver.

There are several ailments that are transmitted through the aerosols of human contact. The common cold is one, another is influenza and also tuberculosis. Doctors believed that the latter was almost always curable; but it has now become more problematic, with the mutation of the tubercle bacillus to a highly resistant form.

There is a real danger in the modern world that rapid travel could transport someone carrying a deadly affliction to the centre of a crowded metropolis and so spread the infection. It nearly happened with Lassa fever during the outbreak of 1976 when a resident from Chicago visited Nigeria to attend a funeral and caught the disease. Once his condition had been diagnosed all his contacts were kept under strict observation and luckily none succumbed. The story might have been different had he returned to the slums of Rio de Janeiro.

Cities have been a focus for diseases from at least Roman times. Potentially the greatest danger to modern man is the rapid growth of conurbations such as Bombay or Calcutta in developing countries .

Some Important Diseases Could be Recreating Themselves

Scourges have beset man from the earliest days when he came down on to the plains and hunted game. Although this was a healthy existence, it was probably the first time our forbears could have been infected by other animals, for it was often the weakest – and probably infected – prey that was caught and killed. The next stage in disease transmission possibly occurred when Neolithic man first learned to grow crops regularly around 10,000 years ago and settled in villages. With closer contact they caught new pathogens in an environment where waste would attract predators and newly cultivated land would unearth its own diseases.

Man has travelled a long way from the ancient settlements; as diseases have multiplied, so in many ways has their cure. To see what the future could hold it is helpful to review some of the major blights that have affected mankind over the past few thousand years. In many ways these have shaped our customs, civic services, and quite often religions.

We should first be aware of the bubonic plague – one of the greatest killers of all time that, as we have seen, has struck the west regularly since the 5th century BC. The next is typhus, a terrible and deadly fever transmitted by ticks which, over time, has done more to defeat armies than actual combat. Then there are the destructive and sinister haemorrhagic diseases such as Ebola that caused such a stir in the 1970s. Originating in Latin America and Africa they literally destroy a body's organs and are often untreatable.

The list should include smallpox, a killer of millions throughout history which now thankfully has been eliminated by the efforts of the World Health Organisation (WHO). The WHO similarly attacked malaria but despite the expenditure of millions of dollars, the effort failed. Sexually tranmitted diseases (STDs) first destroyed hundreds of thousands in the 16th century and were a constant killer until antibiotics started to reduce the numbers after the Second World War; unfortunately STDs have once again become a major problem in the last twenty years. Finally there is cholera: a pestilence that can still destroy the hundreds of thousands who live in squalid conditions with contaminated water supplies and inadequate sanitation.

Bubonic plague. It is thought that the bubonic plague first struck ancient man when out hunting and he caught a diseased animal; nobody told our forbears that eating uncooked meat could cause problems. There must have been many unrecorded outbreaks of the plague through history but the first likely occurrence was in Athens, probably carried by the Halstatt invasions of Europe from Central Asia - which indirectly spread to Spain from the Ukraine. The next incursion was by the Huns when they carried the plague into lower Egypt in 540 AD at the time of Justinian, from whence it spread around Europe and the Mediterranean.

The plague is caused by an egg-shaped bacterium called *Yersinic pestus,* which is carried by rodents and spread by fleas - both of which are energetic travellers. The bacteria were carried everywhere by the black rat living aboard ships and around the refuse normally associated with human dwellings, where fleas spread the bacteria to humans. In a warm climate the sickness begins with a fever, then on the second day the lymph glands swell creating buboes in the armpits, groin and neck. As the fever rages the nervous system becomes infected, causing a manner similar to drunkenness and at least half the victims die within five days. Even more die during the winter when the disease, carried by the breath, moves to the lungs and becomes pneumonic when patients often die choking on their vomited blood.

One of the worst hit areas during the first outbreak was Constantinople at the time of Justinian, where 10,000 people died every day and bodies were stacked like logs on buildings until the stench became so horrendous they were piled on rafts and set adrift at sea. In all some 40% of the inhabitants perished. For six years the plague struck cities in Italy, Spain, France, the Rhine valley, Britain and Denmark – and re-occurred quite regularly. Historians believe England was so weakened by the halving of its the population that the people gave way easily to the Saxon invasions; it also helped destroy resistance to the first Islamic Jihad around the Mediterranean. The plague spread eastwards to India, China and Japan.

The next invaders after the Huns were the Mongols early in the 13th century. Europe's natural immunity had been impaired by the famines following the atrocious weather in 1317–8 and many people were no match for the Black Death in 1348. The plague was regarded as a divine punishment for past wrongdoings and even the Pope's exoneration did not help as millions died and had to be buried in mass graves. The story of the *Flying Dutchman*, a ship manned by corpses condemned to sail the seas for ever, might well have originated from reports of vessels drifting around the coasts with dead crews. Some, however, came off lightly: the city of Milan was almost untouched, as were Jewish people whose higher cleanliness standards discouraged rats. It did not do them any good for they were demonised as poisoners and the ensuing pogroms drove them into eastern Europe.

The Black Death destroyed from one quarter to half the population where it struck in Europe, North Africa and the Islamic world. It was also spread by the Mongols to China where half the population was wiped out. There were occasional outbreaks thereafter, the best known being the Great Plague of 1665 which hit London particularly badly; this was thought to have been eliminated by the Great Fire of 1667. The ending is likely to have been more natural – possibly the black rats may have been killed by the brown rats which did not carry fleas.

There was, however, a silver lining to the Black Death – or 'great dying'. A shortage of manpower led to freeing the serfs in England and perhaps unfairly, a weakening of the church's power – after all nobody else apart from the Jews seemed immune! A further blow to the authority of the Pope was dealt by the Reformation which encouraged Europeans to be more self-reliant. There were other benefits. Several individuals such as Dante, Petrarch and Boccaccio survived the pandemic and were prominent in creating the Italian Renaissance.

Typhus in 1919 killed more men than died in the trenches. Fleas and ticks were also responsible for one of the worst scourges to afflict people in the cramped insanitary, ill-fed conditions found in prisons, slums or some armies. It is thought that typhus was responsible for pestilences in Greco-Roman times but it is difficult to separate individual diseases when several are present, such as dysentery, typhoid, fever, smallpox and scurvy. The new epidemic was noted when Spain employed Cypriot mercenaries in 1489 to fight the Turks. The soldiers went down with a headache, high fever, body rash and often a swelling of the face; the end came after delirium, sores and gangrene that literally rotted the victims. In the campaign against the Turks, of the 20,000 who died, only 3,000 were lost in action.

Typhus was rife amongst the Spanish and French armies in the 16th century. In one case the French siege of Naples had to be called off when half of the besieging troops died within a month. The Spanish took typhus, smallpox and measles to the New World – infinitely more Aztecs and Incas died from transmitted diseases than from military action. During 1577 in England one typhus-infected prisoner in an Oxford court wiped out 510 people including two judges, a sheriff, an under-sheriff, six magistrates, most of the jury and hundreds at the university.

The disease probably took its greatest toll against Napoleon's army in the Russian campaign of 1812. After starting with 500,000 men, by the Battle of Borodino over 350,000 were infected and only 90,000 made it to Moscow, where thousands succumbed to disease and hunger. By the end of December 1812 only 35,000 returned to Germany and of these only 10,000 were capable of fighting. Typhus killed many more allied troops than the Russians in the Crimea and on the Eastern Front in the First World War; out of the 20 million Russians who died during the subsequent revolution over 3 million died from the disease. By the Second World War the armies had learnt their lesson, but even so there was an outbreak among soldiers in Italy and many allied prisoners held by the Chinese died after the Korean War.

Haemorrhagic fever. Opening up new pastures for additional grain and beef has introduced man to diseases that were previously dormant. One such was in Argentina during the Second World War when ploughing the Pampas disturbed the natural habitat of a fieldmouse, *Calomys musculinus,* which harbours the Junin virus (named after the Junin river). The disease causes high fever, internal and external bleeding, shock and death – it is caught from inhaling contaminated air or from infected food. Every so often these mice surge in population only to crash with the virus. In this state the Junin virus spreads to humans who breathe in the dust from dried faeces and urine.

A similar outbreak occurred in Bolivia when, in an effort to grow more corn and vegetables, the country people cut down dense jungle in the flat areas above the Machupo river flood-line. The cultivation again released the Calomys mouse which thrived with the increased food supply. As in the Junin outbreak, the mice urinated on both food and house dust which was either eaten or inhaled. The saga of how the outbreak of the virus was dealt with is the stuff of a detective thriller.

The story began in 1962 when a Middle American Research Unit (MARU) was set up by an American team of physicians, including Karl Johnson, who had studied virology after becoming a doctor. Called upon by Bolivia's minister of health to investigate what he called 'El typho negro' – or black typhus – Johnson and MacKenzie, an epidemiologist, were flown to La Paz, the capital, and thence by plane, canoe and horseback to the stricken area, a village called San Jonquin. Realising the potential danger from the epidemic, the two men took blood samples from those stricken with symptoms similar to the Junin virus and returned to America.

The American response was to create a mobile laboratory at San Jonquin which included 'glove' boxes, which were sealed units kept at a slight vacuum within which experiments could be carried out at minimum risk to the analyst. Within these boxes, possible animal or insect carriers could be checked for the virus and experiments could be carried out on the immunity of other creatures.

After making detailed enquiries from all the affected households, autopsies were carried out on victims. The team were horrified to find the extent to which the virus had consumed the victims' insides, including the brains. Unfortunately, the black typhus did not just affect the villagers, both the researchers started to display the feverish symptoms after a village fiesta and were flown back to an isolation hospital in Panama. Both were also aware that there was no known cure and from their own experiments they knew that the virus could not be quelled by antibiotics. However, they were attended by army doctors with experience of similar wartime viruses, who stabilised their fluid balance to allow the natural immune systems to work. Fortunately this was successful.

After recovering, Johnson and MacKenzie, plus other analysts, set to work to isolate both the virus and its carrier. After exhaustively working through a very large sample of creatures they defined the carrier to be the Calomys mouse that ran freely in the village; the cats had all died from DDT – which had been liberally sprayed over the infected areas! The researchers divided the village into two: in one half they set mouse traps. Within days it was evident that the risk of infection in the mouse free areas was much less than the other areas and the outbreak was quelled.

Another rodent, a rat, *Mastomys natalensis*, carries a similar virus that was discovered in a village hospital at Lassa in Nigeria where several patients were found to have encephalitis (fever, headache, inflamation of the brain, lethargy, seizures), haemorrhage and shock. It did not just affect the patients – half of the Africans carry Lassa antibodies – but also the expatriate staff. Two nurses and a laboratory worker – who had direct contact with infected patients' blood, tissue or excreta – died to the tremendous sorrow of a tightly-knit community. However, some staff, having contracted the virus, survived by being injected with the antibodies from someone whose immune system had successfully fought off the infection. As reported earlier, the real danger from Lassa and other viruses is carrying the disease outside the community.

Perhaps the most deadly outbreak occurred almost simultaneously in Zaire by the Ebola river and in southern Sudan during August 1976. At a mission hospital in the village of Yambuka in Zaire a man was admitted with terrible diarrhoea and was treated with an injection of antibiotics through a needle that had been used several times. After two days the patient discharged himself despite haemorrhaging and dysentery.

Unfortunately, many of the other patients started exhibiting similar symptoms of acute diarrhoea, terrible headaches and bleeding from the gums, bowel and stomach. The Sisters in charge of the mission (there being no one medically qualified) treated the patients with antibiotics but nothing worked. Of those who contracted the symptoms, some 90% perished. Soon the hospital was engulfed by a scourge that turned apparently healthy people, including the nursing Sisters, into bleeding convulsed wrecks within a very few days. Ebola was identified as the second most lethal disease in the

20th century after rabies. Samples of the victims' infected blood were sent to the world's top high-security laboratories.

Dealing with lethal samples to isolate and test the virus's potency is potentially very dangerous to the analyst despite the most stringent precautions. As with other outbreaks, glove boxes were used in pressurised rooms and slowly the information emerged. The virus looked like a series of question marks in a line; it was deadly for almost any creature affected, the source was not known and there was no definite cure. One survivor was Geoffrey Platt, a researcher at Porton Down in England who, despite stringent precautions, to his horror pricked his thumb with a sample containing the virus when conducting an experiment. For six days there was no indication but on the seventh Platt's temperature shot up and he was rushed to a secure unit; thankfully he survived after being treated by large doses of the drug interferon and plasma flown in from Zaire taken from another person who had survived the virus.

Just to prove that virus infections don't just happen to poor people there was an outbreak of an unknown disease in Marburg in Germany when three men in the Behringwerke AG, a subsidiary of the huge pharmaceutical giant Hoeschst, suddenly went down with a fever some ten years before the Ebola outbreaks. The symptoms were similar to the virus infections described earlier with fever, inflamed spleens, bleeding and a marked drop in the white blood cell count. Later the patients had to be fed intravenously and their whole bodies reddened as thousands of blood capillaries blocked, so denying oxygen to millions of cells. After the tenth day they died, vomiting blood. To this day no drugs have been found to counter either Ebola or Marburg and their so-called reservoir and method of transmission remains unknown. However, having taken their toll, both outbreaks died out after the known contacts had been isolated.

Despite a huge effort malaria has still not been eradicated. Clearing scrub and growing crops on new ground has also created new opportunities for the female mosquito of the genus *Anopheles gambiae* to lay their eggs in stagnant pools. There are several thousand species of mosquito and this is one of the 10% that infect people. Before laying eggs, the female needs to gorge herself on sucked blood and in the process infects her victim.

Malaria is a protozoa that attacks the red corpuscles in the blood causing feverish paroxysms. Tremors follow which become violent, the face becomes a livid colour and the shaking of the limbs and jaws becomes uncontrollable. The body, which has started dry and cool, then begins to sweat and the patient either dies from exhaustion or falls into a deep sleep from which there is a recovery. The problem is that once infected the victim can suffer recurrent bouts which cause anaemia, darkening of the skin, or enlargement of the spleen leading possibly to liver cancer.

Mosquitos can only fly two miles, they seek prey at night and prefer not to fly high above the ground. This is why people build their houses on mounds wherever possible and the surrounding land is drained; upper storeys are used for bedrooms and are lit, and people sleep under mosquito nets. Over the course of time mankind has had to come to terms with malaria – or swamp fever – which became endemic in Italy during the Roman era. Rome itself was malarial until around 1900 and was only rid of the disease when Mussolini cleared the Pontine Marshes. The disease badly hit the colonial Jamestown settlement in 1607 and was still a grave problem in the southern states of the USA in the 19th century. The cotton plantation owners either went abroad or moved to the coast in the summer allowing the slaves, who were generally immune to malaria, to manage the business.

The only known cure before antibiotics was quinine, prepared by grinding the bark of a cinchona tree and mixing it with white wine. Originally grown in the north Andes the bark was shipped in small quantities at very high prices to Spain where the disease was rife. Shrewdly the Jesuits had procured a monopoly of the bark, which enraged some Protestants who called it the devil's powder.

Malaria strictly limited the advance of colonialism, for only a few white people were immune. In 19th-century India it killed a million babies annually under one year old and another million between the ages of two and ten. To remain on station the British army in India needed 750 tons of bark a year – more than was available from the Andean supply; Henry Hobhouse in *Seeds of Change* reports that to prevent 2 million adults dying every year would require 15 million pounds of quinine a year and to prevent recurrent fever would need a total of 150 million pounds. Supplies could not keep up with the colonial demand of the British and Dutch, who decided to grow their own cinchona in the Nilgiri Hills of India and in Java.

The plants were transferred from the Andes to Kew Gardens and then to Calcutta sealed in a special cabinet designed by a Dr Ward which ensured quarantine for the plant on the long journey by sailing ship. The exercise was a success in India, where by 1880 quinine production was greater than the total produced elsewhere and was mainly used in the sub-continent. The Dutch however were more commercial and the bark was sent to Europe for processing in Amsterdam and London.

Between 1958 and 1963 $430 million was spent on failed attempts to destroy malaria and a further $793 million until 1981. The bill was mainly paid by the United States, where a million soldiers had suffered from the disease during the Civil War and it had been a major killer in the south up to the 1930s. Another half a million American soldiers were at risk during the Second World War. The treatment after the war was still quinine but then DDT was used in the fight against mosquito in their swampy habitat.

Operating on a ten-year cycle of attacking or eliminating mosquito swamps and treating patients with chloroquine, malaria was slowly eliminated from many areas, but then the programme broke down. The 'green revolution' for expanding agricultural production opened up new lands and provided ample opportunities for mosquitos to breed. Although these and other pests were attacked strenuously with DDT and similar pesticides, the inevitable happened and chemically resistant bugs emerged. As insects became immune, in South America and Thailand the disease itself became resistant to the then universal cure of chloroquine and doctors went back to the old staple, quinine.

Man is solely responsible for sexually transmitted diseases (STD). Venereal diseases have been one of mankind's greatest scourges, eliminating whole swathes of the population from around the 16th century. Humans are particularly good at spreading these germs because our eroticism is unmatched in nature except by dolphins; both species apparently have a similar sexual excitability, not limited by season.

The syphilis bacteria was the greatest sexual scourge before AIDS, striking indiscriminately, irrespective of class, gender or race through the 16th century. Once widely believed to have been brought by the Spaniards from the West Indies, syphilis is now thought to have existed for several thousand years as a complaint called yaws. This ancestor of the bacillus first lived on decaying matter, which then passed to primates, and on to children and young adults who suffered a disfiguring skin infection and sometimes infected bone marrow. The wearing of clothes reduced direct infection but the germ gained access by the mouth and genitals, and spread more rapidly with increased opportunities for coitus in urban life. With more rapid transmission, the disease progressively attacked the nervous system and other organs.

The link between syphilis and the West Indies was originally made in 1495 when Charles VIII of France besieged the Spanish in Naples with 50,000 mercenaries supported by camp followers. His troops, from many parts of western Europe, overcame the defences then sacked the city and raped the population. Syphilis then spread throughout Europe through the returning troops and their 800 women. The new plague was horrible and could attack within months or years. It first appeared at the genitals then spread as a general rash over the body into abscesses and sores; it went on to destroy the nose, lips, eyes, genitals and finally attacked the bones.

By 1500 it had spread to France, Switzerland, Germany, Denmark, Sweden, Holland, England, Scotland, Hungary, Greece, Poland and Russia. It was also carried by troops and sailors to Calcutta, Africa, the Middle East, China, Japan and much later to the Antipodes. It felled hundreds of thousands but was not confined to the laity. It is reported many priests including bishops and popes succumbed. Gonorrhoea, a less severe disease than syphilis, may also have been present several thousand years ago in Europe and Asia. It affects primarily the urinary tract (and for women their ovaries) but the infection was not identified until 1827 as an independent bacterial disease. Before 1947 over 10,000 Americans were dying every year from syphilis, but with the advent of penicillin, (which cured both diseases), the number dropped to 6,000 per year by 1949 and in the 1950s was still declining.

But these two scourges were not eradicated. The advent of the birth control pill increased promiscuity and by the early 1980s over 2.5 million were contracting gonorrhoea annually, with syphilis ranking behind chicken pox as the third most common infectious disease in the USA. Another complication arose in the late 1970s when a penicillin-destroying mutation of gonorrhoea appeared amongst infected American men serving in the Philippines, which then spread back to the United States where strains even more resistant to whole families of antibiotics were reported.

The numbers of what were known as pelvic inflammatory diseases (PIDs) were increased by two organisms – herpes and chlamydia. Herpes (HSV 1) has a long history of causing cold sores which at some time had infected over 90% of older residents in America and Europe. By 1980 antibodies had been developed but in the same decade a more dangerous strain of herpes appeared called (HSV 2); this is a sexually passed virus infecting nerve cells and causing painful sores around the mouth and genitals. Between 1966 and 1981 the numbers treated by American doctors suffering from HSV 2 had increased ninefold and by 1986 60% of men living in key American cities were infected. By the early 1990s chlamydia, another PID, creating female infertility within a year if not treated, was the most infectious disease in the USA after the common cold.

Venereal diseases were not confined to heterosexuals. The gay community was becoming more sexually active so that by 1974 80% of the 75,000 San Franciscans being treated for STDs were homosexual men. From 1974 to 1979 the incidence increased by 250% and a random survey reported that 20% of homosexuals had gonorrhoea, 10% carried herpes and a smaller proportion were infected with syphilis. There was also a three-fold increase in hepatitis B (HPV), which can become liver cancer. In one form or another, hepatitis has infected humans throughout the centuries but today it infects some 5% of the world's population (around 200 million people) mostly in South America and Africa but it is also increasing in the United States and Europe.

By the early 1980s the first cancer clinic in San Francisco's general hospital was asked to treat a young male homosexual prostitute with purplish-blue splotches on his skin; a survey showed that twenty-six men from California and New York all had the same complaint. Within a relatively short time apparently normal healthy men had died, a number of them from pneumonia. One of the west-coast researchers plotted the rise in the number of men back to the first-reported similar case in 1977, forecasting that by 1985, 40% of gay men would be similarly infected. Despite medical warnings, the numbers grew progressively. By mid-1982 it had been established that the American epidemic was contracted mainly from two sources: male homosexual activity and intravenous drug use. Tragically, haemophiliacs had also caught the disease through infected blood.

It was not until 1982 that the AIDS virus was identified as a disease infecting the immune system. It seems that while the body's cells recognised the virus, the active T-cells were so disrupted that they were unable to respond in fighting the intruder. At the same time doctors were diagnosing people with similar conditions in Europe, the disease being imported from America, Haiti and Africa, either homosexually or through blood products. It was thought that Gaetan Dugas, a promiscuous Canadian flight attendant, was the main link in the spread of AIDS between Africa and America.

Research as to the origins of AIDS continues but it is thought that the mutating virus could have been carried for centuries by green monkeys in the Lake Victoria region, encompassing Rwanda, Uganda, and Tanzania. It was harmless to the monkeys but possibly through a bite it spread to humans; it must have stayed local until the region was disrupted by wars following Idi Amin's dismissal in Uganda and the invasion from Tanzanian troops. Every disease needs a period of 'amplification' before it becomes a pandemic and this was the virus's opportunity.

In Africa AIDS was initially spread heterosexually through troops and then by prostitutes along the trading routes. In the United States and Europe, the amplification stage was the surge of homosexual activity and drug usage in the late 1970s and early 1980s. Unwisely in the west, a great deal of attention was given to preventing the spread amongst heterosexuals, among whom it is relatively rare.

By the mid-1990s, as people have learnt to change their habits, the rate of AIDS increase is diminishing. In the west, Spain has the highest incidence of HIV-positive persons with 58 per 10,000 of the population. By the early 1990s two thirds of the world's 13-14 million carriers are found among Africans, although in 1995, for the first time, more people contracted HIV in Asia than anywhere else. In India the disease is spreading through widespread prostitution and along burgeoning trade routes.

Cholera and other water-borne diseases. Unlike the pestilences considered earlier, cholera and typhoid are carried by polluted water and thrive in conurbations with indifferent sanitation and water supply and tight living conditions. Cities like Calcutta were prime targets with rapidly multiplying ill-nourished people, piles of dung and rubbish from animals and humans and putrid air conditions. The first cholera outbreak, reported as a new disease, infected the Ganges delta region in 1817.

It is believed that the bacteria *Vibrio cholerae* has been around for over 2500 years. The bacilli thrive in polluted water, which then transfer to the human gut and are then recycled back into the water. The disease can also be caught by eating infected fish, vegetables washed in contaminated water, from flies or soiled towels. Once swallowed, the bacillus multiplies in the intestine, releasing a strong toxin causing violent vomiting and diarrhoea which rapidly depletes the body of fluids; this in turn causes muscle spasm, circulatory collapse and often death. If untreated, cholera causes up to 50% fatalities within days – even hours. An epidemic can be sparked off by a carrier's faeces being absorbed by fish or water. From the first outbreak in Calcutta, which felled hundreds of thousands including 5,000 British soldiers, it then spread throughout India, China, the East, Arabia and Africa but stopped short of Europe.

Moscow was the first European city to suffer higher casualties from cholera than from the Black Death; it spread to Germany, England and elsewhere. In the 1830s, the bacillus was especially dangerous to poor people with inadequate sanitation and low immune resistance, and thousands perished. It was then carried to America via migrants, particularly from Ireland, where the same disadvantaged groups of people succumbed. After a decade with only a few fatalities, cholera struck again in 1848 taking 11,000 lives in England but this time it prompted reformers, led by Edwin Chadwick, to overcome insanitary conditions. Chadwick, a zealot for cleansing the unwashed multitude, was appointed commissioner for the board of health.

By the time the next epidemic struck in 1868, Chadwick's health reforms, preventative medicine and public refuse collection saved many lives; he was helped by a London doctor called John Snow who, while analysing an outbreak around Broad Street in London, narrowed the source of infection down to a public pump. He asked for the handle to be removed and the outbreak stopped.

Chadwick's work was so admired that public health legislation, improved sewage and clean water systems were introduced in Europe and America markedly reducing cholera and other diseases. Among these was typhoid fever caused by the bacteria, *Salmonella typhosa,* which caused diarrhoea, headaches, intestinal inflammation and dysentery. It was not until Louis Pasteur, Robert Koch and others led research to isolate the bacteria that it could be treated by antibiotics. However, cholera is still a danger, for in 1991 bilge water, thought to have been pumped from a Chinese freighter in Peruvian waters, infected the marine environment. Within two years of the release 500,000 cases of the disease were reported in Latin America which cost the Pan American Health Organisation $200 million to eradicate.

The Cycles of Disease

Several earlier chapters have described drought cycles that we know cause malnutrition and lead to a reduction in the body's immune system. We have seen how civil wars such as those in Chechnya and Bosnia create huge numbers of refugees and if these were on a bigger scale, the problems would be almost insurmountable. In the past refugees with a disease immunity could be carrying an infection to their host country. There is also the possible collapse of the debt cycle, which after an outbreak of disease could endanger vital spending on public health, sewerage and clean water systems, even in the developed world.

Drought has created tremendous difficulties for mankind throughout history. Quite apart from making people more susceptible to disease, it forces them to choose between starvation or moving. Dr Iben Browning, whose work is mentioned in Chapter 2, believed the period through to the next century would create the conditions whereby those who usually had excess would have enough, while the people with only sufficiency would starve. Famine conditions not only affect people. Several of the disease outbreaks described earlier have been caused by animals driven from their natural habitat by drought or attracted to the rubbish normally surrounding dwellings. Browning also drew attention to the 800-year cycle of disease (already mentioned) going back at least to 1200 BC. We can corroborate the scourge that hit

Athens in 443 BC, the plague carried by the Huns in the 5th century AD and the Black Death transported by the Mongols in the 13th century. It is now 800 years since Genghis Khan struck.

We have noted that wars create huge problems both for combatants and for civilians. People displaced against their will suffer the double disadvantage not only of carrying disease (from which they themselves may be immune) but also of being open to infection where they settle; if there is inadequate sanitation then cholera or another fever could be rife. Unfortunately, wars tend to destroy, or leave inoperable, public health systems, so compounding the danger.

The Cycles Only Exaggerate What is Happening Already

Man has had notable successes in eliminating disease. Smallpox has been eradicated, public hygiene improved and antidotes found for such ancient killers as the plague, typhus, cholera and syphilis. To some extent man is a victim of his own success in that there is a general belief that modern medicine has the capacity to cure everything, even though the damage may have been self-inflicted through smoking or excess alchohol, drugs or sexual permissiveness. However, some areas are rapidly becoming out of control, which the cyclical pattern will only worsen.

While killers have been removed, strains of mosquito are emerging that are immune to DDT and the parasites that cause malaria are developing resistance to chloroquine. Tuberculosis, which was thought to have been beaten, is now returning with a mutation resistant to mainline remedies, and new mutations of gonorrhoea are expensive to treat. In addition, new strains of influenza are arising all the time. Perhaps the most dangerous are the potentially untreatable scourges, like the haemorrhagic diseases described earlier, which have no known reservoir or vector. Already it is reported that hantavirus, a potentially fatal disease spread by rats and mice, is sweeping the war-torn terrain of Bosnia.

To make the prognosis even more disturbing, hospitals are becoming once more a focus for incubating bugs. A survey produced by the *Journal of the American Medical Association* showed that half the patients in 1500 European hospitals were on antibiotic treatment for infections they had *acquired as patients*.

The unhealthiness of cities has already been noted but it is not new. For example, in ancient Rome there was an expectation that only one third of the population would live to the age of thirty, compared to 70% in the countryside. During the plague years, those who could afford it always fled to the country hoping they would escape death. This did not always work. More than half the population of the village of Eyam in Derbyshire died during the plague when infected fleas escaped from a bolt of woven cloth delivered from London.

The migration from the countryside to the cities has accelerated since the Second World War. Countries like Russia and China had 75% to 80% of the population living in the country until the 1930s with only a small proportion in cities. Now the percentages have switched dramatically. In 1950 there were only two megacities, London and New York. By 1980 they had been joined by Buenos Aires, Rio de Janeiro, São Paulo, Mexico City, Los Angeles, Beijing, Shanghai and Tokyo; of these it could be said that only two were wealthy enough to update their sanitary systems regularly – quite apart from keeping the malaria mosquito at bay.

By the year 2000 it is estimated that 3.1 billion people (around half the world's population), mostly from developing countries, will live in these and other cities, including Osaka, Manila, Jakarta, Dhaka, Madras, Bangkok, Calcutta, Bombay, Karachi, Tehran and Cairo. It is easy to extrapolate figures, it is horrific to conceive the possible consequences should one of the age-old scourges re-occur - or indeed new ones emerge. In addition, there is danger from the rapid movement of people by air which, as we have seen, could spread a disease like Lassa fever rapidly from Africa to North America. The increase in the size of cities – particularly in developing countries – must give rise to the greatest concern. Until 1960 the vast majority of cities in the world were between 40 and 60 degrees north with a mean temperature of between 45 and 65 degrees Fahrenheit. They were in relatively wealthy countries, able to afford modern sanitation and cool enough to discourage mosquitos. The new cities described earlier will be in danger from malaria – as indeed will be conurbations such as Tokyo, Los Angeles and Washington, should global warming bring the mosquito zone further north.

History Has Something to Say About the Outcome

It is the contention of this chapter that the real danger to millions of the human race will come from hunger allied to disease which is unlikely to be contained by international agencies. It is true that many, sensing the danger from STDs, will not just take better precautions but practise abstinence like our Puritan forbears; this could well be coupled with a religious revival. As other chapters have shown, there is a move away from cities in the west, as modern technology enables those with a skill to practise their trade or profession away from a central office.

We should also be comforted by the expanding science of biotechnology which seeks to identify the human genes whose malfunction is responsible for a specific disease. Once recognised they can be potentially replaced through a treatment called 'gene therapy'. The techniques can also be used to test whether a patient either has, or is at risk, of contracting an ailment, in time for corrective steps to be taken. Experts in this science also believe biotechnology can be used for testing drugs much more rapidly than at present by creating organic systems that closely resemble human metabolisms.

Even if there were a catastrophe on the scale of the 5th plague or the Black Death, nature seems to have a way of compensating the human race, and modern medicine is far from being defeated. True, those weakened by disease are often themselves so debilitated that they fall prey to other diseases but there are compensations for the survivors. From the Black Death emerged the Italian Renaissance and in England, at least, freedom for the serfs. Nothing is permanent. Man's spirit will always overcome tragedies – perhaps in ways never dreamt of by his contemporaries.

CHAPTER 13

THE CYCLES OF TECHNOLOGY AND INNOVATION

It would be most surprising if technology and innovation did not also run in cycles. Indeed the great economist Joseph Schumpeter, in his book *Business Cycles*, believed that the Kondratieff cycle was almost certainly controlled by the 'bunching' of innovations at the beginning of the upwave that gave impetus to each recovery. He then went on to argue that once these new innovations pass the growth climax, their decline then triggers the next downwave. Schumpeter's ideas were then expanded by other economists, but they all left out of their calculations that the threat of war, or combat itself, has often triggered innovations without leading to a recovery. For example, the re-arming of the 1930s encouraged a number of developments including the telex, jet-powered aircraft, FM radio, helicopters, the coding machine and radar. None of these generated a recovery but they considerably assisted the post-war upwave.

As technology and innovation play such an important part in western culture, this chapter examines whether they work in cycles and how, in combination with other rhythms, they may develop in the future.

The S-curve pattern of technology

There have been innovations from the dawn of mankind, when the first flint was fashioned into a hammer and then, by sharpening an edge, into a crude knife and a weapon. While these developments took place over hundreds (or thousands) of years, modern innovations have been shown not to be constant over time but advance in what has become known as a series of S-curves. The French sociologist Gabriel Tarde in 1890 was the first to explain that anything new starts with a slow advance. This is then followed by a rapid and uniformly accelerating progress which slackens off until it finally flattens and probably declines following the shape of a flat S.

The idea was then applied to product cycles in 1950, when the economist Joel Dean suggested that the length and shape of a product's performance was governed by the rate of technological change, market acceptance and the ease of competitive entry. Later researchers went one further arguing that the S-curve has four fundamental phases:

Introduction: a new product has a slow start when first brought to the market; there is no established demand and sometimes it has to be proved technologically. Some pharmaceutical products like thalidomide come into this category, or Clive Sinclair's first electric car.

Growth: this occurs when the new product is accepted, demand begins to accelerate and the size of the market grows rapidly. This can happen even during a recession like the 1930s when refrigerators became popular for preserving food.

Maturity: this is the stage when demand slackens and products are bought as replacements, and competitors crowd into a diminishing pool of demand. Domestic appliances probably reached this stage in the 1970s; then twenty years later respected marques like Hoover felt obliged to offer foreign travel as a sales inducement.

Decline: when a product loses appeal the sales drift downwards. This was the fate of the stage coach when replaced first by the train and then by the motor car. To ensure continuity the next product should be introduced before the old becomes obsolete. This may not always be easy to achieve technically. For example, Rank Xerox failed to introduce an electronically controlled photocopying machine before the electro-mechanical design patents had run out. When Canon introduced new machines the company had the choice of either losing the market or to retool their photocopiers completely.

The idea of the S-curve applies to international trade. For example, a technology such as machine-driven spinning and weaving started in England during the 18th century and found ready overseas markets for many decades. Despite a strict export embargo, machines were smuggled into America but could not be worked until much later, when the migration of skilled individuals showed how the plant could be used. India also bought machinery for their own production and once underway demanded protection from cheap imports. Most advanced countries are now importers of textiles from the nations with a lower-cost base but have access to the same machinery.

The same sequence is now being felt in several advanced countries which, having introduced and manufactured products, find the cost of production excessive and start manufacturing or subcontracting work abroad. These firms still retain the marketing, and probably the technological expertise but progressively all the production is transferred abroad so that the parent company now becomes a designer, importer and distributor. Chapter 8 describes some of the many alternative ways of sub-contracting components for cars, aircraft and electronics, or services, such as handling insurance or accounting. Even head offices are being moved from high cost and taxation areas to locations of lower expense.

Simon Kuznets, the economist whose name was given to the 18.6-year American real-estate cycle, applied S-curves not just to products but also to industries. He found a growth series in agriculture, mining and a range of manufactures where innovations revived obsolete technology, so creating a new life cycle. For example, the principle that power could be transmitted through a piston started with Newcomen's steam engine in 1712, was perfected by James Watt and found new application in boats and locomotives by using higher pressures. Nikolaus Otto then showed how power could be generated in the internal combustion engine so continuing a cascade of S-curves that has lasted nearly 300 years.

S-curves govern population growth, changes in affluence and even nations. Once an innovation has been introduced, its successors lead to such things a lowering costs, increasing efficiency or improving reliability. Once an industry reaches an optimum of performance it is usually superseded; for example, oil has largely succeeded coal as a fuel and natural gas has taken over from coal gas for cooking and heating.

The History of Technology

Perhaps the most important cycle applicable to technology is Raymond Wheeler's 500-year cycle. As the technology of the day originated either in Europe or in the East, so it was duly transferred, sometimes through war. The Arabs learned about papermaking from Chinese captured after the Battle of Tallas River. Gunpowder and the movable-type printing press were probably transferred from China through trading contacts.

In our 20th-century arrogance, we are inclined to believe that there was little technological development before the year 1500. Professor Gareth Price of St Andrew's Management Institute goes further. He believes the Industrial Revolution was inevitable given the knowledge available in the 16th century.

Until the year 1000 AD and well into the next millennium, technology was largely dependent upon the needs of warlords wanting either arms or better personal protection for themselves and for their troops. This created work for many trades, including armourers who used wrought iron smelted with charcoal, then tempered to harden the blades. In the 14th century iron was used to produce sledge-mounted cannon that were so unwieldy they could not be used on battlements. First used at Crécy by the English, cannon were later employed to devastating effect by the French to destroy the English-held castles during the Hundred Years' War. It could be said that if the king controlled the supply of cannon he could destroy local feifdoms – perhaps one of the contributors to the modern nation state.

This same ironwork was used for making the first clocks for churches early in the 13th century, although most were still constructed of wood. The iron workers used powered hammers driven by water-wheels which were still in use in the 19th century. By the 16th century, cannon were becoming increasingly reliable and coal was used in reverbatory furnaces to make glass. People had become used to imported spices and peppers but after the Turks had cut the eastern trade routes, voyages of discovery became essential. These were made possible by the magnetic compass, with latitude being defined by the sun and pole star.

New technologies were also appearing in everyday life. Canals were being dug for transport, with locks to cope with the different levels; the networks were further improved by road building with bridges being built at river crossings. The techniques of digging and clearing were also applied to land clearance, the additional grain supplies being ground in wind and water-mills. The art of communication was immeasurably improved by Gutenberg's printing press.

Life 500 Years Ago Must Have Been Exciting

The 500-year cycle also applies to technology. These are some of the developments by 1500:

Fuel. Wood was the predominant fuel with its derivative, charcoal, as the essential ingredient for smelting iron; however, wood was becoming somewhat scarce in England due to competing claims from construction and heating. Coal had been used for smelting in the Bronze Age and in England could be picked off the beach at Newcastle-upon-Tyne for shipping down the coast to London or elsewhere by river and canal. Coal was also used by the 11th-century monks to fire their forges, producing beautiful ironwork and in glass-making. Wood was used for heating and cooking until the invention of chimmneys in Elizabethan England allowed coal's noxious fumes to escape. Hard coking coal had also been discovered in Shropshire and was used in malting barley.

Early metals. The first use of copper alloys for making weapons, tools and ornaments goes back to the early Egyptians who wrought bronze. Copper alloys dominated metal production before 1200 BC when one of the 800-year cyclical incursions from cental Asia (mentioned in Chapter 12) brought in the aggressive Boat People who cut off the tin supplies and forced the development of iron.

Iron initially was probably an unwanted by-product of bronze to be beaten out of the incandescent mass. However, by cutting tin imports the Hittites forced the ancient metal workers to reconsider the use of iron. The problem was that even when using a bellows it was difficult to reach the melting point of iron at 1537 degrees centigrade. Yet their efforts must have been successful, for one of the first iron artefacts discovered was a beautiful dagger with golden hasp found in the tomb of Tutankhamun. Modern metallurgists were amazed by its quite untarnished condition over the centuries.

It is thought the Hittites based in Anatolia (present-day Turkey) were responsible for discovering three fundamental qualities of iron: first the increase in strength and toughness when alloyed with around 1% of carbon to become steel. Secondly they discovered that hardness could be increased through heating then quenching in water and finally they found that the brittleness, induced from working, could be relieved by tempering – or re-heating to allow stess relief.

Iron was made until the 14th century by intensely heating a mixture of charcoal and iron ore for several hours. Using increasingly efficient bellows the ore became an incandescent sponge forcing out the dross into the outer layers, leaving the refined metal inside; the glowing ball was then pulled out and beaten to remove as many impurities as possible. As the demand for iron increased in the 1500s, the furnaces grew larger and a stonger blast was needed to penetrate the initial blend to produce something similar to present-day pig iron. The more malleable wrought iron was made by stirring the melt with hazel twigs which provided a source of oxygen to reduce the brittle carbon.

Communications. People have been able to pass messages to each other from earliest times – it is thought prehistoric man used to convey meaning by beating hollow logs with sticks. His vocabulary increased when skins were stretched across a hollow to make simple drums able to express warnings, pre-arranged signals – even emotions. Beacon fires communicated the fall of Troy over 500 miles to Queen Clytemnestra in 1084 BC and the same techniques were used to signal the arrival of the Spanish Armada to London. Smoke signals could convey different meanings but the technique was severely restricted by the weather.

One of the greatest breakthroughs occurred around 1448 when Johann Gutenberg of Mainz formed a partnership with a goldsmith, Johann Fust, to exploit his invention of a movable-type printing press. The partnership came apart when Fust, demanding repayment, took possession of his stock and the invention. Although discouraged, Gutenberg went back into business with another partner, Conrad Humery, and produced the first printed Bible (known as the Mazarin Bible) after its discovery in the eponymous Cardinal's library.

Although manual type-setting took as much time as hand copying, the time for the printed copy was reduced by 99%. Marc Faber in 'The Gloom, Boom and Doom Report' states that by the year 1500 more than a thousand presses throughout Europe had produced about 10 million copies of 35,000 different titles. In around fifty years, more written material had been printed than in all the years since the Sumerians first developed writing around 4000 BC.

Warfare. Down the ages there have been principally two classes of weapons: those that deliver a shock, blow or slash and those that are delivered from a distance. With time, the aim of technology has been to reduce the risk of the one discharging the weapon from retaliation and to improve the terminal accuracy by guiding projectiles during the time of flight. The history of weapon technology has been either to overcome enemy defences or to improve one's own security in a game of deadly counterpoint. The first weapon was the club, to be rapidly followed by the throwing spear, the sling and then in the later Stone Age, the bow and arrow.

The ability to discharge an arrow accurately remained the most important 'distant' weapon over many centuries. Its precision and range made it a formidable tool in the hands of Saladin's cavalry who used it to good effect against the Crusaders. To counter this, the European armies introduced the crossbow, an accurate weapon firing short 'bolts' but the rate of fire compared poorly with the bow. Genghis Khan's cavalry used short and immensely stiff bows made from bone to outrage their opponents, their aim being steadied by the first use of stirrups. Edward I was so impressed by the Welsh longbow that he adopted it as the standard arm of his yeoman infantry; it had a range of 250 yards and a much higher rate of fire than the crossbow. So important was the longbow that even in Henry V's day, the yeoman were required to practise archery after church every Sunday on the village green.

Mobility became more important to the Egyptians when the more wealthy used chariots to hunt or ride into battle; once in position, combat was often still hand to hand. Cavalry appeared after around 1000 BC when the warriors could either fight mounted or, like the charioteers, dismount. Little has changed in principle. Three thousand years later the tank has replaced the mounted warrior, and the armoured personnel carrier the mounted foot soldier.

Siege warfare became important at about the time of Alexander the Great when the Persians could discharge missiles from siege machines over a range of some 500 yards: the first of these was a fearsome weapon firing spears, the second was the trebuchet – or catapult – that could project rocks into a fort, or even a dead horse to contaminate the water. The catapult had been invented by the Chinese in the 6th century BC and taken up later by the Mongols. It was used by both besiegers and defenders for its ability to hurl several hundred pounds of rocks at 90 mph over 150 yards; at one famous siege on Kenilworth Castle during the Wars of the Roses opposing missiles collided in mid-air, a most unusual occurrence. They were also used to reduce the opposing side's morale by firing the heads of decapitated prisoners! In one such siege in 1345 the Mongols fired prisoners' bodies containing the deadly bubonic bacteria into the Crimean fort at Kaffa.

As weapons became more proficient so did protection. Expensive armour, only affordable by knights, was one way of protecting the body, but armour proved inadequate with the introduction of gunpowder. This mixture of sulphur, saltpetre and charcoal was known to the Chinese and was used both as a noise maker and in rudimentary rockets in the 12th century. Two hundred years later it was discovered in Europe by Roger Bacon and a German monk, Bertold Schwartz. Its first accepted use on the battlefield was at Crecy where iron jugs fired darts.

Although the aristocratic knights still ruled the battlefield for a time, their days were numbered by the advent of more efficient firearms. Initially these were the infantry weapons introduced in the 15th century known as 'fire sticks' or 'hand cannons' with a two to three foot barrel and a bore of half an inch. To start with these were strapped to a pike handle but later a butt enabled them to be fired from the shoulder, often with a support for the barrel. The loading procedure of the 16th-century firearm would have been familiar to the infantry at Waterloo: first the powder was poured into the barrel and retained by a paper or cloth; tamping was followed by a lead or iron slug. Unlike Waterloo, when the muskets were fitted with flintlocks, the piece was fired by a slow match, a cord or twisted rag soaked in saltpetre, which ignited powder in a pan and thence to the charge through a touch hole. The effective range of these pieces was barely 100 yards, but they could penetrate armour.

It was thought that a renegade European introduced the Turks to the cannon, who made it into an effective siege weapon consisting of a cast or wrought iron tube sometimes encased by hoops. They were moved around on ox-drawn sledges and had to be set on earth mounds or log platforms to absorb the recoil. The early pieces usually fired stone cannon balls but neither the bores or balls could be accurately machined and so had to be matched before action. By 1453, the Turks were able to mobilise seventy heavy pieces for the siege of Constantinople, one particulary effective weapon was a 19-ton monster able to fire a 1500 pound stone ball a distance of one mile; its rate of fire was slow with only seven discharges possible during a day but it frightened the life out of the defenders.

The French made excellent use of cannon cast by the Bureau brothers during the latter part of the Hundred Years' War. The walls of castle after castle were surprisingly quickly battered into rubble without the defenders being able to reply, which contrasted with the difficulty Henry V had of investing Rouen and Cherbourg around 1419 without cannon – four years after the Battle of Agincourt. The French supremacy continued with the design of a field gun mounted on two wheels which could be towed into position by horses and quickly brought into action. A further refinement was the development of the trunnion allowing the barrel to be adjusted for elevation.

The Rate of Change Quickens

Innovations accelerated during the 16th century with the need to improve the efficiency of the military adventures that accompanied the voyages of discovery. Technology, which had been divorced from science since the age of the Romans now converged to produce remarkable advances:

Fuel

As suggested earlier, the development of coal for cooking and heating was only made possible by the invention of the chimney in Tudor times and by 1600 was rapidly replacing wood for its higher calorific value. Coal is a remarkable fuel formed from the decaying rain forests that covered the European and American latitudes around 350 million years ago. As these ancient plants thrived they absorbed carbon from carbon dioxide in the atmosphere. House builders learned to add chimneys to houses to discharge coal's unpleasent gases and to contain the warmth by heat-resistant bricks. Coal then created its own industrial demand when Abraham Darby first adapted the techniques of malting coke to smelt iron in the 18th century. This growing demand was met firstly from surface outcrops and then from buried seams. The mines were likely to fill with water and needed to be pumped out by the newly invented Newcomen steam engine, described later in the chapter.

In 1814 the use of coal was further extended when the National Light and Heat Company heated coal to produce the first gas for street lighting; its luminescence for buildings was greatly enhanced by the invention of the gas mantle in the 1890s. Coal gas was only replaced by electricity – itself generated from coal-burning boilers – when, in middle of the 19th century, it was discovered that light was emitted when a current was passed through a filament. At first the only practical lamps were carbon arcs requiring a mechanism constantly to adjust the striking width, but then two innovations took a hand before electric bulbs replaced gas: the first was the Sprengel mercury pump which allowed the glass envelope around a filament to be evacuated, so avoiding metal deposits; the other was the ability to draw brittle tungsten into a filament.

Coal driven transport did not depose the horse for mass transportation until railways replaced the stage coach from the 1830s onwards. Coal was still used in ships even after the invention of the turbine but by the 1920s most vessels were converting to oil; not only did the liquid have a higher calorific value per pound, but it needed fewer stokers and was infinitely less dirty. Remarkably, coal was still used by locomotives in the west until the 1960s and is often still the railway fuel in China and India. As coal superseded wood so oil-firing replaced coal, the successor being formed not by decayed plant life but in the oceans. When plankton and other molluscs die they are normally oxidised to carbon dioxide when falling to the sea bed; however, if they are preserved in an oxygen-deficient environment, the matter builds up on on the sea bed, decays and is duly covered by rock formations which can later be tapped. Oil has about 25% higher calorific value per pound than coal, but apart from some viscous crude being found naturally in areas such as Java and Trinidad, unrefined oil was not used as a fuel in the west until Scottish shales were distilled in the middle of the 19th century. Oil was first drilled in Pennsylvania around 1860 but it was not until 1913 that Standard Oil introduced thermal cracking to break down crude oil through a distillation process. Apart from its use as a fuel, oil products now serve as raw materials for detergents, man-made fibres, plastics, fertilisers, pharmaceuticals, synthetic rubber, etc.

Iron and steel

The real breakthrough in iron-making came in 1709 when Abraham Darby smelted iron ore with coke (instead of charcoal) at Coalbrookdale, Shropshire – so paving the way for the Industrial Revolution. His invention was important, economically and industrially. For centuries charcoal has been formed by the charring of wood in an oven. However, Britain was running out of trees from the competing demands of shipbuilding, construction and heating. Using a supply of coking coal – reputedly from an outcrop in the grounds of a monastery – Darby was able to produce material that answered the second industrial need, plentiful cast iron.

Darby used techniques, developed by brewers, to smelt iron by firing alternate layers of coke and ore. By 1722 Darby's ironworks were casting iron cylinders for Newcomen's steam engines and in 1770 was the only foundry in the world capable of producing the cast sections for the famous iron bridge crossing the Avon in Shropshire. The whole edifice, weighing 378 tons and 10 hundredweight, spanned over 100 feet and used woodworking methods of joining the material – such as mortise and tenon joints.

Steel, which is iron with 0.1% to 1.5% of carbon, had first been made in a crucible in 1740 by Benjamin Huntsman, a Yorkshire clockmaker, at Abbeydale near Sheffield. To a wrought-iron melt, he added small quantities of carbon to produce steel which was then beaten into scythes, sickles and reaping hooks, using water-wheel-driven hammers. Over seventy years later the process was brought into batch production by Alfred Krupp of Essen who held sway until Henry Bessemer perfected a rapid conversion furnace in 1856 for converting pig-iron into steel. Amazingly, it only required a decade to bring this invention into operation and by 1910 half the world's output was produced in this way and was only phased out in the 1960s. Larger batches of steel were made possible through the Siemens-Martin open-hearth furnace which started operating only four years after the Bessemer process, to reach a peak of nearly 100% of world production by the Second World War. The demand for steel in the USA rose dramatically by over 41% during the Civil War but declined to around 3% in the 1920s. After rising to over 4% in the Second World War, steel demand fell despite cheaper steel from electric furnaces and oxygen lancing. In the 1990s steel is barely holding its own against substitutes such as aluminium, plastics and carbon fibres.

Engines

The Marquess of Worcester in 1663 was the first to describe a steam engine which turned a combustible fuel into mechanical work – although the earliest patent was taken out by Captain Savary thirty-five years later. Necessity being the mother of invention, Thomas Newcomen patented the first practical beam engine to pump water out of mines only a few years before Abraham Darby created the huge demand for deep-mined coking coal.

Newcomen, a Devon ironmonger, brilliantly used the principle of a French academic called Denis Papin to harness atmospheric air pressure to provide the power stroke for his engine. Steam from an external boiler was admitted to the underside of a 21-inch piston head which, through a huge rocker arm, lowered the pump head. The steam was then shut off and water spray admitted to the driving cylinder to condense the vapour; this created a partial vacuum allowing air pressure to make the return stroke. Newcomen also devised the switching gear which allowed the engine to perform 12 to 14 strokes a minute automatically. Quite soon these machines were used throughout the industrialized world despite being highly wasteful in fuel. Instead of the discharged steam being condensed for recirculation as in modern engines, it was discharged to the atmosphere.

James Watt, a Scottish instrument maker, noted the opportunity for improving Newcomen's engine when repairing a model of the original beam pump. Two radical improvements were made: the first was to admit steam on both sides of the piston so improving the stroke rate. The second was to fit a separate condenser which recovered the spent steam and returned it to the boiler – a major improvement in thermal efficiency. Structurally Watt's engine employed a beam, like Newcomen, but instead of driving a pump it was linked to a crank.

But the design required a whole range of machine tools to manufacture the crankshaft, valves, connecting rods and so on to create the machine-tool industry. This included James Wilkinson's borer – originally perfected for smooth-bore cannon – and Henry Maudslay's screw-cutting lathe. Other tools were needed, such as machines for grinding, turning, slotting, planing and cutting. The royalty on Watt's engines was calculated as a third of the coal saved compared to Newcomen's machine and the combination of steam raising and coke for iron-making created a huge demand for coal.

Innovations followed rapidly after Watt's patents ran out in 1800 allowing higher pressure engines to be designed for propelling vehicles and ships. William Symington built the first steamboat in 1802 which, had it been adopted by France, might have allowed an invasion of England on a day when Britain's three-decker sailing ships were becalmed. Increasing thermal efficiencies allowed George Stephenson to built the first colliery engine in 1814, then the 'Rocket' in 1829 for which he won a prize of £500. He and others solved the technical problems of improved boiler draught by discharging the steam through the funnel; they also perfected the technique of traction friction for cast – or wrought – iron rails.

As so often happens in history, the career of George Stephenson's son, Robert, paralleled that of Isambard Kingdom Brunel. This remarkable man, who started his career digging tunnels under the Thames, created the Great Western Railway by designing trains that could pass through tunnels, over bridges and along cuttings. The GWR was one of the wonders of the age with a seven-foot gauge (compared to Stephenson's four feet, eight and a half inches) designed to link London to the south-west of England and later to Wales, at speeds not possible at that time. The two great rivals, almost contemporaries, died within weeks of each other in 1859.

Although steel rails were not available in quantity until after the Bessemer furnace was in production in the late 1850s, railway building caught the public's imagination in England during the 1830s when George Hudson formed numerous partnerships to build lines. The speculative mania attracted people from all walks of life who wanted to invest in even the meanest branch line. Although he lived to 1871, Hudson's enterprises crashed in the depression of the late 1840s. In America, the Civil War spurred the building of railroads, created a huge demand for steel rails and a fortune for Andrew Carnegie. The two coasts were linked at Promontory Point Utah on 10 May 1869 with the meeting of the Central Pacific and Union Pacific Railroads.

The steam engine allowed factories to be sited well away from the rivers or streams that had earlier driven water-wheels, yet it had several major shortcomings. The first was that it had a limited rotational speed for driving the newly invented dynamo. Michael Faraday had discovered in 1830 that an electric current could be generated by passing a conductor through a magnetic field, but it was not until thirty-seven years later that Siemens developed a practical generator which benefited from a high rotational speed.

Initially, faster steam engines provided the rotary power but the answer was the turbine invented by Charles Parsons in 1889; this used higher steam pressures bearing against impellers that were similar in shape to water-wheels. The steam was first directed against impulse blades then, as the steam expanded, on reaction blades. Higher pressure steam also improved the power to weight ratio – the second major problem of the steam engine.

Although reciprocating steam engines were ending their useful life, the piston engine was the focus of a powerful new product cycle. A patent had been taken out in England in 1871 for a hot-air pumping engine that burned vaporised paraffin but the first working internal combustion engine was designed by the Belgian inventor, Jean Lenoir, in 1860. Other inventions followed, including Nikolaus Otto's four-stroke engine in 1876. Later Gottleib Daimler applied the four-stroke cycle to motor vehicles in 1886.

The rest, as they say, is history. In the short space of less than thirty years, Henry Ford had set up an assembly line for the

Model-T using the remarkable techniques of F. W. Taylor. Taylor had the genius to see that most so-called skilled operations could be broken down into discreet simple motions or activities – an idea first mooted by Adam Smith. He also perceived that these could be readily taught and a specific skill mastered in a relatively short time. In the opinion of the management guru Peter Drucker, Taylor was largely responsible for the huge rise in American production during the Second World War – something Hitler believed would not be possible.

Communications

There was little advance in distant communications from the bonfire beacons used in Tudor days until in 1792 a French physician called Claude Chappe invented a telegraph consisting of a shutter array able to be read over six miles away; these were then organised in a series to link coastal stations with Paris. The system was improved by an English bishop, George Murray, and his technology was still in use linking New York to Philadelphia until 1846. The electrical breakthrough came in 1835 when Cooke and Wheatstone devised an electric telegraph which could move a simple galvanometer. A few years later this was upgraded when a six-wire set of galvanometers could transmit twenty letters and ten numerals. The development went across the Atlantic when Samuel Morse devised his code which was the only method of sending written messages a long distance until the early 1930s when the first teleprinter was introduced. The Morse system was used by Paul Julius Reuter using land lines and later transatlantic cables after setting up his first pigeon press service in 1849. The first military line was used in the Crimea and some ten years later was in extensive use during the American Civil War.

In parallel with cable messages came the telephone, made possible when Michael Faraday induced currents to flow in a coil when passed across an electro-magnet. Graham Bell was the first to apply Faraday's ideas to speech transmission; in 1876 he patented the earliest telephone which to start with could only be used in direct lines before the techniques of speech 'chopping' made possible multiple transmissions on a single cable. The invention of the vacuum tube just before the First World War increased the range of telephones, making transatlantic calls possible.

Telegraph transmission peaked around 1913 when Guglielmo Marconi's invention of wireless communication removed the need for a physical connection. The principle of electro-magnetic waves had been established earlier by several physicists including Maxwell and Hertz. Later William Crookes created a telegraphic system that needed no wires or cables and another English physicist, Oliver Lodge, invented a device that could selectively tune frequencies.

Marconi's genius, like that of Newcomen, was to assemble all the previous work on the subject and arrive at a practical solution. His first successful experiments were held in Bologna before he moved to England; in 1896 Marconi made a successful transmission between Penarth and Brean Down – a distance of nine miles. Subsequently, after starting Marconi's Wireless Telegraph Company, he created a radio link between England and France in 1898 and across the Atlantic between Poldhu, Cornwall and St John's, Newfoundland, three years later. It is held that the first use of wireless to apprehend criminals was the arrest of Dr Crippen on a transatlantic steamship.

Despite the Depression, the 1930s were a fruitful time for innovations, possibly associated with German re-armament. The teleprinter came into use early in the decade; Telefunken introduced frequency-modulated radio (FM); Baird sent the first television pictures; Watson-Watt experimented with the RDF which later was incorporated into Britain's Chain Home-Low (CHL) system; and AEG of Germany produced the earliest magnetic tape-recorder. The first code machine was produced in 1931 to increase bank security which the Germans adapted to the Enigma.

The Second World War and the subsequent Cold War accelerated the ability to process and transmit information. The first electronic computers were designed to break the German and Japanese codes; these used vacuum tubes but the breakthrough in reliability and power came with the invention of the transistor by Bell Telephone in 1951. The silica chip also made it possible to reduce greatly the weight and increase the reliability of mobile radio equipment. One of the greatest wartime inventions was the cavity magnetron, a brilliant device designed by researchers at Birmingham University which, with much higher radar frequencies, made possible the precise detection of submarines, ships and aircraft.

Innovation and War

Earlier parts of the chapter showed how warfare triggered the advance of weapon technology. From 1500 onwards there were great leaps forward, not only in design but also in usage. Spain led weapon development in the 16th century by standardising the common calibre arquebus (musket). Another advance was the adoption of match and wheel-locks operated by a trigger to control the time of firing. There was considerable experimentation with artillery, the Spanish setting the design for nearly two centuries with a long-barrelled gun called a culverin, two shorter pieces and a mortar.

There had been little change in sea warfare since the Romans employed galleys rowed by fifty-four oarsmen, which attempted either to ram and sink, or to close and board their opponents. The Venetians also used galleys but mounted a cannon as a bow chaser. Galleys were used by both sides at the Battle of Lepanto where the Turks were disadvantaged by being unable to use their small lateen sails. Further west on the Atlantic coast, the new maritime states such as Spain and Portugal led the development of the square-rigged galleon which maximised the amount of canvas. The vessel was designed with upperworks built like castles to conduct a land-style battle fought by soldiers; the Dutch brilliantly modified the shape of a trading vessel to make a warship.

Henry VIII's shipbuilders converted a floating soldier carrier into a warship by mounting cannons on small wheels where the recoil was absorbed by rope and tackle; allied to the French invention of the gun-port, a warship now became a floating gun battery. A well-trained crew could reload and fire their piece fairly rapidly during the action – something the Spanish vessels could not. Unfortunately for the Armada, the Spanish ships carried field guns which could barely be reloaded in action. These innovations totally changed naval tactics, enabling English ships to stand off from their Spanish, Dutch and French enemies and better them into submission.

At about the same time, the development of navigational instruments made possible the extraordinary voyages of discovery needed after the Ottoman Turks had cut the eastern trade routes in the Second Jihad. Gemino Fresius developed a celestial globe for finding stars in 1508 and the astrolabe then converted these to right ascension and declination. Latitude was measured by the forerunner of the sextant, a cross-staff with a stick graduated in degrees which had a moving arm aligned between the object and the horizon. At first it was only possible to measure latitude from a polar star or the sun at noon; longitude could not be measured without accurate time. Sir Isaac Newton explained the matter simply in 1714:

> ... for determining the longitude at sea, there have been several projects, true in theory, but difficult to execute ... one is by watch ... but by reason of the motion of the ship ... variation of heat and cold ... such a watch hath not yet been made ...

England was the leading clock-making country in the 18th century and many attempts were made to produce a reliable chronometer, for many men and cargoes were being lost for want of accurate longitude.

The problem came to a head when a British fleet commanded by Admiral Sir Cloudesly Shovell was wrecked off the Isles of Scilly in 1707. Forced by the navy and merchant interests, the government offered a prize of £20,000 (equivalent to £1 million today) for the person who could define longitude to within half a degree (30 miles at the equator). The solution was found not by a clock-maker, but by joiner's son called John Harrison, who by the age of twenty had made a long-case clock entirely from wood. Encouraged by the Astonomer Royal and by George Graham, the leading clock-maker of the day, Harrison produced the first shipborne chronometer which considerably improved the accuracy of navigation but not to the required standard. However, aided by his son William, and after many arguments with the 'Board of Longitude', Harrison was eventually awarded the prize in 1773 only three years before he died.

While weapons remained similar in construction, they were changed in detail to widen their scope and improve their accuracy. One of the leading figures was Gustavus Adolphus of Sweden, called the father of modern field artillery, who developed pieces which could be rapidly manoeuvred to support infantry and cavalry. Adolphus also halved the weight of a musket to around eleven pounds and introduced an early cartridge where the charge and ball were consolidated in one unit so allowing one round to be fired per minute. Adolphus's further brilliant stroke was to mount a bayonet in the muzzle as a defence against cavalry. Formerly around half the infantry had to be pikemen as a defence against mounted troops but the advent of the bayonet, which was later mounted separately, allowed the piece to be fired with the bayonet fixed. This led to the pike becoming obsolete and doubling the number of musketeers.

The manoeuvrability of fleets was considerably improved by the introduction of flag signals from 1647 which, by the 19th century, had expanded by a system of single flag codes. Signalling made possible the introduction of 'standard practice' fighting codes. Naval ships had developed from the galleon into a series of vessels ranging from the 2,500 ton 1st rate carrying a hundred or more guns in three decks, to the 6th rate, or frigate, carrying as few as twenty-five guns. Over the course of time, British ships perfected the timed broadside and the ability to spend weeks – even months – at sea while being supplied with essentials.

There were few technical breakthroughs during the Napoleonic Wars at the start of the 19th century despite innovations like Krupp's steel forge and steam-propelled vessels. Little changed during the Crimea War but the American Civil War brought in a host of new designs. For example, the Confederates used some of Joseph Whitworth's breech-loaded, rifled field guns which outranged the Union's smooth-bore cannon. Another innovation was the Marling carbine, which was the first to use a lever repeating action to fire cartridges loaded into a butt magazine; Richard Gatling began work on his revolving battery-gun in 1861 where gravity magazines fed ten rotating barrels driven by a hand crank. This weapon was later used to good effect by the British in the Zulu Wars.

The real impact of war on innovations is evident in the period before the two World Wars. In the armament race of the first decades of the 20th century there was a spate of breakthroughs: among these being the submarine by the US Navy, rubber vulcanisation by the Diamond Rubber Company, the military aeroplane in France, the dreadnought battleship in Britain, the gyro compass, the vacuum tube by AT&T, the Ford assembly line, thermal cracking by Standard Oil, synthetic fertiliser by BASF and stainless steel developed by Thomas Firth.

The inventions before the Second World War, briefly mentioned earlier, were even more impressive occurring as they did in the Depression of the 1930s when, according to some theories, they should have been *leading* the recovery. The list includes the gas turbine by Brown Boveri, PVC from IG Farbon and synthetic rubber from DuPont. AEG in Germany introduced the magnetic tape-recorder, radar was developed by Watson-Watt to defend Britain and later two Birmingham physicists designed the cavity magnetron oscillator; the helicopter was introduced by Focke-Wulf and jet aircraft by Messerschmitt.

The Cycles of Technology

The idea that wars run in rhythms of 142, 57, 22 and 11 years is not wholly satisfactory for it fails to identify the Second World War. Perhaps more tenable was the 179-year cool cycles of liberation explained in Chapter 2. The other cycle is the long wave with the peaks and troughs alternating between international and civil wars. One would expect to find a spate of innovations *before* a war of aggression and *during* a civil war. The preparation before the two World Wars are examples of the first, and the innovations during the American Civil War, of the second.

We have noted earlier the many and varied innovations during the 1930s in preparation for the Second World War. Cycle theory suggests these should have pulled economies out of recession; but they failed and the war itself triggered the recovery. As the history of weapons shows, there is little doubt that the prospect of war concentrated the minds, first of kings then presidents, ministers and dictators. This was particularly true around 1500 and before major conflicts.

Joseph Schumpeter, the Austrian-born economist, argued that innovation has been responsible for the Kondratieff and Juglar cycles. Schumpeter subsequently migrated to the USA where, amongst other works, he wrote his treatise on business cycles. Schumpeter's ideas can be summarised as follows:

> The act of innovation is 'doing things differently' whether this be exploiting a previous invention, opening up new markets or sources of supply, changing work practices or modifications to existing products or services. Although basic innovations such as Abraham Darby's use of coke happen relatively seldom, to be successful they need the

addition of a potential market and the necessary financial backing. Because innovations occur internally, Schumpeter believed that they were responsible for his observed cycles – effectively ruling out influences such as changing climate.

Innovations do not occur evenly through time. They come in 'swarms' when, after the recessionary period of the long wave, the bravest entrepreneur finds the courage to risk a new venture; others follow and so lead the economy into potential growth. Schumpeter argues that the steam locomotive, electrical and chemical industries meet the criterion. As the boom continues capital investment increases which encourages further growth. As more competitors are attracted into the market the price of the resource rises but profits are eroded as price rises stall through competition. As the economy falters, deflation sets in as leveraged companies no longer can pay their debts, the recession begins and continues until the bad debts are wrung from the system.

These ideas have worked at times. For example, the railroad network in America took off when Henry Bessemer developed cheap steel for rails and other construction, but it is debatable whether the rising prosperity might have triggered the rotary press or anaesthetics which occurred at the same time. It is also hard to determine the precise turning points when, as Chapter 2 pointed out, there is a plateau phase which could be interpreted as just a continuation of the upwave. They have also not worked to revive nations from a recession. As we have seen, the diesel-electric locomotive, synthetic rubber, colour photography, etc., invented at the depth of the Depression failed to bring the west out of a slump. In fact most British innovations (as judged by patent applications) have occurred during recessions.

In his work *Stalemate in Technology* the German economist, G. Mensch, adapted Schumpeter's ideas by suggesting that basic innovations give rise to new industries at the beginning of the Kondratieff long wave; these thrive following the basic S-curve shape, then reach their maturity before declining to cause recessions. Small innovations may be tried to maintain growth but these are to no avail. At the low point of the ensuing recession, entrepreneurs feel confident enough to take risks and a new set of innovations/industries then take over. Mensch believes that lack of innovation is the main cause of depressions which, as we have seen from evidence of the 1930s, is questionable. The economist is on firmer ground when he suggests that recessions force innovations as we saw from General Motors' introduction of the record-breaking diesel-electric locomotive.

Another theory has been put forward by the veteran economist, W. W. Rostow, suggesting that as the timing of agriculture and raw material innovations was necessarily tied to such determinants as population growth, they went in fits and starts over a cycle of some fifty years. For example, innovations such as McCormick's reaper and binder or nitrogen-based fertilisers were encouraged by high grain prices but their introduction created a huge excess of capacity. Prices fell until population growth caught up and shortages appeared once again, forcing prices up and creating the next round of innovations.

Rostow has also put forward the idea that the type of investment varies between the Kondratieff up- and downwave. Consumer goods investment and production lead the recovery while money is put into the infrastructure during the decline – so making possible the next recovery. For example, canal building in Britain during the late 18th century made possible the first upwave in the 1790s to around 1815. Likewise the investment in railways during the downwave ending in 1848 triggered the recovery during the 1850s and 1860s. The American railroad investment in the 1850s and onwards made possible the huge increase in agriculture in the upwave and the rapid movement of men and military supplies during the Civil War.

In Britain there was considerable infrastructure investment to expand the unloading and distribution of refrigerated meat and food imported from America and New Zealand. The first successful refrigerated dock warehouse was set up in London in 1882 and frozen stores made it possible to remove abbatoirs from the cities. Food conservation took another step forward when tomatoes were canned in California and New York State making it possible for retailers to offer a wide range of 'out of season' fare. There were similar innovations during the Great Depression when refrigerated trains made possible more efficient food distribution, and Roosevelt's New Deal greatly increased federal funding in new roads, harbours and hydroelectric programmes.

Are There Cycles or Patterns of Innovation?

On the face of it, there seems to be a loose 500-year cycle described by Raymond Wheeler. For example, the Greek trireme of 500 BC gave way to the Roman coriba, a sail-driven Mediterranean cargo vessel in the 1st century AD. The Chinese introduced the junk in around 1100 and the square-rigged ship came into use for ocean voyages around 1500. The Roman army probably reached its peak about the birth of Christ and 1000 years later the Chinese invented gunpowder.

Wheeler's ideas that east and west changed domination every 500 years could also be appropriate. For example, the Chinese invented paper made from rags, bark or fibrous material in around 100 AD but the west was still using papyrus and parchment until over a thousand years later. The last half millennia has belonged to the west with the Spanish and then the Portuguese and English navigating across the Atlantic and around the Cape of Good Hope. To defend themselves for these adventures the ships had to be adapted into armed galleons. The Spanish were also the leaders in standardising cannon size and their military employment. The 1500s also encouraged visionaries such as Agostino Ramelli, a French military engineer, and Leonardo da Vinci, who both produced designs for machines that were developed later.

The shortage of charcoal (in line with W. W. Rostow's raw material cycle described earlier) was almost certainly the trigger for Abraham Darby to produce pig-iron from coke and iron ore. The 'swarm' theory of innovation could then have encouraged Newcomen to invent the beam engine (using Darby's castings) for pumping out new deep coal mines. Some seventy years after Newcomen's patent was taken out James Watt created the configuration of converting reciprocating to rotational energy. The piston engine, initially powered by steam then driven by gasoline or diesel oil, has stood the test of over 300 years. This innovative 'swarm' in turn created a new cluster of coal-based inventions around the internal combustion engine, the dynamo and the chemical industry.

Rostow's infrastructure ideas depend on people's prosperity and the critical size of the nation. Britain's canal system was built in the rising affluence of the Industrial Revolution, followed by the railways in the 1830s and 1840s. American railroads were the mainspring for opening up the newly joined states after the

Mexican wars of the 1840s. Britain's system of food generation expanded rapidly during the recession of the 1880s and 90s. The USA borrowed heavily to build up roads, docks and hydro-electric systems during the 1930s Depression. If there is to be another Kondratieff type depression of the late 1990s and into the next century only a handful of countries have the resources to rebuild the eastern states of Europe, embark on any major infrastructure programmes or take measures to prevent epidemics described in Chapter 12.

Mention has been made of the pattern of conflicts around the 179-year sun retrograde and Kondratieff cycles. There were wars of liberation in the mid-17th century and then later after 1810, and if history repeats itself one might expect similar armed struggles today of which Chechnya and Bosnia could be the unfortunate foretaste of more extensive clashes.

There is a pattern of conflict in the Kondratieff cycle at the troughs and peaks of the succeeding rhythms. At the low points were the French Revolution, the 1848 rebellion, the Boer War and the Second World War while the 1812 War, the American Civil War, the First World War and the Vietnam War happened at the cyclical peaks. The combination of both cycles suggests a strong likelihood of an increasing number of civil or limited conflicts into the next century.

What Innovations can be Expected into the 21st Century?

The Kondratieff downwave of K4 almost certainly started in 1990 and we are likely to feel the impact of the sun retrograde cycle in a rising number of civil conflicts; we are also feeling the impact of Wheeler's 500-year cycle in the political uncertainties that afflict almost every nation. If these three rhythms follow their previous patterns, we can pull together the strands of this and other chapters to consider future technological trends listed under six headings:

Conflicts. If there are to be civil disturbances and wars of liberation then it is likely these will not be fought with nuclear weapons. More sophisticated conventional weapons than exist at present will be designed to inflict the maximum damage to the opposition's will to continue but with minimum danger to one's own side. To achieve this, remotely aimed robotic tanks, artillery and even infantry weapons will be needed and there could be headway in new armaments designed to put individuals temporarily out of action without them being killed or wounded.

Probably the greatest advance is likely to be in information gathering and processing, requiring remote sensors that glean information on enemy movements to be automatically fed back to command positions. At the same time electronic markers will identify the position of allies.

The individual. The switch from the status of an employee to self-employment has been identified in other chapters. Apart from the likely reduction in the power of central and local government, individuals will require a self-contained place in which to live, work and bring up their family with only minimum support from public services; they will also be the main beneficiary from the electronic revolution. The house will need more security than is available at present with sensors and devices designed to deter – or temporarily incapacitate a would-be intruder. There will also be increasing support from private crime prevention services.

The housing renaissance and the role of the individual. In addition to the danger of a housing meltdown, the position is complicated in the 1990s by the advent of Toffler's Third Wave. As the Industrial Revolution gives way to the Cybernetic Revolution several things happen: first, traditional employment, that was the norm for most people, declines as firms become less labour intensive. Next, as self-employment rises so the home will become increasingly a place of work – just as it was in the early 18th century. Finally, as the cities reduce in economic importance the unemployed city dwellers add to the lawlessness so further forcing businesses and their employees out of the cities into the country – effectively reversing the trends of the Industrial Revolution.

These changes will represent a considerable challenge to the house owner, lenders and to the construction industry. Builders will be faced with a marked decline in new construction but a growth in modifications – or remodelling; the housing stock will have to accommodate a work area and probably space for elder relatives who can no longer count on state support. In addition, homes in the future could be expected to be more self-contained than at present, with their own communications and possibly their own water recycling, waste disposal and food growing areas.

History never quite repeats itself which is why the forecast housing crash will probably be deeper than in the early 1930s but more constructive for it will be accompanied by a shift in population. The movement is already happening in the US called the Valhalla Syndrome where white middle-class Americans are detaching themselves from the suburbs of cities like New York and Philadelphia.

Although many of the migrants tend to be over 55, they will be still wanting to work in the diaspora of new industrial and commercial centres. While there would also be significant numbers of people working from home, local offices would also be needed – probably shared by non-competing firms wishing to use the skills of people who have drifted away from head office. These areas would be fitted with modern communications for conference meetings and provide the social support for those wanting to work with others.

Any steep fall in house prices would be accompanied by great changes in the role of dwellings: as suggested earlier they would be a place of work. Next they could be a place of learning where grandparents and other close relatives would have an important supporting role in running the home and training children while the parents were working. If, as suggested elsewhere in the book, the state would no longer be able to run education and medical services, then the home could also be equipped to supply schooling and first-line medical services, using a whole range of modern communications and diagnostic equipment.

Modern homes could also be more self-supporting than at present if the forecast water shortages drastically increase the price per gallon. They could be equipped with their own water recycling and waste disposal systems; they could also grow much of their own food using self-contained hydroponic or permaculture programmes. Houses would also need greater security arrangements and probably have their own power generation and satellite communications. As more people become self-employed there will be a spate of new devices aimed to give the individual's output greater added value; these will be micro-processor based devices allowing a product or service to be supplied while the individual is elsewhere.

All these adjustments would provide some compensation for a construction industry gravely weakened by a steep decline in house prices and building. New alliances would be formed as training, security, medical, food growing, recycling and other services would be offered along with traditional building skills. The new role for the home could partly make up the losses suffered by lenders who have traditionally lent on the security of the dwelling, by offering loans based on the combined security of the house plus the cash flow of the home-based business.

If the analysis of decentralisation is correct some new use will have to be found for many of the offices and factories in towns and cities that will no longer be needed. Commercial and industrial real estate suffered badly during the downwave in the early 1930s, at the beginning of the plateau in the mid-1970s and now in the 1990s. If the pattern continues then large office blocks could find a use as accommodation. Quite a reversal from the accepted wisdom earlier in the century!

An ageing working population. Individuals will be obliged to continue working well beyond their normal retirement date without the present level of state support from medical and social services and pensions. They will also need to be kept fit and well which will encourage new drugs, fitness routines and devices to reduce the load of the self-employed. This could prove a golden age for retired people where their knowledge and experience and support for their family will prove invaluable to succeeding generations.

Industry and commerce. The probable deep recession will force businesses to subcontract as many services as possible in an effort to convert fixed to variable costs. This will attract a large number of specialist support operations, many of them able to work remotely – or abroad if necessary. This drive to reduce cost and save inventory will attract manufacturing machines able to convert raw material directly into finished goods without many of the present processing techniques such as casting, rolling, forming and machining.

Energy. The cycle of fossil fuels that has served mankind for the last 500 years may be ending with the prospect of cold fusion. The original experiments into the feasibility of fusing atoms of duterium to generate heat have now been confirmed and the inventors hope to have a practical source of power generation into the next century. If the process does indeed prove sound then there is a good chance that this source of energy could be applied down to small units that could power houses – or even cars. The 'swarm' of innovations accompanying such a breakthrough can only be imagined.

Food production. There could be a problem if land continues to be taken out of production in areas of China and Russia. This comes at the same time that the 'green revolution' (using cultivars, fertilisers, additional irrigation and better cultivation) can no longer keep pace with demand, particularly with the supply of water. Anticipate considerable innovations in techniques such as hydroponics and permaculture where the available water is continually recycled with replenished plant nutrients. In addition new plant and animal hybrids will be needed to take account of changing climatic conditions.

Disease prevention. The increasing need to plough new lands and the migration from the cities will give a new life to cures for previous scourges. These will include diseases such as the plague, typhus, cholera, tuberculosis, plus the newer Lassa and Ebola fevers.

About Innovation

As we have seen, most innovations rely only on a relatively small scientific content. For example, it was said that to produce the nuclear reactor for USS *Nautilus*, the first true submarine, was 90% technology and 10% science. The physics of operating a pressurised water reactor were known and understood but the real skill was in making it work within the confines and safety considerations of a manned submarine. When one is considering the cycles of technology it is wise to remember that there have been few really earth-shaking inventions that owe nothing to the past. For example, James Watt's steam engine was a brilliant adaptation of Newcomen's atmospheric mine-pumping engine and the gas turbine owed its antecedents to the water-wheel and Parson's turbine.

There will surely be similar practical breakthroughs in the future similar to those of Darby, Newcomen, Harrison, Whitney, Edison, Bell and Marconi. Despite large organisations setting up their own development divisions, Du Pont reports that of the seventy most important inventions in the first part of the 20th century, over half were produced by individuals contributing such innovations as cellophane, bakelite, the ballpoint pen, the cyclotron, the gryo-compass, the jet engine, xerography and so on.

Individual contributions have continued in the latter half of the 20th century. In many of the rapidly changing modern markets, innovators such as the founders of Apple Computers and Microsoft will increasingly flourish – putting to shame some large powerful organisations which are unwilling or unable to change. Perhaps many large companies will find it more economical to devolve developments to individuals or small groups then license these for commercial exploitation.

In an age when individuals become increasingly significant we will see the real growth in technology applied to help people achieve greater personal independence.

CHAPTER 14

THROUGH THE WHIRLWIND TO RECOVERY

The themes and events in this book flow directly from a highly singular confluence of important cycles that are reaching their low point in the 1990s and into the 21st century. Three of these are dominant: first there are the major upsets that occur every 500 years; next there are the climatic and historical changes that arise from the 179-year drought cycle. Finally there is the downwave phase of the 45 to 60-year long wave. Taken singly each has the capacity (and by late 1996 is already starting) to cause a major discontinuity in the affairs of mankind; in combination they could be devastating for those unaware of what was occurring. However, it is a cardinal principle of cycles that the following upturn into the next century will be full of exciting new opportunities.

The impact of these rhythms has been described in previous chapters. First there are individual sections covering important executive areas such as business management, politics or investment. Finally there are descriptions of how cycles concern other fields such as war, technology and disease – for each of these will become important in the recovery phase. It is recognised that all of these subjects are important in their own right and demand a much greater treatment than is possible in one volume.

Kept until last have been the most important questions: what is likely to happen, how will we know when an event is near and how can we respond as individuals to discontinuities? There have been many discontinuities in history. There is a story told that on 24 October 1929 the Church of St Margaret's, Wall Street, was full of people on their knees who had lost their jobs and capital; as far as they were concerned the world had come to an end. They wanted help. The rector might have told them they were all important in God's eyes and had been given talents which could be adapted into other channels. Although it did not occur to them at the time, they were the lucky ones who had a training and the education to adapt. Unfortunately, the majority of the 25% unemployed in the US had little of either to fall back on.

Planning for discontinuities is difficult even using cycles, for unforeseen influences can affect the timing – but seldom the events themselves. To recapitulate, these are the most significant cyclical pressures on the western world in the 1990s and through to the 21st century:

The 179-year and other drought cycles have been an important feature in war, history and politics – and for similar reasons. Poor harvests create food shortages and those people who could not afford to be properly nourished have taken to the streets. There have been riots and rebellions putting governments at risk, launching civil wars and overthrowing oppression.

The long wave has created the richest material for cyclical events – affecting such important activities as politics, housing, investment, technology, warfare and also disease; it has also been an important influence on business and non-commercial organisations. From what has been written earlier, it is evident that what worked for the upwave is seldom successful in the downwave.

At the end of this five hundred years: During the 1990s downwave most governments have borrowed too much and are becoming increasingly authoritarian; this is because of their belief in the 'nanny state' or their observation of international treaties. Many Americans believe the federal government is operating in the first category, many British consider the European Union is imposing unacceptable rules in the second; but the trend is against these high-handed politicians. In addition to the difficulties encountered by governments increasing their borrowings, many of the electorate are reluctant to pay more taxes and are arranging their tax affairs to minimise state levies.

As we move towards the end of the century the role of the state is being challenged on fundamental grounds – just as Luther challenged the church in the early 16th century and Thomas Jefferson disputed with Alexander Hamilton. For not only will the state start to run out of money but the post-industrial revolution of Toffler's Third Wave will render most large organisations obsolete. As we saw in Chapter 6, a combination of high real interest rates and the downwave is the worst possible combination for corporate bankruptcy. While more is asked of central and local governments they will be able to deliver less – so firms or individuals will need to take responsibility, returning once again to the doctrine of personal accountability.

If this is indeed a reasonable hypothesis we now have to prepare ourselves mentally and socially for a new range of situations – what the psychologists call a *paradigm shift*. Paradigm is a Greek word which has the modern meaning of a model, a theory or a perception. Stephen Covey in *The Seven Habits of Highly Effective People* describes it as a way in which we 'see' or perceive the world. However, within the context of the major cycles there will be scenarios requiring their own paradigm shifts.

As we move from one set of conditions, principles or circumstances to another there will be numerous breaks with tradition. This happens often in wartime as the British army found in the Boer War. Centuries of tradition were dumped when red coats provided too good a target and were discarded for the more practical khaki. There could be also be prosecutions on matters of principle, such as when Galileo postulated that the earth was not the centre of the solar system. The cluster of cycles described in other chapters will almost certainly break with tradition – a discontinuity which will be felt not just in one dimension but many. There are a number of people who can deal with a change in one set of conditions; coping with several at the same time will be much more difficult unless we adopt the right attitude and prepare for them.

Adapting to a paradigm shift will require a changed set of references. This we might achieve by creating a framework – or scenarios – whereby we will not be unduly surprised by changed circumstances. In this way we can partly anticipate, and think through, different conditions. Next we will need to develop fresh personal values to provide the flexibility to cope with what lies ahead. Finally we can look forward to a new golden – but different – age.

Anticipating Events

The famed Shell method of scenario planning, now practised by the St Andrew's Management Institute, presents planners and decision makers with up to two or three overlapping hypotheses, the optimum number for which contingencies could be reasonably planned. However, using cyclical analyses the implications of these can be extended. For example, one of the scenarios presented to the board of Shell in the early 1970s was a strong chance that there would be a rapid increase in oil prices. Had the team been aware of the 22.4-year drought cycle they might also have encouraged the board to take account of other rapidly rising commodity prices, rising interest rates, inflation, then a rapid fall into a sharp recession.

The major cycles can now contribute to creating some of the alternatives. The first scenario is that the debt deflation of previous long wave cycles will be replicated; the second are the implications of the 180-year and climatic rhythms. Events stemming from these would seem the most logical pattern of events but others could emerge to modify the underlying trends. The prefix D is used to signal the implications for the downwave scenario and U for the upwave.

Implications for the Downwave

The following items are not necessarily in sequence although the latter are more likely to extend into the next century. The passages in bold describe the action, the others are the leading indicators and a guide for decisions:

Implication D1. Plan for rising commodity prices in 1997 and into 1998 during the downwave deflation which the central banks will try to delay as long as possible. If governments hold interest rates down, this could cause stagflation to be followed by a financial crisis, a collapse of the bond market and later by a stock-market crash. This was explained in Chapter 9 – but close account should be taken of political action which will decide the timing of the outcome and the unlikely (but

possible) Implication D2. The leading indicator for such a move would be initially the CRB index (explained in Chapters 2 and 9) breaking out above 270 and a rapid rise in insolvencies. The outcome ultimately would be a deep recession.
Managers should learn how to prepare themselves by reading the historical precedents suggested later in the chapter and then re-read Chapters 4 to 9 for the detailed operations. Assemble advisors to monitor the position then prepare contingency plans for dealing with rapid swings in costs, commodity prices, currency exchange rates and markets.

Implication D2. Although commodity prices rise there is little or no inflation as governments clamp down on prices by raising interest rates and balancing their budgets. This would be highly deflationary leading to a deep recession. The only benefit compared to Scenario D1 would be the preservation of the bond – and possibly the currency – markets.
Despite this being an unlikely course some governments may be courageous enough to act. Watch for commodity prices and interest rates to be high initially but then to decline as the recession bites.

Implication D3. A deep recession would cause the default of poorly rated national, corporate and personal debt. At this stage most governments, unable to raise debt, would be forced to cut back severely on their own budgets – so deepening the recession. One might then expect a slow recovery into the next century as bad debts were purged.
Take advantage of a rapid rise in inflation to eliminate debt as interest rates will inevitably rise before a crash – after this cash will be at a premium. Towards the end of the inflation, shorten supply but lengthen sales contracts and take steps to secure payments. After the crash, budget for sales volumes substantially lower than 1994 levels – see Chapters 6 and 7. Those who have preserved their cash will be able to buy cheaply the subsidiaries of failed companies.

Implication D4. A recession would accelerate cost reduction programmes and increase unemployment. There will be worries about rising crime and disease in cities.
Anticipate a rapid rise in part-time working, self-employment and unemployment as organisations are forced to downsize using modern technology. At the same time expect an acceleration of operations moving away from cities as people are no longer prepared to brave

public transport and rising crime. *These moves will require a radical reassessment of communications and transport.*

Implication D5. An increase in self-employment and a reduction of government support implies a reduced standard of living for the majority. The unsupported elderly will require families to adopt the Confucian-style responsibilities described in Chapter 10.
Chapter 4 describes why the housing market will probably collapse. However, the construction industry will need to refurbish dwellings to house three generations, to convert homes as a place of work and to install added security; anticipate a rise in demand for rented accommodation. Houses will be more self-contained than at present.

Implication D6. Rising nationalism in Russia forces a much greater awareness of increasing conflicts in areas such as the Balkans, Russia and eastern Europe. These could only be made worse by the threat of malnutrition and breakdown of civic order creating mass migration to the west described in Chapters 11 and 12. By early 1996 there were 65 million people (25 million of them Russians) who, with the break up of the Soviet Union, were living away from their place of origin and could be radically displaced in the event of severe shortages. Any disruption of the fuel reserves would send the price of oil rocketing and with it possible dangers, once again in the Middle East. However, the threat to the west of millions of refugees would create untold problems for national stability.
Anticipate that the armed services will be used to counter mass migration and possibly dealing with disease epidemics.

Implication D7. The recessions accompanying the downwave described earlier are likely to increase nationalism and so create tensions and possible disintegration within trade and political unions. Anticipate competitive devaluations and selective trade policies similar to the 1930s. This would end the European Union and lead to secession within several federations.

Implication D8. Anticipate an increase in limited wars not only in countries like Russia but also in China and other areas of tension. The west may not become directly involved unless they are the target for the mass migrations described earlier.

This will place most governments in a dilemma. They will have run down their armed forces in the 1990s to cut costs but, as in the 1930s, preparation for war creates innovations and stimulates economies.

Implication D9. If there is a prolonged recession then governments, unable to increase their revenue from taxation and debarred from borrowing from a collapsed bond market, will be forced to unwind state-run services. Anticipate privatisation of health, education, social services, regular policing, benefits, pensions, etc., and a rapid increase in voluntary organisations that already thrive in the US – and to a lesser extent in Britain. The Swiss practice of devolving responsibility to the community (described in Chapter 10) could be used elsewhere to cut the costs of local authorities and encourage voluntary agencies.

Anticipate many different local initiatives to provide schools, health care, crime prevention, help for old people, welfare and unemployment services. The new communities will experiment with many different organisations. They will also embrace many different ethics and standards from a new Puritanism to a Kibbutz-type socialism.

Implication D10. The rising tide of self-employment could have a serious impact on the nature of capitalism. While the free market of goods and services will not be in doubt, the uncertain nature of many stock and bond markets will encourage individuals to invest, not in other companies, but in their own enterprises. After a financial crash the flow of cash into pension funds, private investment and unit trusts could be seriously reduced. This would mean a return to the more family-orientated approach towards saving and enterprise practised in the east. Individuals with spare cash would be more likely to invest their funds in ventures supporting them into old age.

Implication D11. The expected cool and dry period in the upper latitudes in the northern hemisphere could last well into the next century creating severe water shortages in some areas. If this occurs food scarcity will raise prices, forcing many people either to move or to become more self-sufficient. Historically, a cooler climate has pushed people into fundamental faiths, stricter moral codes and demands for independence.

Anticipate many new initiatives for helping people to grow their own food using techniques such as hydroponics and permaculture. There will also be a need for new hybrids to cope with a changing climate.

Implication D12. The high price of grain from food shortages will reduce the disease immunity of many people, particularly those living in the conurbations described in Chapter 12. Most of these cities are in developing countries with inadequate water and sanitation, making them open to existing and new pathogens.
This is not just a danger to these cities. Rapid communications enables chronically sick people to travel around the world within hours. Anticipate that the public health authorities in developed countries will tighten migration procedures. Individuals will take their own precautions, by avoiding where possible, public places and transport.

. . . And Into the Upwave

It is an important cyclical truth that out of adversity comes strength and for every misfortune there is advantage. The upwave is no exception, for much of the distress caused in the downwave has its own beneficial counterpart. This list of recovery scenarios is clearly not complete but there should be the latent energy and foresight in mankind to make the most of the many advantages offered. The list will include the growth areas identified by management guru Peter Drucker who identified health care, security and the environment as being the market leaders into the next century.

Implication U1. The component parts of many large collapsed corporations will be in private hands with the owner/managers anxious to make a success of their new acquisitions. They will have many advantages such as a slowly expanding market, cheap credit and a pool of skilled individuals to supply the services not provided in-house. Unlike the rush to seek a listed quotation in the 1980s, there will be a determination of many businesses to remain in private hands.

Implication U2. These new independent activities will form the core around which many of the new communities will locate. Being privately owned these businesses will be rooted in the community generating initiatives to reform local services such as children's and adult education, health care, crime prevention, local unemployment, welfare and care for the environment. There will be no one pattern; each community could grow in a different way.

Implication U3. There will be many new industries among them being biogenetics and cold fusion, the controlled power behind the hydrogen bomb. Both will revolutionise our lives, although cheap power from 'heavy water' is still some way ahead. Should it become a reality then it would be available not only for the electric grid but for individual manufacturing plants, offices, houses and probably vehicles.

Implication U4. The techniques that created the Cybernetic Revolution which forced organisational downsizing will be adapted to create millions of new businesses. The self-employed will be enabled to make rapid gains in productivity from simple tasks. This will be of the utmost importance for the unemployed for they will receive little governmental help.

Implication U5. This is the converse of Scenario D5, described earlier, when the majority of people will be working for themselves and demanding dwellings to house several generations. These will be a place of work with excellent communications and often be self-contained and need additional protection from a likely period of increased lawlessness.
A prolonged period of a cool dry climate will encourage the demand for specialist foods to be grown within or around each household.

Implication U6. An increase of infectious diseases will create a demand for personal and home protection. To counter this, expect an increase in home fitness programmes plus diagnostic equipment enabling households to be on line to a local medical centre. In this way a general 'flying doctor' type of self-help service would be available for first-line remedies.

Personal Qualities

Creating the scenarios is just the first stage. Much more important will be for people to develop the mental, emotional, moral and physical stamina needed to guide not only themselves but others. Those men cramming into the Wall Street church after the calamity in October 1929 were not only losing their status; collapsing wealth would hit their family life and they might lose their friends and be forced to take up menial jobs. There were stories of British officers after fighting in the First World War selling matches on street corners wearing masks – ashamed to be recognised by their friends. During the early 1930s very respectable people in America would politely ask passers-by whether they could 'spare a dime'.

One of the first to recognise a hierarchy of needs were the followers of Abraham Maslow, himself a disciple of Carl Jung. They worked with seven levels of needs ranging from the basic homeostatic through to the highest aesthetic level. The psychologist argued that once the basic need for food, clothing and shelter had been satisfied then at the next level people would require safety and security – hoping presumably they will never have to return to the lowest level.

The next level is love and belonging, then further up is esteem – something that was obviously the main concern of the frightened people in St Margaret's and the officers selling matches. After esteem Maslow believed people need self-actualisation, a process of inner attainment, then above that the more cultivated levels of understanding and finally aesthetic appreciation. In essence, people are given the opportunity to propel themselves up the scale on the upwave. They worry about sinking during the downwave

Intellectually understanding such a heirarchy is one matter, being emotionally able to accept a decline is quite another – particularly if there has been a struggle to reach a certain level. Maslow's scale of success primarily described society during the Industrial Revolution when attainment and the associated levels of success were quite finely drawn. In an effort to build on his work, SRI International, an offshoot of Stanford Research Institute of California, and Taylor Nelson of Britain, have worked on psychological stereotypes in an effort to help explain the attributes and needs of society – particularly business – into the next century.

Francis Kinsman in his book *Millennium, Towards Tomorrow's Society* describes these classes as 'sustenance', 'outer directed' and 'inner directed':

The *'sustenance'* driven people are impelled primarily by job security. Although many are comfortably well-off they tend to be clannish, conservative and resistant to change. Their voting patterns are faithful to their working-class agricultural roots.

The '*outer directed*' individuals may be classed as the 'yuppies' of the 1980s whose motivation is esteem and status – i.e. something outside themselves. These are materialistic people concerned that their car, house, job, children's schools should all reflect well on them. Kinsman describes these as being hard working, intelligent and continually striving to better themselves although they can change direction if it suits them. They usually vote conservative.

Finally the '*inner directed*' are described as the 'children of the trans-industrial age'. They are largely indifferent to what the world thinks of them while retaining their own sense of values and goals. They usually have a wide range of interests, a good grasp of current affairs and are tolerant of others. Although not indifferent to wealth, they are more concerned with spiritual, emotional and cultural values as a means of self-expression. They tend to vote liberal.

Which group will now become dominant and most capable of coping with the paradigm shifts described earlier? Probably none of the above stereotypes, which probably owe more to the 1980s than to the next century. Several combinations will be needed to deal with the required changes. For example, the *outer directed* will be needed to spot and take advantage of the rapid changes as they occur – probably supported by a competent staff group made up of *inner directeds*. The *inner directeds* will be ideally suited to be the new independent suppliers of specialist services working with, and through, networks of like-minded people.

At first glance the *sustenance* group will be the most disadvantaged of all, clinging to their security at the lower level of an industrial society. But this again is too stereotyped because, having the least to lose they can take on the more menial jobs or learn the simple trades that the inner and outer directed groups would regard as beneath them. This is why an out-of-work executive could be more vulnerable than a bricklayer. There will, however, be a fourth class of people who have not the training, attitude or inclination to be anything other than labourers. They had a manual role in an industrial society working on an assembly line or as janitors but they no longer have any economic value in Toffler's Third Age, and without support are relegated to an underclass.

Peter Drucker in his *Post-Capitalist Society* lauds the educated person as the social archetype, a cognitive elite. They are the people who define society's performance capacity, and embody their beliefs, values and commitments. They are trained to understand global cultures and within these understand the principle concerns of mankind's motivations, insights and challenges. But these knowledge people are not in the same mould as the present liberal humanists; they would act, not pontificate, about the world's ills. Returning to SRI's stereotypes, they will combine the functions of the outer and inner directed group in interchangeable roles.

With little security now available for any one of the above working groups, how can any of them come to grips with the paradigm shifts set out earlier? Three of these qualities are flexibility, integrity and interdependence:

Flexibility is obviously a key attribute whether moving up or down Maslow's hierarchy; it is also an essential quality during the downwave. To quote Adam Smith in *The Wealth of the Nations*:

> the speculative merchant exercises no one regular, established, or well-known branch of business. He is a corn merchant this year, and a wine merchant the next, and a sugar, tobacco or tea merchant the year after. He enters every trade when he foresees that is is likely to be more than commonly profitable and quits it when he foresees that its profits are likely to return to the level of other trades.

This flexibility was not just applied to trading; Smith suggests that a carpenter

> is also a joiner, a cabinet maker, a carver of wood, a wheelwright, a plough-wright, a cart and waggon maker.

It may not be as easy to switch professions today as in the late 18th century but many entrepreneurs have the ability to set their hands to many enterprises. We can at least anticipate the next moves by thinking through the various scenarios, make contingency plans, monitor progress then implement policies when needed. We also will need strenuous retraining. Adam Smith in his *Theory of Moral Sentiments,* written in 1759, encourages us to adjust to different levels of success (moving up or down Maslow's hierarchy). He states

> the never failing certainty with which all men, sooner or later, accommodate themselves to whatever becomes their permanent situation. This may, perhaps induce us to think Stoically ...

He illustrates this principle by telling of the Count de Lauzun who, when incarcerated in the Bastille, occupied himself learning how to feed a spider.

There is also flexibility of thought if one follows Edward de Bono in his book *The Use of Lateral Thinking.* We rely on deductive reasoning as part of the life process for we no longer have to work out the effect of turning a car's steering wheel or pressing an accelerator; what had to be reasoned as a learner driver now becomes a high probability response. However, the same thought processes can lead to a dead end during a discontinuity. We then need what de Bono calls lateral thinking to achieve a novel solution – and new ideas will be needed to cope with some of the scenarios.

Lateral solutions are low probability for they rely on a given set of facts or opinions arranged or presented in a new way. For example, Einstein considered the existing information on motion and assembled it quite differently to the standard Newtonian structure; he refused to accept the correctness of his solution until it was proved experimentally by observing an eclipse. De Bono believes lateral thinking can be taught and lists four contributory lines of approach:

1. Recognise that the truth may be evident from opposites. De Bono gives the example of Edward Jenner who observed that milkmaids, through immunity from cowpox, did not contract smallpox.

2. Searching for different ways of looking at things often means breaking down what is apparently a whole into

small component parts. In this way what appeared as 'facts' become something different when assembled in different ways. A story is told of a wartime bomber whose hydraulic controls were damaged but spare fluid was not carried; the plane was in danger of crashing but was saved when urine (another fluid) was substituted in the system.

3. Do not be hidebound by deductive thinking and experiment with alternative ideas. One of the best ways to create alternatives is to work out different hypothetical solutions which may be confirmed or denied as more facts become available; this is the principle of taking a fix at sea, the more position lines that are available the more accurate the location.

4. 'Play' with alternatives, with different approaches and seemingly unrelated facts without attempting to deduce a solution. This is called by some the Alpha factor. Those who have experienced it will recall the solution to a problem coming together when least expected almost in an instant with the most brilliant clarity.

Integrity, although not mentioned by the SRI's stereotypes, is probably the most important of all characteristics. Described by *Webster's Dictionary* as being the quality or state of being complete or undivided, integrity also requires a firm adherence to a moral code. Adam Smith typically suggests a market driven approach:

> ... that the real and effectual discipline which is exercised over a workman is not that of his corporation, but that of his customers. It is the fear of losing their employment which restrains his frauds and corrects his negligence.

Integrity need not only be imposed by the market place but have an inner source. Max Weber in his *The Protestant Ethic and the Spirit of Capitalism*, explains how John Calvin and his followers were obliged to live out their faith in diligence to God's laws and in hard work. They could become wealthy provided this was not frittered away with hedonistic delights; their gain was to be either accumulated or given away. Weber explains how some of the most ascetic sects make the best businessmen, citing the Mennonites in Prussia during the reign of Frederick the Great. The story goes that despite their steadfast refusal to fight in his armies, Frederick was obliged to excuse them on account of their hard work and industry.

Benjamin Franklin made a similar point about personal habits when he reminded his readers that time and credit is money. A creditor might well extend a loan if he hears 'the sound of your hammer at five in the morning or eight at night; but if he sees you at the billiard table, or hears your voice at a tavern, when you should be at work, he sends for his money the next day'. He goes on to observe 'for six pounds a year you may have the use of one hundred pounds, provided you are a man of known prudence and honesty'.

Weber cites statistics to explain why pupils with a pious background can be trained to have a good understanding of work, the ability to concentrate, an application to their jobs and a natural frugality. These attributes are obviously not confined to Christians for other groups such as the Jews and Confucians also have a powerful love of learning, a respect for their elders and an application to hard work. Adam Smith would agree with Weber when he discuses the basis of morality. Covering such topics as merit, justice, judgement, duty, virtue, etc., he lauds the religious man whose faith enforces a sense of duty. He is not grateful for the sake of gratitude, not charitable from spirit of humanity, not public-spirited from love of country, or generous for love of mankind.

We have seen already how our national perceptions change with the long wave: in the upwave we become international in our thinking and are prepared to enter treaties for mutual benefit. These principles become strained in the downwave for amid accusations of competitive currency devaluations and the dumping of goods we are inclined to think nationally. Again, Adam Smith:

> The man of public spirit is prompted by humanity and benevolence and will respect the established power and privileges of individuals within the great order and societies within a state. Therefore he will accommodate, as well as he can, his public arrangements to the confirmed habits and prejudicies of the people and remedy, as well as he can, the inconveniences that flow from adverse regulations.

The man of system, on the contrary, is apt to be wise in his own conceit, often enamoured by the supposed beauty of his own ideal plan of government from which he cannot deviate. He seems to imagine that he can arrange the different members of a great society like pieces on a chess board without considering that each one has a set of principles and motion of their own. If the ideas of the ruler and individuals are in harmony there will be a successful outcome. If they are opposite or different there will be the highest degree of disorder. This arrogance is familiar to political speculators who entertain no doubts of the immense superiority of their own judgement – for they hold in contempt the divine maxim of Plato that the state is made for themselves, not themselves for the state.

Interdependence: Stephen Covey (quoted earlier on the paradigm shift), goes on to describe lessons or habits that will increase adaptability by first learning independence then interdependence – the quality of being mutually dependent. First one must learn how to become proactive, or the power of behaving in accord with self-awareness, imagination and conscience. Covey quotes Eleanor Roosevelt who said 'no one can harm you without your permission'. Another saying is 'sticks and stones will break my bones but words will never harm me'. Covey defines this inner worth as a frame of reference for making decisions. Wisdom is a sense of perspective, an ability to balance alternatives for coming to a decision and the driving power for action.

These disciplines are then applied to two groups which he forms into a matrix, relating to their urgency or importance. Covey obviously wants managers to concentrate on the critical issues such as developing relationships, forward planning and recognising new opportunities. However, he realises that urgent/important matters include crises, pressing problems or deadlines which need priority.

Adam Smith's *Theory of Moral Sentiments* would have provided an ideal model of interdependence but he approached the matter in a different way in the *Wealth of the Nations.* Here he suggested interdependent relationships were in reality self-interest when he expressed his famous dictum: 'It is not by the benevolence of the butcher, the brewer, or the baker that we expect our dinner, but from their regard to their own interest.'

The Post-Industrial Individual

Will the stereotypes described earlier be able to steer their organisations through the anticipated discontinuities or will a quite different type of person be needed? The lessons of history suggest that there is a person for every crisis but not necessarily in the right place or the numbers to prevent the destruction of what was previously valuable. For example, it needed Luther to save Christianity, Cromwell to create the New Model Army, Roosevelt to restore America's faith in itself and Churchill to give the free world the faith to beat Germany and Japan.

Like Kinsman, we can group the people we need into three or more categories but not in such stark terms as the 1980 types. These people closed the last stage of the latest plateau phase but are unlikely to achieve the same prominence in the next century. For want of better titles let us classify these people under the headings of leaders, staff officers and the implementers. If Michael White is correct, these will comprise some 40–50% of the population. At the moment the remainder can look forward only to temporary work – a terrible outlook in today's terms, but the clue probably lies in Implication U4 described and will be the subject of another book.

The *Leaders* are those who, having identified a challenge, set up the necessary resources and timetable and go for it – often with the guile of Sun Tzu. They are intelligent, industrious and aggressive individuals capable of communicating their ideas and leading others towards a goal. They are likely to work for wealth, power and prestige but they can also be the leading light of charities and good causes. They will often be highly cultivated individuals capable of working in several areas, such as politics, business or the professions; one might hope that some might also be successful clerics. As suggested by Drucker, a number will be interchangeable with staff officers.

The *staff officers* could be classified as Kinsman's inner directed individuals. These will be the flexible thinkers who will thrive in the next century for they are naturally self-employed and could work for one or more leaders. They will probably change their careers several times during their lives for they are natural learners and will adapt readily to new circumstances. They have a symbiotic relationship with the leaders for neither can operate without the other.

Some *implementers* will bear a remarkable resemblance to Adam Smith's description of a prudent man in his *Theory of Moral Sentiments*; to modern eyes he may appear boring and rather quaint, but would be a good person to have around in a crisis. He studies seriously to understand what it is he professes; he is not cunning or arrogant; he does not assume airs and is not ostentatious or quackish to preserve his reputation; he believes that only the superficial have vanity. He never exposes himself to the accusation of falsehood and restricts his friends to a few well-tried companions; likewise he is not guided by showing off but by modesty, discretion and good conduct. The prudent man is frugal, never sacrificing the future for the present. He always lives within his income and does not go in quest of new adventures or enterprises, preferring the life of secure tranquillity. He is also a man of principle and honour, adhering steadily to maxims.

Today our men of principle have additional qualities. They will be professionals working in many different fields, able to implement the plans prepared by the staff officers and directed by the leaders. They will be completely dependable, averse to taking risks and will not put a foot wrong. They will need to be set tasks and are natural employees although a number will doubtless be happy to work for themselves. They will not be able to work independently of others. Smith then goes on to identify his prudent man as an object of proper respect, deserving and obtaining credibility among his equals. Smith believes that it is the utmost importance for a younger man to maintain his health, fortune and reputation – this is what he calls prudence. Older men appear to need a different agenda!

We learned earlier that ability alone might not carry people through a crisis. In the critical atmosphere described in the downwave scenarios most individuals will be more content to have an income than to worry about status or job titles. As they respond flexibly to their changes, probably their greatest asset could be the inner drive associated with the Memmonites or Puritans so admired by Max Weber. This inner driving work force need not necessarily be Christian as proved by the energy of Jews and Confucians – it could also be in the crusading zeal that Islam has proved so brilliantly over the centuries. The political skills for leading such people will require a combination of qualities seldom observed at present, those aspiring to be leaders would be wise to heed Adam Smith's strictures.

Training for the Downwave

Training for expected scenarios is seldom included in the curriculum of either business or military staff colleges, on the assumption that running a business or a war in the future will be much like that of yesterday. However, cycles teach that discontinuities often confuse those in charge so that for a business to avoid failure (or an army defeat) a new set of people must take charge. One such group of people were those commanding RAF squadrons at the time of the Battle of Britain. Out of an original intake of 50 men in 1920 only one or two regular officers were able to match the needs of the hour and overcame the onslaught – but they went on to become Air Marshals.

It is obviously undesirable that companies should be allowed to fail or armies lose battles just to train future leaders. However, by late 1996 there was enough evidence that the cycles are working as before to encourage case studies to be built around the anticipated scenarios. Business schools, universities and staff colleges should then consider courses to describe and understand lessons from appropriate moments in history for students at least to recognise similar conditions should they reoccur. For business leaders these might include:

- Events leading up to and following the Great Crash of 1929.
- The Great Depression and how businesses were run during this period.
- Case histories of how governments in countries such as the United States, Britain, France and Germany responded to the Depression.
- The events leading up to the Great Inflation of the Weimar Republic, how businesses coped then and when conditions stabilised.
- The reasons for the great commodity explosion of 1972 to 1974. What happened to prices, how governments responded and how businesses were run.
- Events leading to the crash of many US Savings and Loans during the 1980s and the lessons learned from the Resolution Trust Corporation.

It would then be possible to convert past and modern situations into case studies designed to analyse what happened and to learn from the mistakes. Then managers could be taught:
- Warning signs of these conditions reoccurring.
- The planning for contingencies – possibly in the form of scenarios and implications.
- Tracking events for implementing, or modifying the contingency plans.
- Being aware of the pitfalls in any situation, politically, economically, financially and industrially.
- Leading indicators for recovery, the action of customers, suppliers, bankers and shareholders.
- Opportunities once the danger is over.

Most universities and business schools would find it difficult to adapt their present courses to the suggested topics, for most lecturers are used to teaching subjects suitable for Toffler's Second Wave. Military staff colleges are probably closer to dealing with dynamic situations for they teach 'what if' situations as part of a strategic plan around which the forces are trained and organised. It is more likely that these new subjects will be taught as post-graduate courses, possibly from new departments of existing institutions.

Military staff courses, like business schools, are also geared to tackle the staff and planning aspects of past operations. These include interventions like the Falkland War, support operations as in Bosnia and insurgency actions in such places as Panama, Grenada, Borneo, Kenya, Rhodesia, Yemen and so on. Unfortunately, as Simon Hollington of the Leadership Trust points out, in peacetime students are naturally considering their next appointment – hence will tend to offer 'acceptable' solutions (for they are marked on their course work) and avoid innovations which might brand them as possibly 'unsound'. Reverting to the earlier scenarios, likely future case studies for staff colleges might include:
- Dealing with mass migration of people arising from unusually poor crop-growing conditions in the Eurasian land mass.
- Coping with a pandemic disease.
- Building and training citizen forces.
- Disaster relief from unusual conditions such as earthquakes, volcanoes, acute flooding, etc.

How will it all turn out?

Seldom in the way we expect, for there are too many variables that are implicit, but are not the direct cause of the cycles; one of these is the possibility of China attacking Taiwan. How each of us will react to new, and possibly fraught, situations even with training is still problematic; like troops going into action for the first time, nobody quite knows how they will react and often the apparently macho individuals are not necessarily the bravest. The suggested training programme is a help but obviously no substitute for direct experience. Having attended courses the next stage should be for managers to be put in difficult situations to gain crisis experience.

Perhaps we should not worry unduly. Mankind has recovered from difficult situations in the past and will do so again, although it does help if at least some of the likely scenarios have been thought through previously, which, after all, is the whole purpose of this book. Probably the most important result will be not the whirlwind itself but how we deal with the next upwave, for it will be quite different from anything experienced over the last 200 years.

If most enterprises belong to owner/managers, the new shareholders will regard the local community as their home turf. As central and local government can no longer afford public services, these will be provided through local democracy supported by firms who themselves would benefit from sound education, reduced crime and competent health services. In addition, new sciences such as biogenetics and cold fusion could spawn a whole range of innovations just as Darby, Newcomen, Watt and others triggered the Industrial Revolution. One must be optimistic that the Third Wave will not only be fascinating but extremely rewarding; the individual could be provided with a sense of freedom, a renewed faith and a dignity only possible for the minority in the Second Wave.

FURTHER READING LIST AND USEFUL ADDRESSES

Art of War, The by Sun Tzu (Shambhala Publications) 1991.
Avoiding Adversity by William Houston (David and Charles) 1989.
Brook Hunt & Associates Limited, Woburn House, 45/47 High Street, Addlestone, Surrey KT15 1TU
Coming Plague, The, by Laurie Garrett (Virago Press) 1995.
Competitive Strategy: Techniques for Analysing Industries and Competitors by Michael Porter (Macmillan) 1980.
Corporate Financial Distress and Bankruptcy by Edward Altman (John Wiles & Sons) 1993.
Corporate Bankruptcy in America by Edward Altman (Heath Lexington Books) 1971.
Council of Mortgage Lenders, 3 Savile Row, London W1X 1AF
Creating a New Civilisation by Alvin and Heidi Toffler (Progress and Freedom Foundation) (1994).
Cycles of American History, The, by Arthur Schlesinger Jnr (Andre Deutsch) 1987.
De Tocqueville by Larry Siedentop (Oxford University Press) 1994.
Evolution of Technology, The, by George Basalla (Cambridge University Press) 1988.
Exploring Corporate Strategy by Jerry Johnson and Kevan Scholes (Prentice Hall) 1993.
Faber, Dr Marc, 'The Gloom, Boom and Doom Report', 2705 New World Tower, 16-18 Queen's Road Central, Hong Kong.
Foundation for the Study of Cycles, 900 West Valley Road, Suite 502, Wayne, Pennsylvania 19087 USA.

Halifax Building Society, Halifax, North Yorkshire HX1 2RG.
Handbook for Effective Emergency and Crisis Management, The, by Nudell and Antokol (Lexington Books) 1988.
Harrison by Jonathan Betts (National Maritime Museum) 1933.
Hundred Years Ago, A, by Colin Ford and Brian Harrison (Penguin Books), 1983.
Infectious Diseases by Macfarlane Burnet and David White (Cambridge University Press) 1972.
International Franchise Organisation (IFO) 1350 New York Avenue, NW, Suite 900, Washington DC 20005-4709.
Iron Bridge to Crystal Palace by Asa Briggs (Thames and Hudson) 1979.
Isambard Kingdom Brunel by L. C. T. Rolt (Penguin Books) 1957.
Long Wave in Economic Life, The by J. J. van Duijn (George Allen & Unwin) 1983.
Millennium: Towards Tomorrow's Society by Francis Kinsman (W. H. Allen & Co) 1990.
Natural History of Infectious Diseases, The, Burnet and White
Plague's Progress by Arno Karlen (Victor Gollancz) 1995.
Political Business Cycles edited by Thomas Willett (Duke University Press) 1988.
Post-Capitalist Society by Peter Drucker (Butterworth-Heinemann) 1993.
Power Cycles by William and Douglas Kirkland (Professional Communications, Phoenix Arizona 85011) 1985.
Princeton Economics International Inc, 214 Carnegie Center, Princeton, New Jersey 08540 USA.
'Prize Gold Acceptance Speech' by Reginald Howe (Bank Lips AG, Mittelstrasse 10, PO BOX 626, 8034 Zurich) 1992.
Protestant Ethic and the Spirit of Capitalism, The, by Max Weber (Routledge) Reprinted 1992.
Public Spending: a twenty-year plan for reform by Patrick Minford and Paul Ashton (Centre for Policy Studies, 52 Rochester Row, London SW1P 1JU) 1995.
Rats, Lice and History by Hans Zinsser (Little, Brown) 1934.
Recover Myth, The, by Bryan Kavanagh (Land Values Group, Melbourne) 1994.
Re-engineering the Corporation by Hammar and Champy (Nicholas Brealey) 1993.
Riding the Business Cycle by William Houston (Little, Brown) 1995.
Seeds of Change by Henry Hobhouse (Sidgwick and Jackson) 1985.

Seven Habits of Highly Successful People, The, by Stephen Covey (Simon & Schuster) 1989.

State of the World 1996 by the Worldwatch Institute 1776 Massachusetts Avenue, NW, Washington DC 20036, USA

Syspas Ltd, Dyers Hall, 11/13 Dowgate Hill, London EC4R 2SU.

Theory of Moral Sentiments by Adam Smith (Henry Bohn of Covent Garden) 1861.

Thriving on Chaos by Tom Peters (Pan Books) 1989.

Trap, The, by Sir James Goldsmith (Macmillan) 1994.

Understanding Company Strategy by Brian Houlden (Basil Blackwell) 1990.

Use of Lateral Thinking, The, by Edward de Bono (Pelican Books) 1972.

Wealth of the Nations Books I-III, The, by Adam Smith (Penguin Books) 1980.

World in 2020, The, by Hamish McRae (Harper Collins) 1994.

INDEX

Adams, Henry, 189, 190
AEG, 263, 267
agency working, 49, 101, 115
AIER (American Institute for Economic Research), 31–40
Airfix, 74
Altman, Edward, 73, 74, 76, 80
America, 178, 194, 238–9; community society in, 198–200; debt, 157, 163, 164fig, 175, 180, 181, 195–6; election campaigns, 189, 190–1, 191; employment in, 4, 114, 159; gold rush, 18, 58, 145; gold standard, 140–1; navy, 180, 209; political cycles in, 170–81, 189–91; post-war, 179–80; property market, 60–1, 134–5, 136, 137, 138; Revolution, 209; War of 1812, 141, 144, 145, 153, 171, 220, 271; War of Independence, 209; *see also* Great Depression; railways/railroads
American Civil War, 18, 58, 153, 174–5, 214, 220, 271; and disease, 239; and gold standard, 141, 146; and tariff protection, 147; and technological innovations, 261, 262, 266
American Institute for Economic Research *see* AIER
Apple, 150, 276
Armstrong, Martin, 22–3, 143, 156, 163, 189, 190, 193
AT&T, 266
Avery, William, 126

Avoiding Adversity (Houston), 82, 83, 84, 99

balanced budgets, 158–60, 161, 163, 186, 281
Bank of England, 73, 143, 147
bankruptcies *see* failure
banks, 75–8, 142, 203; failure of, 73, 74–5, 145
Barings, 21, 73, 147, 194
Barraclough, Sir John, 222
BASF, 266
BCCI, 74
Beckman, Robert: *The Downwave*, 30–1
behaviour and climatic change, 13–14, 17, 24–5, 55, 168, 221–2
Belgium: debt, 20, 28, 140, 165, 196
Bell Telephone, 263
Bendix Corporation, 47
Bic Pen, 127
Boeing, 4, 149
Boesky, Paul, 56
Bolger, Jim, 198, 202, 205
bond market, 23, 35, 159, 174; collapsed, 156, 179, 280–1, 283; and debt, 160, 163; in downwave, 156; and inflation, 161, 162; in K2, 146, 147; in K3, 148; in K4, 149, 150, 151, 157–8; and long wave cycles, 143, 144, 145; in upwave, 151, 153, 154
bonds, 37, 142–3, 196, 204
Booker, Christopher, 166, 167
Boots, 116

BP, 115
Britain, 57, 142, 184, 189, 209, 212, 220; debt, 157, 186; and disease, 238–9, 243–4; and EEC, 166–7; and gold standard, 140; inflation policies, 162; national health service, 203; navy, 177, 180, 185, 208; political change and cycles, 181–6; property market, 21, 59, 60–1, 133, 135–6, 137–8; unemployment in, 159; and WWI, 26, 185, 215–16; and WWII, 26, 186; Zulu war, 214–15
Browning, Dr Iben, 15, 26–7, 31, 244
Buchanan, James, 174
Buchanan, Pat, 4, 189
budget balancing, 158–60, 161, 163, 186, 281
building *see* property market; housing industry
Bureau for Economic Analysis (BEA), 34
bureaucracy, 26, 51, 165–8, 196–206, 278; *see also* decentralisation
Burnet, 226
business cycles, 9–10, 19, 30–40, 55, 77; four phases, 68–71; management for, 41–66, 67–71; and starting a business, 72–3

Canada, 5, 199, 204; debt, 20–1, 22, 28, 140, 165, 166, 194, 196
Canon, 99, 249
Carnaux Metal Box, 126
Centre for Franchise Marketing (CFM) Consulting, 98
Chamberlain, Neville, 9, 159, 186
Champy, James, 81, 85, 102, 118, 121–2
Charmin Paper Company, 46
Chrysler Corporation, 74
Churchill, Winston, 123, 180, 293
Cigma healthcare, 114–15
Cirrus Technologies, 130
cities, 281–2; and disease, 7, 230–1, 243, 246, 247, 275, 281, 284; workers move away from, 272, 273, 274, 281–2
Clausewitz, Karl von, 207, 213
Cleveland, Grover, 176
climatic change, 2–3, 7, 9, 10–12, 28, 126, 145, 176; and behaviour, 13–14, 17, 24–5, 55, 168, 221–2; and business cycles, 55; and commodity prices, 28–9, 158, 161–2; cycles of, 24–8, 168, 188,

208, 280; extreme cold, 2, 12, 13; and historical events, 14–15, 15–17, 207–8; and investments, 153; and Kondratieff long wave cycles, 44–50; planning for, 283–4; and political change, 170; and recession, 75; and self-sufficiency, 283–4, 285; and wars, 207–8, 220, 221; *see also* drought
Clinton, Bill, 191
Colorol, 55, 74
commodity prices/markets, 28–9, 35, 64, 147, 196, 283, 284, 295; in American Civil War, 174; in Britain in 1900s, 183–4; and climatic change, 161–2; in downwave, 161, 188; and innovation, 269; investment in, 141–3; and long wave cycles, 58, 143, 144, 149, 150, 158, 160, 164; planning for rise in, 280–1; in upwave, 151–2, 153
Commodity Research Bureau (CRB) Index *see* CRB
communications technology, 193, 253–4, 262–3; *see also* information technology
communities, 29, 192, 283; as basis for society, 198–206; and businesses, 193–4, 284–5, 297
competition, 70, 126–8, 131–2
computer forecasting, 31, 35
computers *see* computer forecasting; Cybernetic Revolution; information technology
Confucianism, 25, 198, 204–5, 206, 282, 291, 294
Connelly, John, 125–6
construction industry, 57, 59–61, 152, 272–4, 282; *see also* property market
consumer demand, 48, 49, 116–19, 126; *see also* customers
contract work, 4, 54, 99–101, 115, 250, 274; *see also* outworking
Control Data, 149–50
Coolidge, Calvin, 178, 190
Covey, Stephen, 279, 292
CRB (Commodity Research Bureau) Index, 164, 281
credit, 75, 79, 154, 155, 164, 291
'credit vortex', 3, 4, 22, 64
crop yields, 64, 145, 227; and climate, 2, 10, 12, 15, 28, 35, 153, 278
customers, 48, 116–19, 120–2, 124, 125–6

Cybernetic Revolution, 4, 53, 113, 131, 168, 205; and unemployment, 192–3, 197, 272, 285

Daimler Benz, 3, 50, 261
de Bono, Edward, 289–90
de Tocqueville, Alexis, 191, 192, 198–200, 205
debt, 12, 13, 22, 23, 28–9, 64, 86, 138; 'deadly anomaly', 163, 164; defaults, 160, 163, 196, 281; deflation, 280–1; as economic indicator, 36, 37; factoring, 63, 79; and GDP, 20, 22, 162–3, 181, 186, 196; and long wave cycles, 58, 149, 157; monetising, 158, 160, 162, 163, 196; national, 5, 20–1, 33, 160, 162–3, 165–6, 180, 181, 194–5; *see also under individual countries*
decentralisation, 85, 98–9, 198–206, 272–4
deflation, 161, 162, 186, 188, 196, 280–1
derivatives market, 21–2, 155–6, 157
Dewey, Edward, 208, 218, 220, 221, 222, 223
disease, 7, 8, 271, 282, 285, 296; and cities, 7, 230–1, 243, 246, 247, 275, 281, 284; cycles of, 225–47, 244–5; drug-resistant, 7, 8, 227–9, 230, 239, 240–1, 242, 245; and migration, 222–3; transmission of, 229–31, 232, 242, 246, 284; and war, 183, 226, 233–4, 244–5
Dow Jones, 148, 156, 179
downsizing, 105–12, 192, 281, 285
downwaves, 51, 130–1, 205–6, 206; and failure, 72–93; investment during, 139–64, 269; management policies for, 114–38; planning for, 280–4; and property market, 133–8
drought cycles, 2–3, 6–7, 11, 15, 35, 160, 277, 278, 280; and commodity prices, 158, 161–2; and disease, 244; and wars, 221
drought and plenty cycles, 14
Drucker, Peter, 131, 132, 194, 196–7, 262, 284, 288
Du Pont, 147, 267, 276
Dun and Bradstreet, 75–6, 79

earthquakes, 11, 28, 164
East India Companies, 142, 143
economic indicators, 31–40, 41, 64, 68–70, 160, 280–5, 296
EDI (Electronic Data Interchange), 120–1

Edison, Thomas, 147, 275
EEC *see* European Economic Community
Efficient Customer Response (ECR), 121–2
Einstein, Albert, 289
Electronic Data Interchange (EDI) *see* EDI
Emerson, Ralph, 189–90
employment, 36, 37, 54, 151; full, 114, 186, 193; full-time, 4, 54, 193; part-time, 4, 281, *see also* contract work; self-employment
England, 17, 26, 218, 219, 232; Civil War, 13, 15, 169–70, 221; Renaissance in, 14, 15; Tudors, 15, 26, 142
equities, 139–40, 160, 163
European Commission, 51
European Economic Community/ European Union, 26, 166–7, 195, 201, 278, 282; and free trade, 2–6, 52, 53
Evans-Pritchard, Ambrose, 167–8
Exter, John, 139
Exxon, 148

Faber, Dr Marc, 143, 149, 150, 254
failure, 98, 153–4, 163, 279, 281; cycles of, 72–93, 94; training to avoid, 295–6; warning signs, 7, 72–3, 93
Fairbridge, Rhodes, 168
farms and farming, 19, 57, 73, 149, 157, 173, 176
Federal Housing Association (FHA), 59, 134
federal society, 198–206
'federated' structures, 115–16
First Capital Holdings, 73–4
Fisher, Irving, 30
fixed to variable costs conversion, 70, 89, 95, 115, 132–3, 274; and employment, 97, 99, 100, 101
'flattening the organisation', 94–112, 115, 129
flexibility, 20, 56–7, 288–90, 293; *see also* Just In Time (JIT) techniques
Ford, Henry, 147, 178, 261–2
Ford Motor Company, 102, 123–4, 148, 266
forecasting *see* computer forecasting; indicators
'Forecasting Business Trends' (AIER), 31–2, 34
Forward, Gordon, 129, 130

Foundation for the Study of Cycles, 37, 38, 39, 143, 207–8
foundry group case study, 82–3, 86–7
France, 3–4, 26, 145, 191, 198–9, 209, 210; debt, 28, 157; state benefits, 5, 51; unemployment in, 159; in WWI, 215–16
franchising, 49, 51, 92, 95–8, 108, 109–12, 115–16; investment in, 160; of manufacturing, 102–5
Franklin, Benjamin, 291
Fukuyama, Francis, 2

Garrett, Laurie, 226
GDP and debt, 20, 22, 162–3, 181, 186, 196
General Dynamics, 149
General Electric, 147, 149
General Motors, 47, 48, 53, 116–17, 269
Germany, 5, 136, 145, 178, 185, 191, 197; debt, 28, 157; in downwave, 3, 20, 188; post-war recovery, 26; rearmament, 263; social security costs in, 51; Third Reich, 25, 191, 207; unemployment in, 3, 50–1, 159; in WWI, 178, 215–16; *see also* Weimar Republic
Gingrich, Newt, 190, 198, 204, 205
Gladstone, William Ewart, 184, 214
glass company case study, 89–92
gold, 139, 140, 141, 145, 149, 176
gold standard, 6, 18–19, 33, 52, 139, 140–1, 146, 157, 171, 180, 186, 195
Goldsmith, Sir James, 130
Goodyear Tyres, 147
governments, 8, 22, 53, 64, 74, 135; balance budgets, 161, 163, 186, 281; bonds, 23, 196, 204; bureaucracy, 165–206; debt, 4, 5, 20–1, 22, 145, 158, 162–3, 165–6, 194–5, 244; *see also under individual countries*; decentralisation of, 198–206; in downwave, 3–5, 20, 157–62, 205–6, 278–9, 280–4; impose restrictions, 50, 51; inability to maintain welfare state, 22, 29, 51, 159, 193, 195, 206; and inflation, 160–2; monetise debt, 162, 163, 196; spending, 194–8, 206, 244, 269, 297; in upwave, 153
Great Crash (1929), 23, 156, 295
Great Depression/Recession, 18, 23, 113, 147–8, 149, 156, 157, 159, 179, 271; innovations during, 266–7, 268; and property market,

58, 133, 135; as training aid, 295
Great Inflation *see* Weimar Republic
Greenspan, Alan, 140

Hale cycles, 11, 15, 28, 64, 74, 94, 153; and wars, 221; *see also* drought cycles
Hamilton, Alexander, 171, 190, 279
Hammer, Michael, 81, 85, 102, 118, 121–2
Handy, Charles, 115–16
Hanson Trust, 43, 46, 125
Harding, Warren, 178, 190
Harrison, John and William, 265, 275
high-tech glass company case study, 89–92
historical events and climatic change, 14–17, 26–8, 207–8; and cycles, 1–2, 23–4, 277; *see also* nation cycles; political change; war
Hobhouse, Henry, 226, 238
Home Owners Loan Corporation (HOLC), 58–9, 135, 136
Home Shopping Network (HSN), 122
home-working, 100–1, 247, 272, 273, 274, 281–2, 285
homes in the future, 272–4, 282, 285
Hoover, Herbert, 179
hose and fitting manufacturer case study, 88–9
housing industry *see* construction industry; property market
Hunt, Simon, 162
Huntington, Elsworth, 13

IBM, 100, 149, 150
Ifo Research Institute, 50–1
imports *see* tariff protection
Index of Bank and Company Shares, 145
indicators, 31–40, 41, 64, 68–70, 160, 280–5, 296
individualism, 6, 8, 20, 24, 131, 205, 276; lifestyle for future, 272, 274, 279, 285; of nations, 188
Industrial Revolution, 1, 14, 113, 168, 192, 251, 258, 286; innovations during, 250, 256–63, 267–8, 269, 270–1
inflation, 64, 74, 143, 153, 161, 163–4, 191; in Germany *see* Weimar Republic; and government action, 160–2; and planning, 280, 281; and upwaves, 188; in war periods, 153
information gathering, 66, 126–8,

129–30, 272
information technology, 4, 8, 53, 101, 113, 169, 193; and customers, 117; and direct selling, 50; and disease, 247; and re-engineering, 84, 85; in retail, 120–2; and stock market, 149–51
infrastructure investment, 197, 269, 270, 271
innovation: 'bunching' of inventions, 12–13, 151, 248, 268, 270, 275, 297; and climatic change, 47–8; cycles of, 146–7, 248–76; political, 189–90; to avoid failure, 122–33, 130, 131; and war, 251, 264–7, 283
insolvency *see* failure
Intel, 114, 143, 150–1
interest rates, 4, 5, 23, 74, 162, 280, 281
Internet, 5, 192
inventions *see* innovation
inventory, 62–3, 71
inventory cycle *see* Kitchin cycles
investment, 6, 23, 53, 69–70, 160, 206, 283; in downwave, 139–64; early, 141–3; in gold, 139–41; in infrastructure, 184, 197, 269, 270–1; strategies for downwave, 157–64
Ireland, 53, 114–15, 136, 182, 184, 222; potato famine, 57, 145, 183
Italy, 5, 189, 238; debt, 20–1, 21, 22, 28, 140, 165, 196; Renaissance in, 14, 233, 247

Jackson, General Andrew, 171, 172
Japan, 26, 40, 42, 49, 53, 123, 141, 197; debt, 157; in downwave, 3, 4, 188; Kobe earthquake, 11, 28; pensions, 5; post-war recovery, 26, 180; property market, 133; and quality control, 119, 132; *see also* Just In Time (JIT) techniques
Jefferson, Thomas, 170, 171, 190, 279
Jenner, Edward, 227, 289
Johnson, Lyndon, 51, 180
Journal of the American Medical Association, 245–6
Juglar cycles, 13, 18, 23, 31, 44, 64, 74, 94; and innovation, 267
Just In Time (JIT) techniques, 54, 63, 117, 119

K1, 19, 57, 73; and investment, 143, 144–5; and political change, 170–3, 182–3; and wars, 220
K2, 19, 23, 33, 58, 73; and investment, 143, 145–7, 151, 159; and political change, 173–6, 175fig, 183–5; and wars, 220
K3, 19, 33, 58, 73, 153, 157; and investment, 143, 147–9, 151; and political change, 177–9, 177fig; and wars, 221
K4, 20–2, 28, 33, 38, 40, 73–5, 94, 115, 130, 277; future impacts, 271–5; and investment, 143, 149–51, 153, 157–64, 271; and political change, 180–81, 186–8, 180fig; strategies for, 55–6, 59–61; and wars, 221, 224
Karlen, Arno, 226
Kinsman, Francis, 286–7, 293
Kitchin cycles, 13, 30, 33, 38fig
Koch, Robert, 228, 244
Kondratieff, N. D., 17, 18, 31, 157, 190
Kondratieff long wave cycles, 6–7, 17–22, 30–1, 33, 72–3, 190, 278; and business cycles, 30–40; business strategies for, 44–66; and climatic change, 44–50; and failure, 72–93; and innovation, 47–8, 248, 267–9, 267–71, 271–5; and investments, 143–64; and management strategies, 41–66; planning for, 284–5; and political change, 168, 170–91, 188–9; upwaves and war, 208, 220–1, 267, 271; *see also* downwaves; K1; K2; K3; K4; plateau stage
Kuznets cycles, 15, 18, 64

League of Nations, 188
Leeson, Nick, 21, 194
licensing, 51, 98–9
Lincoln, Abraham, 174
Lloyd George, David, 186
Lloyds Bank, 44
long wave cycles *see* Kondratieff long wave cycles
Louisiana Purchase (1803), 18, 57, 144, 171, 172
Ludendorff, Erich von, 215
lunar cycles, 10, 15
Luther, Martin, 24, 279, 293

Mackie, Bill, 72, 93
management, 64–6; change of style, 55–7, 123, 131, 132–3; forward planning, 280–5; policies for a downwave, 114–38; strategies, 6, 38, 40, 41–66, 79–86; tactics,

67–71; training strategies, 295–6
management buy-outs, 8, 82–3, 155, 284, 297; at Raleigh, 132; at SRI, 107, 108–9, 112
Manufacturers' Agents National Association, 101
manufacturing, 35–6, 53–4, 114, 274
market regulation *see* tariff protection
marketing, 47–50, 69, 70, 71, 124, 124–5
Maslow, Abraham, 286, 288
Maxwell, Robert, 56
Maynard Keynes, John, 3, 179
Meltdown (Houston), 137
Mensch, G., 268–9
Mexico, 40, 140, 161, 172–3, 178, 218, 229; war, 58, 270–1
Microsoft, 150–1, 276
migration, 7, 27–8, 57–8, 58, 282, 296; and disease, 7, 226, 243, 244, 245, 246, 275, 284; and war, 222–3
Milken, Michael, 56
Mill, John Stuart, 190
Modelski, George, 24–5
Moltke, Helmuth von, 213–14, 215
money supply measures, 35–6, 37, 64, 70
Monroe, James, 170, 171
moon, 10, 15
Motorola, 150

Napoleon I, 57, 170, 171, 183, 198, 210–11, 227
National Bureau of Economic Research (NBER), 32
National Home Owners Relief Fund (NHORF), 137–8
National Recovery Administration (NRA), 180
nations: cycles of dominion, 25–6, 270
Netherlands, 17, 25, 238–9
Netscape, 151
New Economic Plan (NEP), 188
new technology, 193, 272–3, 281, 285; *see also* information technology
New York Stock Exchange, 146
New Zealand, 9, 116, 158, 163, 165, 198, 202–4
Newcomen, Thomas, 7, 250, 258, 259, 260, 270, 275
Newton, Sir Isaac, 140, 265
niche markets, 48, 49, 70, 116–17, 129, 188
Nixon, Richard, 33, 141, 181

OECD, 4, 157
Olympia and York, 73
OPEC, 60, 153
outsourcing, 114–15, 130, 192–3, 250, 274
outworking, 99–101, 115, 116

Pampers, 121–2
Pan American Health Organisation, 244
paradigm shift for the future, 279–97
Pareto Rule, 83, 85, 102
pensions, 5, 51, 157, 185, 274; pension funds, 22, 194, 206, 283
Perot, Ross, 4, 189
Persons, Warren, 32
Peters, Tom, 56, 117, 118, 119, 120, 123, 132–3
plateau stage, 18, 19, 21, 38–40, 48; investment during, 153–6; recessions in, 33–4; strategies during, 46–7
political change, 6, 17, 54, 170; cycles of, 50–1, 168–206
Polly Peck, 55, 74
Princeton Economic Institute, 22–3, 143, 156, 163, 189
Proctor & Gamble, 46, 121–2
production, 36, 37, 69–70, 71, 114, 250
profitability, 75, 80, 94–5, 115, 119
property market, 3, 19, 44, 57, 58–60, 163, 250; collapse, 21, 133–8, 179, 273–4, 282; in upwave, 152, 153
protectionism *see* tariff protection
Pugsley, John, 163, 164

quality, 119–20, 132; quality control, 54, 71

railways/railroads, 19, 73, 145, 146, 269, 270–1; and innovation, 260–1, 268; stocks, 145, 147, 148, 173, 175
Raleigh Cycles, 85, 131–2
Rank Xerox, 99–100, 149, 249
RCA, 148–9
Reagan, Ronald, 51, 167, 190
rearmament, 47, 58, 164, 222, 248, 263, 266
recessions, 9–10, 18, 19, 33–4, 38, 40, 75, 147, 281, 283; and innovation, 268–9; investment during recovery, 151–3; and nationalism, 282; and new technology, 122; sales methods during, 49–50

306

recovery period, 34, 38, 40, 72–93
re-engineering, 81, 84–6, 95, 102;
    Agile Engineering, 129
Rees-Mogg, William, 206
religion, 17, 23–4, 26, 54, 199, 290–1
rescue operations, 79–92, 95, 123,
    135–8; case studies, 86–92;
    Raleigh, 131–2
Resolution Trust Company, 75, 135,
    295
Riding the Business Cycle (Houston), 1,
    2, 10, 13, 25, 168, 221
Roosevelt, Franklin D., 18–19, 135,
    136, 138, 224, 293; New Deal,
    58–9, 179–80, 197, 269
Roosevelt, Theodore, 58, 147, 177,
    190
Russia, 2, 7, 25, 215–16, 222, 243, 275,
    282; Russian Federation, 189

S-curve of technology, 248–51, 268
Savings & Loans, 55, 75, 134, 135, 295
Schlesinger, Arthur, Jr, 189, 190, 191
Schumpeter, Joseph, 7, 30, 151, 248,
    267–8
Second Wave, 296, 297
self-employment, 4–5, 8, 46, 97,
    98–101, 283; as future trend, 272,
    273, 274, 281, 282, 285, 293
self-sufficiency, 29, 283–4, 285
Shell Central Planning Group, 45,
    280
Siemens, 259, 261
Slater, Jim, 61
Slater Walker Securities, 43, 74
Sloan, Alfred P., 47, 116–17
Smith, Adam, 181, 197, 262, 288, 289,
    290, 291–2, 294
speculation, 9, 21–2, 44, 144, 145,
    153, 288; in boom, 139–40, 172;
    derivatives markets, 156; land, 18,
    19, 157, 172, 179; in property
    market, 133
SRI International: stereotypes, 286–8
SRI (System Resources Inc), 105–12
stagflation, 5, 75, 163, 280–1
Standard Oil, 147, 148, 176, 258, 266
statistical indicators, 31–2, 34–40,
    68–70
stock market, 142–3, 145, 174, 283;
    crashes, 156, 179, 280–1; and long
    wave cycles, 143–64
sun retrograde cycles, 13–15, 28, 45,
    169–70, 221, 271–5
Sun Tzu, 41–3, 55, 65–6, 293
sunspot cycles, 10–11, 13, 15, 220

Sweden, 5, 191; debt, 20, 20–1, 22, 28,
    140, 165, 196
Swissair, 53, 114
Switzerland, 8, 165, 192, 196, 198,
    202; government model, 205–6,
    220–2, 283
Syspas Ltd, 77–8, 80, 94

Taffler, Richard, 76–7, 94
tariff protection, 4, 46, 52, 130–1,
    206; in Britain, 53, 159, 181, 184,
    185, 186; and downwaves, 157,
    188; legislation for, 172, 176, 177;
    in US history, 147, 171, 174–5,
    176, 179
taxation, 4–5, 161, 186, 206, 278–9,
    283
technology cycles, 7, 12–13, 17,
    248–76; *see also* information
    technology; innovation
Texas Instruments, 114
Thatcher, Margaret, 51, 187
Third Generation techniques, 49,
    94–112
Third Wave, 4, 113, 131, 168–9, 192,
    193, 197, 205, 206, 272, 279, 297
Thorn EMI, 98
tile company case study, 102–5
Toffler, Alvin, 4, 113, 131, 168, 192,
    193, 197, 206, 272, 279, 296
Toffler, Heidi, 168, 192
trade protection *see* tariff protection
trade unions, 54, 152–3, 174, 175,
    184–5, 186, 193
training for the downwave, 288–9,
    295–6, 297
tree rings, 12, 16, 27
Truman, Harry S., 180, 217

unemployment, 3, 53, 96, 159, 191,
    272, 285; alternatives to, 130–1,
    197–8, 224; as economic indicator,
    36, 37; future levels, 50–1, 114,
    193, 272, 281, 293; in past, 149,
    159
United Nations, 188, 195, 216, 217,
    223, 224
United States *see* America
upwaves, 18–19, 20, 38–9, 133, 188,
    286, 297; and consumer products,
    47–8; and innovations, 248;
    investment during, 53, 151–3;
    planning for, 280, 284–5;
    recessions in, 33; strategies
    during, 46
US Steel, 147

307

Van Buren, Martin, 172
venture capitalists, 83, 108, 152, 155
Virgin group, 115
volcanic activity, 2–3, 11–12, 15, 17, 28, 145, 170, 176; and commodity prices, 161–2

Wal-Mart, 118, 121–2
Walker, Roger, 100
Wall Street Crash, 278
war, 41–3, 140–1, 153, 164, 185, 208–18; and business cycles, 33; and climatic change, 13, 15, 207–8, 220, 221; cycles of, 1–2, 6–7, 11, 18, 19, 207–24; and disease, 183, 226, 233–4; in future, 282–3; and innovation, 47, 251, 264–7, 279, 283; and Kondratieff long wave cycles, 174–5, 220–1, 267, 271; technology for *see* weaponry
Washington, George, 57, 144, 170, 209
water, 223, 242–4, 245, 273, 283
Way, Michael, 98
weaponry, 213, 214, 217, 220, 267, 271–2; innovations in, 251, 254–6, 264–6
weather *see* climatic change

Weber, Max, 290–1, 294
Weimar Republic, 33, 62, 140, 141, 162, 191, 195, 205, 207, 216, 295
welfare state, 5, 179, 205, 283; inability to maintain, 22, 29, 51, 159, 193, 195, 206, 274; in New Zealand, 202–4
Wellington, Duke of, 170, 183, 210, 211, 227
Wheeler, Raymond, 11, 13, 15–17, 24, 45, 221, 251, 270, 271; battle analysis, 207–8, 218, 223fig
White, Michael, 4, 113, 114, 130–1, 168, 192–3, 226, 293
Willett, Thomas, 190–1
Wilson, Woodrow, 178, 190
Woolwich Building Society, 137
World Bank, 195
World Health Organisation (WHO), 195, 231
World Trade Organisation, 195
Worldwatch Institute, 223, 226

Xerox, 99–100, 149, 249

Z-score, 76, 79, 80
Zenith Radio Corporation, 148, 149
Zinsser, Hans, 226